P9-DEZ-895

THE WOMEN'S CANADIAN HISTORICAL SOCIETY
OF TORONTO
Incorporated
February
14th, 1896.

MONCK

Charles Stanley, Viscount Monck

Viscountess Monck

Sir John A. Macdonald

Thomas D'Arcy McGee

Spencer Wood

Lord Lyons,
British Minister at Washington

George-Etienne Cartier

MONCK GOVERNOR GENERAL 1861-1868

Elisabeth Batt

With a Foreword by W. L. Morton

McClelland and Stewart Limited

ISBN: 0-7710-1157-1

McClelland and Stewart Limited,
The Canadian Publishers,
25 Hollinger Road,
Toronto, Ontario.

Photographs from the Public Archives of Canada and the Monck Papers.

Printed and bound in Canada

Contents

Viscount Monck, from a lithograph in the Public Archives of Canada

Foreword

There was need for this book. That need is well met by the author, a direct descendant of Monck and possessor of the precious portion of his papers which survived, well met in two ways. One is that the 'unknown Irishman', as Monck was called on his appointment is now made known. The other is that a largely unknown Governor General at perhaps the most important time in Canadian history is revealed as a personality, sober yet genial, hardworking yet capable of leisure and good fellowship, independent to the point of self injury in the ideas he held yet capable always of working with others. Above all, this book shows, if with reticence Monck would have approved, the real Monck as a family man, devoted to his wife and children, a very ordinary family yet lovable, and especially to his elder son, the dutiful but ungifted Henry. A distinguished Irish novelist once said to me, in reproachful surprise that I should be interested in Monck, 'the Moncks were not *clever!*' They were not, but they were human and interesting, and I think it well that after all the years and changes that have passed Canadians should realize the family and personal sacrifices any Governor General had to make in presiding over the growth pangs of this nation. 'I did it for the money', Monck wrote in his blunt way to Henry. But the money did little to lift the debt on his Irish estate. That, I think, is worth noting.

Nevertheless, the eight years in Canada made up an experience for the Moncks, one still remembered among their descendants and, having noted the costs, we may well turn to the experience. Part of that, in many ways the liveliest, Canadian readers have already shared through the book, *My Canadian Leaves,* of Frances Elizabeth Owen Cole Monck, Monck's sister-in-law, the irrepressible Feo, a natural comic who enlivens these pages as she did the Monck household on her visits to

Canada. Her stories of a Governor General 'fussed' by the St. Alban's raid of John A. Macdonald, his long hair flying, and the 'calm-faced McDougall', of the same Macdonald, after a banquet, seen wrapped in a blanket 'practising' Hamlet before his mirror, are not exactly the dry dust of history. Confederation was the crisis, the turning point, of Canadian history, and over that troubled period, Monck presided with the patience and the helpfulness befitting what he ruefully called himself 'a constitutional monarch.' But his Irish family found occasions in those demanding times for larks which still amuse.

If, however, Monck was personally largely an unknown Governor General, that is not to say that the part he played in Canadian history has not in general been justly assessed by leading Canadian historians, J. M. S. Careless, D. G. Creighton, Chester Martin, C. P. Stacey, Reginald Trotter. Yet that assessment was based on public papers and the opinions Monck's ministers held of him, not on a private knowledge of his origins, background, ideas and, on the whole, of his personality. That in fact was impossible. Monck's private papers were wholly burnt during preparations for the sale of his home, Charleville, County Wicklow, in 1931, except for the two bound volumes of his letters to Henry, given to the Public Archives of Canada by the present Lord Monck, and a small but valuable portion which was salvaged from the fire by a friend of the family. These Monck papers greatly helped to make this book possible, and copies have been graciously given by the author to the Public Archives.

Yet Monck, if now so incompletely known, played during his years in Canada, with an assiduity few Governors General have shown, the delicate role of 'constitutional monarch' in the complicated politics of Canada from 1861 to 1864. By proving his impartiality, always genial but always unvarying, among politicians and political parties, as the author shows, he won the confidence of all sides. He was thus able in June, 1864, to defer a grant of dissolution and to request his ministers and the leaders of the opposition to take time to consider whether a coalition of parties might not be formed to end the deadlock of Canadian politics. Out of the exercise of constitutional discretion came the Great Coalition of 1864. It was a clear mark of Monck's personal influence based on trust that he was able to give this subtle but decisive turn to the course of Canadian politics.

Monck was also influential in soothing the vexed relations between Great Britain and the United States during the civil war and in preserving the neutrality of Canadian territory. This he did largely through his correspondence and friendship with Lord Lyons, the British Minister at Washington. His strong but private support of the North may also have helped. To maintain Canadian neutrality and for the defence of

Canada in the event of war Monck persuaded, even 'prodded,' reluctant ministers to reform the Militia Act of Canada and to vote more money for the training and equipment of the Militia. In doing so he pressed to the breaking point in public speeches the limits of his office, but without provoking controversy or lessening his Ministers' trust in him.

After 1864 he became a valuable middleman between the Colonial Office and all the provinces in assisting the negotiations and manoeuvres which led to the carrying of Confederation. That great change he read out in the Speech-From-The-Throne in 1865 as the creation of a 'new nationality' and himself saw as an event that would put the new nation in the way of defending itself and of becoming, should it choose, an independent power.

A man so unknown could do so much because in fact he was in many ways prepared for the duties of the high office which came to him so unexpectedly. A resident and an improving Irish landlord, a Peelite Liberal in politics, he had served in Irish public affairs since 1846 and in the British House of Commons from 1852 to 1857. From 1855 to 1857 he was a Junior Lord of the Treasury, or political 'whip' for the Irish supporters of Lord Palmerston's Ministry. He thus, unlike most Governors General, knew much of Parliamentary affairs and politics and had many friends, some in high places, such as Delane, editor of *The Times*. Moreover, he was a friend of John Robert Godley, the colonial reformer who believed in colonial self-government and colonial self-defence, with ultimate independence if desired by a colony. These ideas Monck made his own and in their light played his part in advancing Canadian Confederation.

After his return to Ireland in 1868 he took up his first interest, the reform of the land law and of the established Church of Ireland. He advised Prime Minister Gladstone on and helped carry the disestablishment and disendowment of the Church of Ireland in 1869 and the first Land Act, that of 1870. He was Chairman of the Temporalities Commission which disposed of the endowments of the Church and which began the policy of land purchase by the farmers of Ireland. Monck also assisted Gladstone with the Land Act of 1881 and became a member of the Land Commission under that Act. That he was both a son of the Church of Ireland and a landlord shows the quality of his liberal principles. But Home Rule he opposed both as degrading to Ireland in giving it a subordinate legislature and as harmful to the United Kingdom. Ireland was not a colony such as Canada but, in his view, an integral part of the nationality of the United Kingdom. He himself sought, with John Bright, a middle way in the setting up of an Irish Committee of the House of Commons for Irish affairs.

To assist his Irish estate and his numerous family, he entered business in London until illness forced his retirement. Crippled with arthritis, he died at Charleville in 1894.

It is to this plain, modest, and always honest man and to his life and family in Canada that Elisabeth Batt has devoted this book, and in doing so has thrown further light, personal and revealing, on an important page in Canadian history. Her book makes a little known actor in that history a living and a lively person for both reader and student.

W. L. MORTON

Chapter One (1861)

In the late summer of 1861, the affairs of British North America formed the chief topic of conversation in London clubs and provided front-page news in the English press. Because of Britain's persistent neutrality in the American civil war, her relations with the United States were at an all-time low; and Canada's proximity to the United States made her, for the time being, Britain's vulnerable point. The situation resembled a barrel of gunpowder in which the smallest spark was liable to cause an explosion. If this should occur, Canada's three thousand miles of virtually undefended frontier would be the obvious point of attack. It was an awkward time to appoint a new Governor General.[1] Though Canada had been self-governing since 1848, the position of the British Sovereign's representative was no sinecure; among administrative posts the appointment ranked second only to that of Viceroy of India. As one Canadian paper said: "It is impossible to say how much depends on the new Governor General. Would it not be wise to look for the ablest statesman and truest patriot of the day, and, at such a crisis as the present, place him at the head of the Executive in Canada?"[2]

Consequently, there was no enthusiasm, on either side of the Atlantic, when Viscount Monck of County Wicklow in Ireland was chosen to fill the post. "This unknown Irish nobleman", as he was described by Edward Watkin,[3] had had no administrative experience and (equally serious at the present juncture) no military experience. Lord Palmerston the British Prime Minister was accused of nepotism in the appointment, as it was known that Monck was a protégé of his.

Some of the London papers were actively hostile, and most of them showed surprise; yet the London *Morning Chronicle* defended the appointment: "Lord Palmerston, knowing well and esteeming highly a person whom the public does not know at all, has thought proper to entrust him with a post of some responsibility and distinction." On the other side of the Atlantic, the Montreal *Herald* suggested that: "the London journals are disturbing themselves a great deal more than the occasion requires respecting the qualifications of our new Governor General . . . What we want is an honest man, who has no whims of his own to serve, and who keeps himself from such personal friendships and antipathies as will influence his conduct." The theme running through the varying degrees of criticism was – "Who is he?" – which was in itself a criticism in the circumstances. It should not be necessary to ask such a question about the Governor-elect for Canada.

Who, then, was he? Beyond inheriting an unearned title and landed property in six Irish counties, what had he done?

Born in 1819, Charles Monck belonged to that much abused breed described as Anglo-Irish. The family, orginally of Devonshire stock, had not been among those English, Scottish, and Welsh settlers planted in Ireland after the Cromwellian invasions; nor had fertile slices of that country been bestowed on them in return for services rendered to the English monarchy. They had acquired their landed property through purchase and what were then called "prudent marriages". It could almost be said that when they were not marrying their own first cousins, they married heiresses. Charles Monck's three-times-great-grandfather, a cousin of the General Monck of Restoration fame, was joint Surveyor-General of Customs in Ireland in 1627, and a survey of the northern ports, written in his own hand, is now in the British Museum. He had a seat in Parliament, as had several of his descendants. Charles's grandfather married his cousin, Anne Quin, thus bringing a strain of true Irish blood into this hitherto Anglo-Irish family. He was connected by marriage with Lord Hawarden and the Duke of Portland, both prominent politicians, who helped and influenced him in his career. Unfortunately, they were both strongly in favour of the union of the English and Irish Parliaments. This grandfather was made an Irish peer in 1797; but it is suspected that the subsequent Viscountcy, awarded him in 1801, resulted from his support of the Act of Union, passed in 1800. This last is a matter on which his descendants prefer not to dwell; but it is only supposition, and nothing definite is recorded of the facts which caused him to be given either title.

Neither rumour nor guess-work has ever been able to penetrate the mystery surrounding the next family honour. The Earldom of Rathdowne was bestowed on Henry, the 2nd Viscount Monck, by George IV in 1822, following that monarch's only visit to Ireland. So far as is known, the King was not entertained at Charleville, the Monck's Wicklow home; nor did Henry Monck contribute, financially or otherwise, to any political party. However, there were several incidents during the King's four week visit that have not been officially recorded, such as the banquet at Powerscourt, home of Henry Monck's nearest neighbour, at which the King did himself so well that he was unable to carry out the rest of the day's program. He had to be discreetly conveyed to the royal yacht by Lord Powerscourt and his friends. Henry Monck's earldom must have been the outcome of one such incident.

Henry's brother, Charles Joseph Kelly Monck, had fought in the Napoleonic wars under General Wellesley, later to become Duke of Wellington. Having been wounded in the Peninsular War, he left the army on half-pay, married Bridget Willington, the daughter of a Tipperary family, and settled in that county. There his son, our Charles Monck was born, and there he spent his boyhood. Being the son of a younger son and the eldest of a family of eight, Charles was brought up to make his own way in the world.

Unlike his uncle and grandfather, who had followed the family tradition of Eton and Oxford, Charles's education took place entirely in Ireland. In 1835, aged sixteen, he entered Trinity College, Dublin. He travelled abroad during vacations, but spending these formative years in Ireland instead of at an English public school and English university greatly influenced his character and future career.

His father had been appointed an officer of health in the parish of Templemore, and as such was responsible for raising money locally for "the payment of the doctor, clothing, flannel and blankets, and medical care of the poor, care of orphans and foundlings, and payment of fares of foundlings to the Foundling Hospital in Dublin, costs of burial . . . sometimes contributing towards the cost of fares for those emigrating to America."[4] For the majority of the Irish population, the standard of living was then seldom higher than near-starvation level, and the small-tenant farmers, subject to the abuses caused by absenteeism, had no resources from which to meet the periodical bad harvests or failures in the potato crop. In "caring for the poor", the officers of health were literally saving the destitute from starvation; and through his father's involvement in this work, the young Charles Monck grew up with a greater awareness of the misery around him than was usual in children of the Anglo-Irish landlord class. Far from sharing the complacent attitude of some of the so-called "ascendancy class", he never forgot that the Monck's landed property, whether acquired by purchase or by marriage, had formerly been wrested from the Irish owners during successive invasions of Ireland.

His Trinity Professor of Political Economy was Isaac Butt, who had originally opposed the campaign for the repeal of the Union (of the English and Irish Parliaments) but eventually became the founder of the Irish Home Rule Party and a champion of the Irish nationalists. Like his former antagonist, Daniel O'Connell, and several other nationalist leaders, Butt would not contemplate complete severance from England. He and other like-minded men influenced Monck. Like Butt, he had no faith in sporadic rebellions and demonstrations of violence. He took a longer view believing that the evils resulting from centuries of English misgovernment of Ireland could best be cured by Irishmen who have earned the right to have a say in Irish affairs. It was his strong sense of public responsibility, rather than personal ambition, which sent Charles into politics.

Meanwhile, he took a degree in law and entered the Irish Bar in 1841, after completing his legal training in London. He worked very hard at his profession at that time, but he was also involved in public affairs, and his friends and associates were reformers and thoughtful politicians. He never wavered in his allegiance to the British Crown, but his personal sympathies were with the Irish people. His letters of that period have been lost, but those he wrote in later years show that he had always strongly opposed the political, agrarian, and ecclesiastical injustices perpetrated by the British Government. He made no secret of the fact that he deplored the results of the Union.

During the "Great Famine" of 1845-1847, when the entire potato crop was destroyed by disease, Charles Monck was one of those who worked tirelessly for the relief of the starving population. While pressing for immediate relief, he and his friends were equally insistent that temporary amelioration of the present distress was only a part of the task which lay before them. Their main objective must be to change a system that created the need for charity. This could only be done by being in a position of authority, even if it meant becoming involved in politics. Monck, John Robert Godley, and William Monsell[5] formed the nucleus of a committee calling themselves "The Irish Party", which they described as "an attempt to combine classes, creeds and interests in Ireland". In 1847, the Irish Party, which included the nationalist leader William Smith O'Brien, presented a memorandum to Parliament. It contained a clear, well-informed summary of the situation and proposed "a short-term plan to cope with the famine, and a long-term plan to restore the national economy."[6] The memorandum was stopped by Parliamentary debate, its sponsors had to admit failure, and "The Irish Party" was disbanded.

To Charles Monck, established tradition and vested interests were no excuse for injustice. He had convictions; yet he was no uninformed fire-eater. He delved into history – political, religious, legal, agricultural – and he kept his eyes open to events around him.

It was inevitable that Sir Robert Peel should be his political father figure at this time. Charles Monck had seen Irish corn and beef shipped to England in order to fill the pockets of absentee landlords, while the tenant-farmers and labourers who produced it were literally dying of starvation. There was a threat of famine in England in 1845, yet the Corn Laws banned the importation of foreign grain lest farmers and landlords should be forced to lower their prices. Peel as Prime Minister succeeded in abolishing the Corn Laws and establishing Free Trade. He was a man after Monck's own heart. "I am a Peelite and a Free Trader", he declared in an election speech; for he soon realised that nothing but a seat in the British House of Commons would give him the right to a voice in Irish affairs.

There were many obstacles to be surmounted first. He was defeated in 1848 when he stood for the County of Wicklow; and in the following year he became the 4th Viscount Monck, in the peerage of Ireland, through the deaths of his uncle and father within a few months of each other. To quote Monck: "An Irish peer . . . is neither fish, flesh, nor fowl." He was forbidden by law to represent an Irish constituency or to take any part in an election in Ireland and, as an Irish peer, he was not eligible for a seat in the House of Lords. A limited number of Irish peers was elected, from among themselves, to sit in the House of Lords. These were almost exclusively conservative and protectionist, and Monck's extreme liberalism was a threat to all they stood for. The Irish peers let him know that they would elect him to the House of Lords without hesitation if he would mend his ways and join their party. This Monck refused to do, since his main objective in reaching Parliament was to attack the unjust laws which had led to the deplorable state of affairs in Ireland. His hand would be tied if he were pledged to support the *status quo*. However, he had many friends who shared his views and looked on him as a valuable ally. In a message urging him to spare no pains to get into Parliament, Sir William Gregory wrote in 1847 that it was to such "young Irelanders" as Monck, John Godley, William Monsell, and Sidney Herbert "that we shall look hereafter when the time comes to influence English opinion as regards Irish affairs."[7]

Though debarred from the House of Lords except by special election, Charles Monck had one advantage in being an Irish peer; unlike an English peer, he could sit in the House of Commons as representative of an English constituency. Thus, in 1852 he was elected Liberal member for Portsmouth. Although he conscientiously fulfilled his promise to the Portsmouth electorate that he would support their interests "as a real working and speaking member", he always took a vigorous part in debates on Irish affairs, particularly when the subject was land tenure or national education. Parliament was only in session during seven months of the year, so Monck was able to combine his duties as Member for Portsmouth with those of a resident Irish landlord.

Along with the title and the Wicklow house, Charleville, he had inherited considerable landed property in other parts of Ireland. He became an enthusiastic agriculturalist and was one of the original members and supporters of the Royal Agricultural Society of Ireland. Defying family opposition, in 1844 he had married his first cousin, Lady Elizabeth Monck (fourth daughter of his uncle, Lord Rathdowne). Of their seven children only four lived to grow up: Frances (Fan), Louise, Henry, and Stanley. Fan, the eldest, became deaf and dumb at an early age as the result of scarlet fever. Elizabeth made the training and education of her handicapped child a life-work and took her to Paris for a few months every year. At that time Paris led the world in the education of the deaf; Britain lagged far behind in both diagnosis and training, still classing deaf-mutes as incurable idiots.

The annual visit to Paris proved to be rewarding in its results so far as Fan was concerned, but it was expensive; and along with the property Charles Monck had inherited a debt of £90,000 from his uncle. In addition to being a Member of Parliament, he needed a salaried post; and he was appointed a Lord of the Treasury when Lord Palmerston formed his first Cabinet in 1855. Two years later, Palmerston's Government was defeated and Monck lost his seat in Parliament, thereby terminating his appointment. He was offered the Governorship of New South Wales, but he turned this down since he still hoped to get into Parliament and to be offered a salaried Government post that could be combined with his duties as an Irish landowner. When the year 1861 found him still without paid employment, he let it be known that he would accept a Colonial appointment if it should be offered to him, and if no vacancy nearer home should occur. In doing this he was sacrificing his principles, which were strongly against absenteeism; but the estate was still heavily encumbered. Owing to agricultural depression, many of his tenants were behind with their rents. Knowing their desperate plight, he would not press them to pay, nor would he follow the example of some of the other landlords who were evicting smallholders in order to farm the land at a profit. Yet money must be found, and if he could earn none within reach of home, he would have to look for a job further afield.

He was not kept waiting long for an answer. On August 21, 1861, he received a letter from the Duke of Newcastle, Secretary of State for the Colonies, offering him the Governor Generalship of Canada.

Chapter Two (1861)

The offer of the Governor Generalship of Canada did not take Monck by surprise. Sir Edmund Head had long been anxious to retire, and the post had already been offered to, and refused by, Lord Wodehouse, Lord Eversley, Lord Harris, and the Duke of Buckingham. Monck must have been aware of this since the holders and ex-holders of government office formed a closely-knit community and took a lively interest in all new appointments. At the Athenaeum Club, Charles Monck heard all the political gossip and knew there had been difficulty in filling the post. In Canada, according to Robert Lowe, "It is not easy for anyone to be popular much or long." Monck had already been approached unofficially on the subject, so the Duke of Newcastle's formal offer found him sufficiently prepared to be able to write a letter of acceptance by return of post:

Charleville
Enniskerry.

August 23rd, 1861.

My dear Duke,
Your letter of the 21st reached me by the late post yesterday evening.

In reply to it I at once place myself at your disposal and accept the offer you have so kindly made of the position of Governor General of Canada. I trust I may be enabled so to act in that post as to justify the confidence you have placed in me, and as far as depends on me, to conduct affairs so as to advance imperial and colonial interests.

I do not think I could be prepared to start for Canada much before the 1st October, but I will expedite matters as much as I can, and if I find it possible to go sooner I will do so. I propose coming over to London either in the end of next week or the beginning of the week following and should wish very much to have an interview with you if that time should suit your convenience.

Believe me to be, My dear Duke,
Yours most faithfully,
Monck.

Monck had been suggested as a possible candidate by John Thadeus Delane, editor of *The Times*. "*Your* cock fights, where so many turned tail," the Duke of Newcastle wrote to him when he received Monck's acceptance.[1]

Several of Monck's close friends were interested in Canada. Sidney Herbert[2] had been Secretary of State for the Colonies, and Edward Cardwell[3] was to hold that office after the Duke of Newcastle's retirement. Charles Adderley[4] and Chichester Fortescue[5] were to become Colonial Under-Secretaries during Monck's term in Canada. John Robert Godley had travelled in Canada with the object of studying colonial development. Robert Lowe[6] was on the Committee of Enquiry into the Hudson's Bay Company, the Deputy Governor of which was the eighty-year-old Edward Ellice who owned property in the St. Lawrence valley. The latter was looked upon as something of an oracle by liberal politicians and was known to have a high opinion of Monck.

Thus, in one way and another, Charles had heard a good deal about the romantic and picturesque land of great rivers, cataracts, lakes, mountains, and prairies, all of whose natural features were on a gigantic scale, and two-thirds of which was still undeveloped and, to a certain extent, uncharted. A great point in Canada's favour was the fact that she was self-governing, since his belief in self-government, for every country capable of assuming it, amounted almost to a passion.

The Governorship of British North America was a big step forward in the career of a man of forty-two with no previous administrative experience. Yet, owing to Canada's proximity to the now hostile United States, her lack of communications, turbulent politics, and severe climate, the post was not an ideal one for a man with a young family. Monck frankly admitted that he accepted it for the sake of the salary, undeterred by the general opinion that £7,000 per annum was "insufficient to reimburse the unavoidable expenditure of the station", and the work "heavy, irksome and undignified".[7] This was amply born out by the experience of former Governors, all of whom had found it hard to reconcile the somewhat rigid demands of the Colonial Office with the self-conscious independence of a colony experimenting with self-government.

The retiring Governor Sir Edmund Head had been criticised both by the Home Government and by Canadians for favouring the Conservative Party at the expense of the others. After the colony obtained a measure of responsible government in 1841, three successive Governors had caused "friction" by refusing to surrender prerogatives that had belonged to their position, but were untenable in the new regime. There is no record that they were censured for this by the Home Government, which tended to blame the Canadian Ministers for any discord that arose. These three Governors were followed by Lord Elgin, who, like his successor Sir Edmund Head, was said to "rule by a party" – in his case the Reformers. Elgin's conduct of affairs otherwise was approved by the Home Government, but a different view was taken in Canada, where meetings were held passing resolutions asking for his recall. On at least two occasions he was mobbed by an angry crowd, "his carriage almost shattered by stones, and he himself narrowly escaped bodily injury at the hands of the infuriated populace."[8]

There was not very keen competition for an office that appeared to require an almost superhuman degree of tact and wisdom. The extent to which the Governor General was expected to wield a personal influence in the administration was not clearly defined by the Home Government, while any interference was liable to be resented by the Canadian Government.

Monck's letter of acceptance reached the Colonial Office on August 24, and the appointment received the Royal Assent from the Queen on August 30. The Duke of Newcastle wrote to her, recommending Monck for the post and she replied immediately in a private letter that "she most readily sanctions this appointment which she think an excellent one. We have just seen Lord Monck at the Vice-Regal Lodge."[9] According to contemporary reports, Queen Victoria was not in the habit of giving such prompt and cordial assent to appointments recommended by her ministers. The few references to Charles Monck in her letters show that she both knew him personally and approved of him highly, which may account for the absence of the usual delays and objections when disposing of this very senior post.

Meanwhile, the news had leaked out. "I must tell you a piece of news which has excited me a good deal," John Godley wrote to Adderley. "Monck is appointed Governor General of Canada! Very flattering to him in the present critical state of North America."[10] One of Monck's staunchest friends, Robert Lowe, evidently considered that Monck did not carry enough guns, in the diplomatic sense, for such a post. In a letter to Edward Ellice, he described Monck as "an innocent lamb".[11]

Subsequent events proved that Lord Palmerston had known what he was doing when he decided that, in this case, character was more important than previous experience. Charles Monck had plenty of common sense, besides the "thoughtful intelligence" attributed to him by the Quebec *Morning Chronicle.* His broad outlook and ability to grasp the essentials of a situation and go straight to the heart of the matter surprised those who had been deceived by his outward calm. He had a warm, friendly manner and was at ease with all classes of people; his integrity was unshakable and he was not easily rattled. Perhaps his greatest strength lay in his unselfconsciousness and entire absence of personal vanity, so that he did not waste time and nervous energy either in resenting personal slights or in playing to the gallery. All these qualities would be valuable in the Governor General of a colony consisting of self-governing provinces, split by regional, political, and cultural squabbles.

Monck had known and respected the Duke of Newcastle for several years. The Duke, however, was not an easy man to work for. He was conscientious and an able administrator, but ill health and an unhappy marriage had not improved a temper that was naturally irascible and intolerant. His claim to be an authority on Canada and Canadians was based on one visit there in 1860, when he organised the Prince of Wales's tour. He had then made himself cordially disliked by those Canadians with whom he had come in contact. The fact was that he knew a good deal about the country without really "knowing" or understanding its people.

Although the Imperial Government had, in the main, supported former Governors in their efforts to deal with the teething troubles of a self-governing colony, Newcastle was shrewd enough to know that some mistakes had been made. He agreed with the Prime Minister that Monck could be the right man for the job, although some of his reasons for doing so differed from Palmerston's. The Duke thought the various problems could be tackled through back seat government from the Colonial Office. Therefore it suited him to send a Governor General he imagined to be a useful piece of raw material, inexperienced and willing to be guided, rather than an experienced administrator who would have ideas of his own.

He first drew Monck's attention to the most vital problem of the day: Canada's urgent need to increase military defence. With his eye on the Treasury, Newcastle was particularly anxious that the responsibility for this should not fall on the Home Government. Canada's contribution consisted of militia force of insufficient strength and inadequate training that had to be complemented by Imperial troops garrisoned at Quebec, Montreal, Toronto, and London.

Both English and Canadian politicians agreed on the immediate necessity for increasing military strength but differed on the question of who should provide it. Even now, four months after civil war had broken out in America and when the uneasy relations between that country and Britain were approaching a climax, the Canadians insisted that the responsibility for defending their territory lay with the Imperial Government. Canadians had no quarrel with the United States nor with any other nation. Since any threat to Canada was the result of her connection with Britain, Britain had the onus of providing and financing defence. An attempt to introduce a new militia bill had recently led to one of the frequent "ministerial crises" in the Canadian Parliament, where policy was all too often decided by the fear of losing votes.

On their side, the British accused Canadians of demanding all the privileges of local independence without shouldering its responsibilities. Theoretically Monck would have little control over government or legislation. Nevertheless Newcastle impressed on him the vital and urgent need to build up a strong Canadian militia force and to ensure that a militia bill be introduced and carried during the next parliamentary session. He must convince the Canadian ministers that permanent defence was a Canadian responsibility whether or not the taxpayers liked it.[12]

In the event of war, reinforcements of regular troops would be despatched from England immediately, but it would be nearly a month before they could reach Quebec. The Atlantic crossing might take as long as three weeks, after which the most direct route would be by water, up the St. Lawrence River. The only overland route to Quebec was the Grand Trunk Railway, which ran through American territory to Portland, Maine. If Britain were at war with the United States, British troops would have no alternative other than to proceed by ship up the St. Lawrence or overland by New Brunswick. But from late November till early May, the river was frozen and closed to shipping.

Canadians saw the construction of an intercolonial railway as a means of opening up communications with Canada West and eventually with the Pacific coast. The Home Government insisted that the first and most important step was to link the Nova Scotian port of Halifax, on the eastern seaboard, with the city of Quebec.

Both of these projects were now to be regarded as second in urgency to defence precautions. Monck was warned to set about them in such a way as to avoid irritating or arousing the suspicions of the United States Government; and he was instructed to maintain strict impartiality toward the various Canadian political factions, thereby avoiding the mistakes of his predecessors.

Neither newspapers nor contemporary letters commented on Monck's lack of military experience. Like his predecessor, Sir Edmund Head, he was expected to be guided by his Military Secretary and by the General in command of the British garrison in Canada (Sir Fenwick Williams). He employed four of Head's *aides-de-camp,* all army officers, and engaged as private secretary John Godley's young brother Denis, a Captain in the 74th Highlanders. The question of how long Monck was to stay in Canada must have been discussed, though there is no record of such discussions. Head had remained in office for seven years, though latterly against his will. Elgin had remained for seven years. Of the four previous Governors, Lord Cathcart had been a temporary military appointment, and the remaining three had all died in office after holding it for less than three years. Later correspondence indicated that Monck had not expected his own term of office to last beyond 1864, if for so long.

While Charles Monck was being briefed for his difficult assignment, it fell to his wife Elizabeth to prepare for the removal of her family and household to the other side of the Atlantic. A Governor was expected to bring his own domestic staff, horses and carriages, furniture, silver, linen, and china.

It was fortunate for Elizabeth that the complicated preparations left her little time to brood over the future. In those days of frequent wrecks, the thought of the voyage was, in itself, enough to daunt an anxious mother. Iron-built ships were gradually replacing wooden vessels and all were equipped with engines. The earlier paddle-engines had given place to the "screw" or propeller-driven type. But all ships still carried a full complement of sails, to which the engines were a supplement rather than the chief means of locomotion. The perils of the voyage to Quebec were not confined to the actual crossing of the ocean, to the icebergs off Newfoundland, or to the fogs in the Gulf of St. Lawrence. To reach Quebec it was necessary to sail up the St. Lawrence River, and ships were often wrecked in the river itself.

Furthermore, the education of the three elder children presented a serious problem. Henry had only four more terms at Mr. Nind's preparatory school before he was due to go to Eton. Fan, now aged sixteen, would be deprived of the annual visit to Paris and the expert teaching of professors from the French School for the Deaf. Mr. Wilkinson from the staff of the preparatory school was engaged as private tutor for Henry. Henry could therefore accompany his parents to Canada and stay there until he went to Eton. Two governesses, Miss Frend and Fraülein Denneler, would take care of Fan's education and that of her fourteen-year-old sister Louise; and the French nursery maid, Mathilde, was to look after Stanley. The domestic staff would include, among others, Elizabeth's maid Dimsdale, and Brock the steward, with several footmen and a coachman and grooms.

It was especially difficult to decide what to take with them because they had no idea where they were going to live.[13] There was some excuse for the Colonial Office to be evasive on this point because Spencer Wood, the official Governor's residence in Quebec had recently been destroyed by fire. Rebuilding was in progress but was not yet finished. Until recently, the seat of Government had been Toronto and it was there that Sir Edmund Head had had his headquarters. Charles could obtain no precise information beyond the assurance that he would be told where to go when he arrived in Quebec.

Monck had booked their passage for October 11 on the *North Briton,* a three-masted, iron-framed ship of the Allan Line. Sailing from Liverpool, the *North Briton* would put in at Derry for Irish passengers, including the usual large intake of emigrants. The Moncks and their party travelled to this northern port by train. Their party included Denis Godley, his wife, Kate, and the new *aide-de-camp,* Henry Brand. At the railway station, horse-drawn omnibuses conveyed them to the wharf on Lough Foyle, where they boarded a tender, stepping onto the paddles and from there down to the deck. It took the tug more than two hours to reach the mouth of Lough Foyle where the *North Briton* lay. A fresh wind was blowing, and it was choppy in the Lough. With the tug "dancing" and the ship swaying, there was some delay before the constantly slipping gangway could be fixed between them. At last they were all hustled on board where Charles and Elizabeth were ceremoniously received by the Captain. Above the shouting and commotion and the noise of wind and waves rose the voices of the sailors singing "a wild song" as they hauled on the ropes, hoisting the sails.

They had a rough crossing. Charles and Fan were the only two of their party who did not succumb to the violent pitching and rolling of the *North Briton.* Fan's handicapped state had sharpened her other perceptions and made her keenly observant of all that went on around her. She was up early walking on deck and never missed the meals at the Captain's table. She was thrilled by the sight of a whale spouting, and towards the latter part of the voyage, by icebergs. After the first week Elizabeth was able to join her in "long walks on deck" and to take an interest in her fellow passengers – "such pleasant people". She also revelled in the unaccustomed leisure. "It is so nice to read so much in quiet, and not to have to do anything else," she wrote. "I love the sea air, too." After eleven days at sea the welcome words, "Land in sight!" were passed from one to the other. As they entered the narrow straits of Belle Isle, Elizabeth brought little Stanley up on deck and showed him the wild rocky coasts of Labrador and Newfoundland.

Their ship crossed the Gulf of St. Lawrence and steamed up the river, threading her way between islands and the mainland. Through a drizzling rain, the travellers had their first sight of the great rock, towering above the river, on which is built the ancient fortress city of Quebec, crowned by the Citadel. At 9.30 in the morning of October 23, the *North Briton* docked at the Grand Trunk Railway Wharf. In spite of the rain, the new Governor General was greeted by a cheering crowd and a guard of honour from the 17th Regiment. A band played as he and his party disembarked, and a salute of guns was fired. The newspapers reported that Monck "gracefully acknowledged the cheers by bowing repeatedly" after which Colonel Irvine, representing the retiring Governor, conducted the party to a convoy of carriages. They were driven up the steep narrow streets of Quebec between wooden, tin-roofed houses; and all along their route more crowds waited in the rain to cheer them on their way. At the grim, barrack style Parliament House, Sir Edmund Head was waiting to receive them. As Spencer Wood had not yet been restored since the fire, temporary accommodation had been made for them in this building until a more permanent residence could be prepared.

The somewhat prison-like exterior of their temporary home was compensated for by its lofty situation. From the south windows, the Moncks could look down over the roofs of the Lower Town to the great St. Lawrence River with its constant traffic of steamships and across to the vast tracts of farmland on the opposite shore. To the north, the Plains of Abraham stretched further than the eye could see. To the north west, the majestic range of the Laurentian Mountains and the woods in all the blazing colours of the fall surpassed anything they had seen in Ireland.

Chapter Three (1861)

On his arrival, the new Governor was plunged immediately into official business. First, he had to be sworn in as Administrator of the Province, lack of time having prevented the usual formality from taking place before he left England. He must receive and reply to addresses of welcome and meet the Executive Council, headed by M. George-Etienne Cartier as Prime Minister and by Mr. John Alexander Macdonald as Leader of Upper Canada.

Sir Edmund Head left Canada on October 25, which allowed only two days for the briefing of his successor who had landed on October 23, 1861. He urged Monck to write personally to Lord Lyons, British Minister at Washington. Monck did so at once and thereafter Lyons was to prove a valuable source of information, and later, friend to Monck and his family.

Monck's office of Governor-in-Chief was combined with that of Captain-General of all armed forces in British North America. In military matters, Head had relied on the advice and assistance of his military secretary, Captain Francis Retallack, who was willing to stay on in that capacity. But in one of his first letters to the Colonial Office, Monck submitted that the present international situation created the need for a senior officer of the regular army to supplement his own lack of knowledge and experience.

After Head's departure, Monck embarked on the first of a series of conferences with General Sir Fenwick Williams, who, for the next five years was to be one of his most frequent correspondents and closest associates. Born in Nova Scotia, Williams was a general in the British Army who had been created a baronet in recognition of his brave defence of Kars, in Armenia, during the Crimean War. He was already well-known to the Moncks as a member of the Westminster Parliament from 1856 till 1859. During the same period, he was General-Commandant of Woolwich garrison and combined that senior military post with a political career. At the same time he was lionised as "Hero of Kars" by London hostesses. Opinions vary on "Sir Kars," as he was mockingly dubbed by his detractors. In *The Critical Years,* Professor Morton describes him as a "carpet Knight" which according to Chamber's Twentieth Century Dictionary, implies that he was knighted "by court favour ... not on account of his military exploits – hence an effeminate person." Yet in *The Road to Confederation,* Dr. Donald Creighton refers to his "abrupt, explosive, military ways." It was rumoured that he was an illegitimate son of Edward, Duke of Kent, and therefore a half-brother of Queen Victoria. The Duke of Kent, fourth son of George III, had been notorious for his harshness and brutality as a military commander and foppishness to the point of absurdity in private life.

Nevertheless, Williams was a favourite with Elizabeth Monck, the last person to tolerate anything "phony"; and Monck himself respected and liked him as a friend while realising his limitations.

Williams' present post was that of General Officer Commanding Imperial Forces in British North America. During his first conference with the new Governor General, he confirmed the precarious position of Canada in relation to the United States. American suspicion of Britain was matched, in Canada, by strong feeling against the "Yankees". Canadian cities were "swarming with Confederate agents and refugees" and "large sections of Canadian opinion [were] enlisted on their behalf".[1] The most trivial "incident" was likely to result in an immediate declaration of war.

Since the American civil war began, the Northern States had built an army described as having become "almost overnight, the greatest military power on earth".[2] In terrifying contrast, the Canadian forces consisted of a so-called "Active" Militia numbering 5,000 cavalry, artillery and riflemen, and of a "Sedentary" Militia. The latter were practically non-existent, since of later years they had received no training, arms, or uniforms. The Active Militia comprised two classes, "A" and "B": Class A were drilled for a certain number of days each year and received pay for these days. The number of men in that class was limited by law. Any number could join Class B, which received no pay except when called out for actual service, but the category was meaningless, since the Canadian Government allowed only enough money to arm and equip Class A. In the General's opinion, even the Active Militia was insufficiently trained to be put into the field and the Imperial garrison should be increased by a further battalion of artillery from England. However, Sir Fenwick reluctantly agreed with Monck that the arrival of fresh troops from overseas would inflame the already hostile feeling on both sides, and that for the present they must concentrate on increasing and training the Canadian Militia. With regard to numerical strength, their would be no lack of volunteers, since hostility towards the "Yankees" had aroused a martial spirit throughout the province.

Monck was pleased to be able to report to the Duke of Newcastle on the "excellent spirit" of the people of both Upper and Lower Canada, the more so because there were English politicians who believed that the Canadians would welcome annexation by the United States. If this had been true, it was no longer the case. Applications, which poured in daily from companies of volunteers anxious to be enrolled in Class B of the Militia had to be refused because of the lack of arms and of funds to supply them. To the Ministers who composed the Executive Council, Monck expressed his views on the situation in strong terms. They should aim to produce a force of 100,000 militiamen, fully trained, armed, and equipped. The Ministers professed to be in entire agreement with this proposal; nothing less would satisfy them and there would certainly be no difficulty in getting the necessary funds granted by Parliament–as soon as Parliament reassembled. Charles pointed out that short of calling a special session Parliament would not meet until March. This was a national emergency and the Executive Council would be justified in using extraordinary powers. But without a single exception, the Ministers declared such a course to be quite out of the question – the unspoken implication being that it was as much as their seats were worth. They were extremely frightened of the Yankees, but a great deal more frightened of losing votes.

A supply of arms had been promised from England but would not be sent out until the spring. It was now the beginning of November, spring seemed a long way off, and before the end of the month, the St. Lawrence would be ice-bound and closed to shipping. If war should break out during the winter, Canada would be cut off from reinforcements from England but all too accessible along the virtually undefended frontier. Before leaving England, Monck had been warned against any sudden and ostentatious preparation for war. To demand an additional battalion from home or to call a special session of Parliament would come under that heading and might provoke the very "incident" all were anxious to avoid. With this need for caution on the one hand, and his own awareness of their dangerous position on the other, Monck could only hope that events would justify the *mañana* attitude of his Ministers.

The urgent matter of railway communication was closely bound up with plans for defence. A week after Monck's arrival in Quebec, the Hon. Mr. Vankoughnet went to London as a delegate "in reference to the projected Intercolonial Railway." He carried an official despatch from Monck on the defence situation to the Colonial Office. Vankoughnet was to sail in the *North Briton*. But the *North Briton* had made her last voyage. In Monck's next letter to the Colonial Secretary he reported: "... the wreck of the steamer *North Briton* (the ship on which I came out). The ship and cargo was completely lost, but the lives of the crew and passengers were providentially preserved." The wreck had occurred in the St. Lawrence River and the efficient Vankoughnet had managed to salvage official papers and to intercept the next ship for England where he arrived after only a week's delay. Charles Monck added that:

> The loss of this fine ship will not give a very good impression of the safety of the navigation of the St. Lawrence, and affords an additional argument in favour of obtaining, as soon as possible, a secure other route ... the proposed intercolonial railway, connecting Canada with New Brunswick and Nova Scotia, apparently presenting the most feasible means of gaining that end.

Meanwhile, Elizabeth was doing her best to make her family and household comfortable in their makeshift quarters. They must be equipped with suitable clothing for the Canadian winter, which, they were told, would come early this year. Fur coats must be bought for men as well as women, and fur caps – to be worn pulled down over the forehead. They must also order fur robes as coverings in the sleighs, or "carioles," built for them by Gringras, the sleigh-maker.

Her country-bred children enjoyed the novelty of living in a garrison town. Fan could not hear the military bands and the bugle-calls, but there was always something new and interesting to be seen from the windows; the sunlight turning the spire and tin roofs to "burnished gold," the sunsets more brilliant than any they saw at home, and the ships plying up and down the river far below. There were drives into the surrounding country, to the Heights of Abraham above the city, or down to the shores of the river to visit the great timber coves; and for Henry and his sisters there was skating on the covered rink while the band played.

Elizabeth could be happy so long as her children were well and enjoying themselves, but she was not finding it altogether easy to adapt herself to her new life. Entertaining presented a problem in these temporary quarters; they were expected to start giving official dinners immediately, and anyone who came from a distance to confer with Charles had to be put up for a night or longer. Brock was being troublesome and complained ceaselessly of his assistants. Having spent most of her life on her family's country estate, Elizabeth had had no experience with domestic problems and had wondered why they were the chief topic of conversation among the ladies of Quebec. She was careful to keep this and all other difficulties from her husband, who already had more than enough to contend with.

His pre-occupation with momentous affairs did not exempt him from trivial annoyances. While despatches and letters of vital importance passed between Quebec and Washington, and between Quebec and London, a complaint on the social etiquette of Government House was made by a certain Lord Aylmer, who, in a private capacity, had come to live in Canada. He had been a guest at one of the Governor's official dinner-parties, which was also attended by members of the Canadian Executive Council. The table of precedence in Colonial Regulations laid down that Ministers of State should take precedence over all others; and when Lord Aylmer found that he was being "sent out" (sent in to dinner) after a mere "Mister," he was deeply offended and lodged a complaint. At about the same time, Charles and Elizabeth were criticized by two Canadian newspapers for accepting an invitation to visit the Ursuline Convent and Laval University. They were said to be laying themselves open to "undue Papal and French influence."

These pinpricks did not help Elizabeth to feel happier at having brought her young family to a country which might, at any moment, become a theatre of war. Unlike the children, she did not look forward to the freezing of the St. Lawrence when, with the United States hostile, they would be cut off from the outside world. Henry and his sisters had been told of the landmarks in the Quebec calendar; of the date when the last steam-boat should pass down the river and when the "ice bridge" would form and they would be able to walk or drive across the St. Lawrence to the opposite shore. They could hardly wait for the day when they would no longer go about on wheels, and the city would be gay with the sound of sleigh-bells.

Charles and Elizabeth treated their staff officers, whether married or single, as part of their own family. Colonels Irvine and Duchesnay, Captain and Mrs. Retallack, and Captain Pemberton were soon on nearly as intimate a footing with the Moncks as were the Denis Godleys and Henry Brand.

The Governor's private secretary, Denis Godley, has been described as "a hard-working official, adept at making the most of his office and its opportunities, . . . [who] earned the ungracious nickname of 'Almighty' from those who had to deal with him."[3] He shared the views of a group, known in England as the followers of Goldwin Smith and John Bright, who believed that England should sever all connection with the Colonies in general, and with Canada in particular. Godley caused grave offence in Canada by broadcasting this opinion which, he stated, was held by the Governor General. This gave rise to a persistent rumour which later was brought to Monck's notice, whereupon he flatly denied having held or expressed any such view. Some confusion may have arisen from his ardent belief in legislative independence; but to his mind it was unthinkable that Canada, or any other colony, should sever connection with the British Empire, "one of the free-est, strongest, and most progressive of the world's societies. There was no part of the province so remote that the justice derived from Westminster was not available, no part of the Empire, however distant or exotic, in which a native of the province might not serve or settle."[4] To increase the consequence of his own post, Denis Godley tried to insist that his own permission be asked before anyone could approach his chief. Monck detested ostentation, and in Canada earned a reputation for being "easy and accessible". It would be a puzzle to know why he ever put up with Godley's bumptious behaviour but for the fact that he never saw it. In the relaxed and informal atmosphere of the Moncks' family circle, Godley showed none of the pompous bustle that offended those who knew him in his official capacity.

One of the other *aides-de-camp,* Colonel J. G. Irvine, was very deaf, and Elizabeth used to worry about his health; she said he looked as if he might have a stroke and, a few years later, her gloomy prophecy came true. Captain Pemberton was an enthusiastic cricketer and a keen horseman; consequently he was young Henry's favourite among his father's staff officers.

Informal entertaining became easier when the Moncks moved to their new home in the Rue St. Louis where two houses had been made into one. Even so, it was rather on the small side considering that it was to be the temporary official Government House, including offices for Monck and his staff. There was the girls' schoolroom, presided over by Fraülein Denneler, or "Denny," and Miss Frend. The latter specialised in the teaching of deaf-mutes, so Fan's education was her particular charge. In the nursery, French Mathilde took charge of Stanley, and a separate study was provided in which Henry was ostensibly being prepared for Eton by his indulgent tutor, Mr. Wilkinson.

The Moncks' letters communicate some idea of the normal day's routine that formed the background to their social life and official receptions. At the nine-thirty breakfast, extra places would be laid for personal friends dropping in or for a Minister who had come to talk to the Governor. A good deal of the business of the day, either work or outdoor recreation, had already taken place before the family met at the breakfast table, including the family prayers.

Monck and his family were accustomed to walking several miles each day, and in the mild Irish climate, there were few days when they could not ride. During the Canadian winter, the skating rink was therefore a great blessing to them, as was the squash court where Monck and members of his staff played during their rare periods of freedom. During those first weeks, however, most days were fully occupied, either with official duties or with social engagements, both formal and informal.

The officers from the garrison were constant visitors. In their turn, the Governor and his family were invited to the frequent regimental balls, concerts, and amateur theatricals. Besides these contacts, Elizabeth had begun to make friends in Quebec. She greatly admired old Bishop Mountain, whose father had been Quebec's first Anglican Bishop. The present Bishop died early in 1863, but Elizabeth continued to be on intimate terms with his wife and family during the whole of her stay in Canada and afterwards. She also made lasting friendships with Prime Minister George-Etienne Cartier, the family of John Rose, M.P.P., and with Thomas D'Arcy McGee, the statesman and poet. McGee had been an Irish patriot and escaped to America after the defeat of the Young Irelanders' rising in 1848, but he was now a staunch supporter of the British Crown.

In addition to these public figures, Elizabeth and her daughters were on informal visiting terms with several less prominent families, and, in defiance of the more extreme Protestant press, with the French sisters at the Ursulines Convent and at the Hôtel Dieu hospital. Although Elizabeth gradually found many congenial companions, especially among the older French residents, there were some aspects of Canadian society that dismayed and repelled her. The years had taught her to be tolerant, but she had little patience with what seemed to her "bad manners," irrespective of the social rank in which it was displayed. Under this heading she classed the "Yankee" customs and slang that had seeped across the border and been assimilated by some of the British North Americans. Many of these "Yankeeisms" startled old-fashioned people in England during the first quarter of the present century, so it is small wonder that Elizabeth found it hard to adjust to them in 1861.

It was even more difficult for Elizabeth to watch her husband being badgered by the intricacies of Canadian politics on the one hand, and, on the other, by the Colonial Office, which blamed him for the vacillations and inefficiency of those over whom, officially, he had no control. Even Charles himself, who was noted for being "easy-going" and a master of understatement, gave vent to one of his rare outbursts in a letter to the Duke of Newcastle:

I am trying, as much as lies in my power, to push on preparations,

> but I must confess to you the truth, I have never had to deal with men who try my temper so much as the members of the Government here. When I see them, they enter into my views and are quite ready to do whatever I require of them; but when I send for a particular minister to consult him about some matter connected with his department and of pressing necessity, I find he is not to be found, has left Quebec, and it is uncertain when he may return. All this is rather aggravating.

In pre-Confederation days the term Union was used to describe the rather uneasy legislative partnership between Upper and Lower Canada. Government was carried on by a system of dual leadership. Thus, in 1861 George-Etienne Cartier of Lower Canada was Premier, and John Alexander Macdonald was leader of Upper Canada. There was a certain amount of friction between the two provinces, which were themselves divided politically. The Lower Canada *Rouges* and *Bleus* and the Upper Canada "Grits" and "Tories" were respectively the Liberal and Conservative parties. The maritime provinces, New Brunswick, Nova Scotia, Prince Edward Island, and Newfoundland, each had an independent government; and the British Crown was represented in each by a Lieutenant-Governor. In theory the Lieutenant-Governors were subordinate to the Governor General, but they could if they wished make direct contact with the Colonial Office in London.

In order to share in her husband's preoccupations, Elizabeth had to master a new vocabulary; that "Rep. by Pop." stood for representation by population, as opposed to equality of representation of Lower and Upper Canada, and why these two alternative methods of electing members to the Union Parliament were such a bone of contention. Lower Canada had been bitterly opposed in the past to the existing equality of representation, since it had the larger population. Both the *Rouge* and *Bleu* parties had been united in demanding that they send more members to Parliament than the sparsely populated Upper (West) Canada. However, since 1851, more people had settled in Upper Canada and the balance had altered; Lower Canadians were outnumbered by Upper Canadians now, who in their turn were pressing for Representation by Population. She had learned that both Upper and Lower Canadians felt an increasing dissatisfaction with the administration of public funds, and that Monck thought their grievance was not without foundation.

She heard these and other matters discussed in her drawing-room, since Monck was in the habit of inviting one or another of his ministers to spend an evening at his house where they would talk over their problems informally.

Their most frequent visitor was John A. Macdonald, the Attorney General for West Canada and Leader of Upper Canada. In his letters to England, Charles Monck was extremely guarded, particularly since he received a warning from one of his friends there to be cautious when replying to that prolific letter-writer, Sir William Hayter, "Everything you write to him is repeated in the London clubs." It is therefore difficult to learn his personal opinion of individual members of the Canadian Government. It is clear that he liked and admired John A. Macdonald, constantly consulted him, and had a great respect for his sound judgement and statesmanlike qualities. Judging by Macdonald's letters, the liking and respect were mutual. But because of their very different personalities, each held certain reservations about the other.

Monck's breeding and training and an instinctive dislike of ostentation, led him to under-dramatise a situation. The more other people bustled and panicked, the calmer he became. He did not mean to be irritating; it was an unconscious reflex action. In times of crisis, a display of histrionic temperament affected him in the form of that *sangfroid habituel* – later interpreted by Macdonald as being "constitutionally incapable of rising to an occasion." Monck's way of doing things did not suit Macdonald's flamboyant temperament; yet the latter's vivid personality and witty conversation made him a welcome addition to any gathering, and his clear, well-balanced assessment of the political situation was of enormous value to Monck. Macdonald had all the gifts which constitute a great statesman. Wise, subtle, and well-informed, he understood the intricacies of Canadian politics. At the same time, he had an outstanding gift for oratory. But like many another brilliant leader, flamboyant and emotional, he was not entirely reliable. Under the strain of a political crisis, he was apt to take refuge in a drinking bout, the results of which were often disastrous to his colleagues and himself. Sir Joseph Pope, Macdonald's private secretary, wrote after his death: "It would be futile to ignore the fact that there was a period in the life of Sir John Macdonald when excess in the direction I have indicated interrupted his usefulness, gave pain to his friends, and furnished his enemies with a weapon of which they never hesitated to avail themselves."[5] It is only fair to say that he had had much to contend with in his private life; the death of his elder son was followed by the death of his invalid wife.

Charles Monck was accustomed to men who drank heavily, but he could not believe that so intelligent and influential a man as Macdonald would allow such lapses to interfere with his public duties. Elizabeth, too, was a product of the Georgian rather than of the Victorian era, and far from being prudish in such matters; but she showed her displeasure when the Attorney General for West Canada visited her drawing-room at times when he would have done better to remain quietly at home. There is no record that she or her husband ever told anyone of these incidents, but their children were not so discreet – at any rate when they returned to Ireland and regaled their cousins with anecdotes of the lighter side of their life in Canada. According to the descendants of those same cousins, John A. Macdonald got himself into Elizabeth's black books by vomiting on the new chair-covers in her drawing-room. This anecdote is apocryphal; the Irish were ever loth to spoil a good story for lack of a ha'porth of exaggeration.

During these informal evenings, the subject of internal politics would give way to the equally engrossing one of the American civil war. The early victories of the South made it less likely that the Yankees would be able to turn their attention to Canada. If only this uneasy peace could be maintained till the spring, then the untrained Volunteers would at least have guns in their hands, and, if need arose, reinforcements could be sent from England. Charles was exasperated by the refusal of the Ministers to supply arms to the Volunteers, thereby wasting valuable time that could have been spent in training them. It was like sitting on a rumbling volcano, when any jolt or unwary movement might cause an eruption.

Chapter Four (1861-62)

The blow fell on November 18 when Monck received a telegram in cypher from the British Ambassador at Washington.

The incident took place on November 8, but for a week afterwards, the American Government had somehow managed to prevent the news from leaking out. The *San Jacinto*, of the United States Navy, had stopped the British mail packet *Trent* in the Bahamas Channel, boarded her, and arrested two Confederate agents, Mason and Slidell, with their secretaries. The forcible removal of civilian passengers from a neutral vessel was in itself a violation of international law; but to make matters worse, the two Southern envoys had been sent on a diplomatic mission to England to lay the Confederate case for recognition before the British Government. It was also rumoured that Captain Wilkes of the *San Jacinto* had not acted on his own initiative but with the consent and approval of the Washington Cabinet, and that news of the arrest was even now causing "exultation" in Washington. Lord Lyons telegraphed that he was awaiting "orders from home," which implied that he was packing his bags.[1] Monck and his Ministers had little doubt as to the outcome. This was it. War seemed inevitable and Canada would be involved in it immediately.

Monck had arrived in Canada on October 23; he had been in office less than three weeks; yet during that time he had summed up the military situation and had decided what he would do if given a free hand. Now, at the risk of offending his ministers and the taxpayers, he proceeded to put these ideas into action. In the crisis which became known as the "*Trent* affair", he acted quickly, shouldering the responsibility for decisions that might be criticised as unorthodox. The "*Trent* affair" was the first of many occasions when he surprised his associates by his ability to make quick decisions and to insist on their being carried out.

Since lack of equipment was the only obstacle to doubling the volunteer force, he applied to General Sir Fenwick Williams for the issue of the necessary arms, "on tick", from the Garrison ordnance stores. At the same time he demanded that the Canadian ministers pass an Order-in-Council, guaranteeing payment for the arms at the next session of Parliament. Sir Fenwick gave his full support and placed the arms under his control at the Governor's disposal. It was an unorthodox procedure, but Monck was certain that the present emergency justified it. "I take entirely upon myself any risk that may attach to the suggesting and carrying out this arrangement,"[2] he assured the General.

Monck also ordered the despatch of three government steamboats to Kingston to guard Lake Ontario. A treaty signed in 1817 forbade putting armed vessels, from either side, on the Lakes; but the necessary armaments were already at Kingston, and the boats could be equipped with them if war broke out. However, since the canals between Montreal and Kingston were frozen, this plan was abandoned. During the same week, Monck learned that the Americans had withdrawn their own cruisers from the Lakes for service on the Atlantic seaboard. This made the danger less pressing, but he sent measurements of all the locks on the canals to the Colonial Secretary in case it should be necessary to send gunboats from England. Monck suggested that some of these should be conveyed by rail, in sections, to Collingwood and put together there, and launched on the Upper Lakes, above the Niagara Falls.

The Canadian government placed their official engineer under the command of Sir Fenwick Williams. Williams set off for Toronto to plan the construction of earthworks for the defence of Toronto and Kingston and the erection of a redoubt, with blockhouse inside, at the entrance of the Welland Canal to Lake Erie. A *tête du pont* was constructed on the great new Victoria Bridge at Montreal, then a marvel of engineering. The fortifications at the Isle aux Noix near Montreal, then used as a reformatory, were again put into use and garrisoned by soldiers. On Williams's suggestion, the Customs House officers along the frontier were used as intelligence agents to transmit information about movements on the American side. Thirty-eight thousand militiamen, composed of a company from each battalion of the Militia, began training for permanent service. As soon as these could be formed into battalions, a second company was to be withdrawn from each battalion, "and so on, until if necessary the whole population will be in arms and disciplined," Monck wrote to Newcastle. The volunteers were coming forward in great numbers and he aimed to muster a force of 100,000 men. He reported that in Quebec itself, the greater part of the merchants, clerks, *etc.*, were spending all their leisure time drilling, and that it was the same all through Canada, "from one end of the Province to the other." Though still hoping that war would be avoided, he was determined to take full advantage of the present warlike fervour to hasten defence work and train volunteers. At the same time, it was necessary to be on guard lest the excitement in the country should get out of control and lead to the kind of "incident" that would make war inevitable. The Canadians were longing to get at the "Yankees," and so was Sir Fenwick Williams. Monck admitted to the Colonial Secretary that he had difficulty convincing the old General of the fact that "we are not at war."

This was not the only "difficulty" connected with Sir Fenwick. Two weeks after the emergency arose, he offered the services of himself and his staff to reorganise the Canadian Militia. As Commander-in-Chief of Imperial Forces in Canada he had no official connection with the Militia. Before replying to this "most handsome offer," Monck consulted his Ministers and found them so strongly opposed to the idea that he was faced with the delicate task of refusing the offer. He could not afford to offend members of the government before the passage of the vitally important Militia Bill; but no more could he afford to upset the impetuous Sir Fenwick, commander of the British troops on which the immediate safety of the country depended. He compromised by telling Williams he would "hold over" his offer for the present.

The correspondence does not indicate just why the ministers refused to tolerate the idea of Williams in command of the Militia, though there are several possible reasons. He was considered autocratic and opinionated by some people. Others regarded him as a figure of fun and were sceptical about his reputation for gallantry on the battlefield. Edward Watkin, sent out from England to reorganise the Grand Trunk Line and support the project for an Intercolonial Railway, coupled Williams with Monck in his scathing remarks on the present administration of Canada.

> I keep asking myself what *could* happen in case of any breach with the United States with such a Governor and such a Military Chief. The former is a jolly, wellbred Irishman and nothing more; the latter is a worn out old roué who *might* get the 10,000 men the Iron Duke spoke of *into* Hyde Park, but who never could get them out again.

Watkin's prejudice against Williams could not have arisen because he served in the British Army, since no objection was made to Colonel Lysons.[3] He was sent out from England at Monck's request to act as Adjutant General of the Canadian Militia.

Ever since he arrived in Canada, Monck had been pressing the Home Government to send him an experienced military adviser for that purpose and was relieved when he heard that Lysons was on his way. Apart from Lysons' professional value, his arrival saved Monck from having to appoint an Adjutant General "on the opinion of others, and I am afraid even at this crisis other considerations than the public advantage might influence those on whom I should be forced to rely." Monck was determined to prevent the appointment from being treated as an affair of political patronage which might have been the case had he relied on his political advisers. In those days members of the Government were inclined to treat the holding of government office as an opportunity to provide comfortable jobs for their friends. He also wrote of the patriotic enthusiasm which was sweeping the country. No longer hampered by his Ministers' fears of sticking their necks out – "I have *carte blanche* to do what I think right".

Each of his letters home ended with an urgent request for information as to how the news of the "*Trent* affair" had been received in England. The United States' Minister in London reported to Washington that, "English feeling is almost out of control. The people are frantic with rage, and were the country polled, I fear 999 men out of every thousand would declare for immediate war. Lord Palmerston cannot resist the impulse if he would."[4] Lord Palmerston told Queen Victoria that an American general had arrived in Paris to propose that France join the Northern States in war against England, offering in return "the restoration of the French Province of Canada." The same general had stated that the seizure of the Southern envoys had been planned and ordered by the Washington Cabinet.[5]

On November 29, the Foreign Secretary submitted to the Queen the draft of a despatch for Lord Lyons to deliver to William Seward, the American Secretary of State. The British Minister was to demand the release of Messrs. Mason and Slidell – with an apology – within seven days. "In case these requirements should be refused, Lord Lyons should ask for his passports."[6] Russell's despatch, which amounted to an ultimatum, was intercepted and revised by the Prince Consort – the last official action of his life. He modified the defiant wording to an assumption that Captain Wilkes had not acted under instructions, that a mistake had been made, and that the United States Government would doubtless wish to offer "such redress as alone could satisfy this country, *viz*. the restoration of the unfortunate passengers and a suitable apology."[7] This gave the Washington Cabinet time to cool off, as well as an opportunity to climb down without losing face.

On the other side of the Atlantic, Charles Monck shared the Prince Consort's conviction that the fact of being "in the right" did not in itself justify sending thousands of men to their deaths. While urging for the preparations for war, he wrote to the Duke of Newcastle that he sincerely hoped and thought they would prove unnecessary: "I see a great deal of the American press, and it strikes me that their tone generally is not so swaggering as I expected it would have been. They seem inclined to rest on the fact that Captain Wilkes acted on his own responsibility."

Monck told Newcastle that his Finance Minister, Alexander Galt, had been to Washington and, while there had an interview with President Lincoln:

> The latter expressed his wish and intention to maintain friendly relations with England. Someone who was by said rather sharply: "What about Mason and Slidell?" on which Mr. Lincoln turned to him very abruptly and said: "There will be no quarrel about that; I guess we'll fix it."
>
> I am afraid [Monck added], however this cause of dispute may end, we shall have to fight them sooner or later.[8]

Monck was not the only one to hold this view, and his next instructions from the Colonial Office were to prepare barrack accommodation and make provision for a safe passage up the river for eleven battalions of regular troops already on their way from England to Quebec. Welcome though this news was, it raised an immediate problem.

Canada, unlike the maritime provinces, had no winter port. When the St. Lawrence became ice-bound, passengers disembarking at Halifax, Nova Scotia, could only reach Quebec by way of Portland in the United States. In spite of the late winter that year, the passage of the troop-bearing *Persia* across the Atlantic became a race against climatic conditions as much as against a possible outbreak of war. It was easy enough for the Colonial Office to issue orders regarding safety precautions for the passage of the ship up the St. Lawrence where navigation was made dangerous by the numerous islands and submerged rocks. By the time it was known in Quebec that the troops were on the way, the upper reaches of the river were already ice-bound, and it was impossible to send craft down the river to relight the lighthouses which had already been extinguished "for the season." Monck and Sir Fenwick Williams made minute enquiries on the safety of shipping passage to Rivière du Loup, and elaborate arrangements were made there for troop disembarkment. These plans were thrown into confusion when the officer sent from Quebec to assist in the disembarkation reported that the *Persia* had anchored at Bic still further down the river, in spite of:

> . . . the river being (apparently) clear of ice, the day fine, and noth-

ing (as far as I could ascertain) preventing a steamship getting from Bic to Rivière du Loup. At Bic there is nothing deserving the name of a landing place, and the disembarkation was performed with great difficulty not unaccompanied by danger. At Rivière du Loup, there is a fine Pier with Stairs and Slips ... and twenty canoes, with boatmen, brought there expressly from Quebec, were waiting to assist the disembarkation ... and I have no doubt that she [the *Persia*] could have landed the *whole* of the Troops and Stores, and left the river as soon, if not sooner, than she did.

On December 28, Monck wrote to the Colonial Office:

> I think it right to bring before you, in order that, if you see fit, you may have it investigated, the conduct of the commander of the *Persia*. He arrived at Bic where, as I told you yesterday, there are no facilities for landing either men or stores. Immediately that I heard he had anchored there, I telegraphed to ascertain the state of the river and Rivière du Loup. The report was perfectly satisfactory. With the concurrence of General [Sir Fenwick] Williams, I ordered the ship up there .... The Captain of the ship distinctly refused to obey the orders. Yesterday he landed the greater part of the men at Bic ... and put out to sea carrying with him about a hundred officers and men, and the greater part of the stores and baggage. I *believe* the men landed with their knapsacks and blankets, but without their arms. I hear, by another telegram from Father Point, that he has passed that place going eastward, and he will probably be next heard of at Halifax. He may have done quite right in all this, but if he had come on at once to Rivière du Loup on Thursday, he might have landed all the troops there in a few hours, as also the baggage and stores, and so saved considerable expense to the Govt and hardship to the men. I have at the same time the gratifying news that the population around Bic have crowded in this morning with offers of assistance of all sorts. I understand they (the troops) have 1,000 sleighs and horses placed at their disposal.[9]

It was largely due to the prompt cooperation of the civilian population that the British troops of the 62nd Regiment were not left stranded indefinitely at Bic, and the same invaluable assistance was given to those landed at St. John. In the storms and extreme cold of January, 1862, 7,000 men were transported in sleighs from northern New Brunswick, through the snow-choked Madawaska Road, to Rivière du Loup, and from thence to Montreal.

Meanwhile much of their baggage, with the remainder of the troops and a hundred officers and men for Canada, had been dumped at Halifax in Nova Scotia. Sir Fenwick Williams asked Monck's authority to accept a contract offered by Messrs. Allan and Edmonstone, the great shipping firm, to convey the baggage, excluding "warlike stores" to Montreal. Although this involved taking it across United States territory, Monck agreed to the proposal since it was the normal route. This decision, however, resulted in a bombardment of "Lord Lyons to Lord Monck" coded telegrams from Washington:

> Consul at Portland informs me that Mr. Seward has given permission to British troops and stores to land there. I knew nothing of it. I do not think we should ask or avail ourselves of this permission without directions from home.

Monck was puzzled by this communication since there had been no question of sending either troops or army stores by that route and arrangements were already being made for their slow and laborious transport across New Brunswick. Neither had he authorised anyone to apply to the Secretary of State for permission, which would be unnecessary in the case of transport of ordinary baggage. Enquiries showed that the contracting firm had, without consulting the Canadian authorities, applied to Washington for this permission. In reply, they had received the following telegram from Seward who did not share his President's friendly intentions towards the British: "No objection, even for munitions of war or soldiers." Seward's message savoured of arrogance if meant to be taken seriously, of insolence if intended as a joke. Lord Lyons telegraphed: "Does not this unasked favour appear as if intended for a boast or a sneer? Ought we to accept from the U.S. permission to carry through their country warlike stores which we might turn against them?" "Very unpleasant remarks have been made on the subject both in the newspapers and in Congress," he wrote later.

The exchange of telegrams interspersed with despatches, mostly at cross purposes, continued for several days.

The affair having been taken up by the American press, Monck wrote a full account of the proceedings to the Duke of Newcastle, which he concluded by saying:

> I wished to let you know about this as soon as possible as the matter has got into the papers, and you might see some statement in reference to it not founded on fact. ... I have just had a letter from General Williams in which he tells me that the first division of the 62nd Regt had arrived at Montreal, having crossed New Brunswick without any accident or difficulty, with the exception of a few desertions, not numerous as yet.

To Lord Lyons he wrote:

> The troops are now arriving in considerable numbers from Halifax via New Brunswick. The only casualties I have as yet heard of have been a few deserters to which every inducement is held out by the Yankee borderers. Is it possible Mr. Seward may have expected to add a regular body of troops to the U.S. Army by this process?[10]

But Monck had not heard the last of the muddle arising from the "ill-judged action" of the contractors who transported the troops' baggage. It was all part of the day's work to reply to queries and criticisms from the Canadian Ministers, the Colonial Office in London, and the British Minister in Washington; but he might have been excused for showing impatience when he received on February 1, an officious demand for an explanation from that compulsive letter-writer, the Lieutenant-Governor of New Brunswick. The Hon. Arthur Hamilton Gordon is described by Donald Creighton as having "a very large capacity for disapproval and criticism. Finding fault was something he did frequently and well."[11]

Gordon's father, the Earl of Aberdeen, had been Prime Minister in England from 1852 to 1858 and had been greatly respected by W. E. Gladstone and others. For the father's sake, they tolerated the conceited ways and bad manners of the son. Arthur Gordon had been appointed to New Brunswick at the same time that Monck had been offered the Governor Generalship. Gordon, ten years younger than Monck, had accepted the post with enthusiasm, only to find that in a self-governing province, a Lieutenant-Governor had little prestige and less power. During the term of his Lieutenant-Governorship and long afterwards, he was familiarly known as "Thy Servant Arthur" – "from his having given directions that he should be publicly prayed for (in the prayer for the Royal Family) under that appellation."[12] If the Anglican clergy of the province carried out his instruction, it was his only cause for satisfaction, since he detested the climate and despised the provincial politicians who held the reins of government. He nursed a permanent grudge against Monck because he resented being in a (nominally) subordinate position to the Governor General and was irritated by the latter's refusal to quarrel with him. To his frequent provocative and even offensive letters, Charles Monck replied with unfailing good humour and defended Gordon when his troublesome behaviour annoyed the Colonial Office. Gordon did not confine his criticisms to their personal correspondence, but in letters to other people, he accused Monck of being a mere automaton entirely devoid of originality, and a weak character completely ruled by his private secretary, Denis Godley, who was Gordon's *bête noire*. Extracts from Gordon's letters have been published, and his opinion of Monck quoted by Canadian historians who did not have access to a letter from General Sir Hastings

Doyle[13] to Monck describing "Thy Servant Arthur" as "a self-conceited individual, with a good share of *talent,* but no ballast or common sense!"[14]

To Gordon's letter of February 1, Charles Monck replied: "I wish to set you right upon a matter of fact with regard to which I must have expressed myself very clumsily in order to have so completely misled you." This was followed by a brief account of the true facts of the case, ending: "This is the whole story and I should be sorry you continued under the impression that General Williams had had anything to say to the communication with the U.S. Govt."[15]

Before this seemingly interminable correspondence had died down, the original cause of the crisis was removed; on Christmas Day the United States Government released the Confederate agents, and "disavowed" Captain Wilkes – which was the nearest they could bring themselves to making an apology. In writing home Monck expressed his fear that having been made to "climb down" had intensified the Americans' grudge against the British. He was glad to be able to report that the majority of British North Americans shared his view, and that there was no slackening in the efforts to improve defences.

Previously, Monck had found himself between two fires: the Canadian Government argued that defence should be undertaken by Imperial troops, and, if supplemented by an increased militia, that the expense should be borne by the Home Government, the Colonial Office insisted that the defence of Canada should, at least in part, be the responsibility of Canadians. Now, all this had changed and it seemed to him likely that a Militia Bill would be unopposed when the Union Parliament reassembled on March 21. Monck had appointed John A. Macdonald Special Minister for Militia Affairs, to ensure priority being given to revision of Militia law in the next session of Parliament. Defects in the present system were daily brought to Monck's notice. For example, there was no law to forbid the export of military stores, even in time of war.

Monck learned that he had been over-optimistic to assume the ministers shared his conviction that they should continue to be on the alert. In the comparative calm following the storm over the "*Trent* affair," it became evident that they would be reluctant to vote for the amount of money required for the force Monck intended to raise: 50,000 men drilled for a certain period of each year, with "permanent machinery" to enable an additional 50,000 to be in training if the first batch should be called out for actual service. Already a force of 40,000 had been built, absorbing nearly all the past year's receipts from the province, and Charles was informed that it would be difficult to extract "any large increase" from the taxpayers.

With the arrival from England of Colonel Lysons in January 1862, a new impetus was given to defence work. Accompanied by some officers from the regular British army, Lysons became a member of the Commission, sanctioned by the Governor General, to consider the reorganisation of the Militia and to prepare a Militia Bill. Newcastle had written to congratulate Monck on what had already been achieved, at the same time suggesting that the War Office be asked to send out a number of senior officers, subalterns, and drill sergeants to help in training the Militia. Monck replied that though the senior officers and drill sergeants would be invaluable as instructors, he had no need at present for additional junior officers. Already he was receiving applications from retired army officers, now in Canada, seeking employment in the Militia, and it was difficult to find employment even for the officers who had come out with Colonel Lysons. Had war broken out, they would have been indispensable: and there would be plenty for them to do when the Militia should be put on its new footing.

One of Monck's reasons for appointing Colonel Lysons as Adjutant General was to ensure important military posts being filled by order of merit, not for the convenience of politicians. But the officers must be Canadians, not men sent out from England.

Monck had an opportunity for encouraging the Canadians to pull their weight with regard to defence, and in all his letters to England he stressed their readiness to do so. For the time being, however, a certain amount of outside help was necessary, and when Monck next wrote to the Duke, he asked if it would be possible for the British Government to help in providing either arms or uniforms or both – at least in the early stages. This was followed by another letter in which he stated his case even more persuasively. He knew that his request would be an unpopular one and that the British Government was unwilling to contribute to the peacetime defence of Canada. He assured the Duke that the Canadians understood this and had every intention of being self-supporting in that respect; but would it not be possible to meet them half way? They were drawing up a Militia Bill which would necessitate heavy expense, and this was going to be a great shock to Parliament. A concession from England would make all the difference to their reception of the Bill. Once again, he emphasised the willingness of the Canadians to stand on their own feet with regard to peacetime defence; the men were even prepared to pay for their own uniforms; but it was necessary to provide "machinery" which would be called on in case of war, and it was here that help was needed. Canada was prepared to make a supreme effort. Surely she deserved a little encouragement in the initial stage. Finally the Duke yielded, on the understanding that a "strong Militia Bill" would be presented and passed, thereby showing that Canada meant business.

Before the arrival of Colonel Lysons, Monck had depended chiefly on Sir Fenwick Williams for military advice. "His personal kindness to me since I arrived here has been very great, and his self-sacrificing zeal and energy are beyond praise," he wrote afterwards to Newcastle. However, occasional problems arose from his having relied too heavily on the advice of the old General. Before the arrival of Lysons, Monck had instructed some of the more experienced among the regular army officers to examine and report on Williams's plans for defence works along the frontier and waterways. This step had to be explained very tactfully in a personal letter from himself to the General. After examination, the officers stated very bluntly that the General's darling project – the works on the Welland Canal – would, while costing a great deal, be "ineffectual for their proposed object". This put Monck in an awkward position. He was responsible for the defence of the country and, in this case, for the proper use of public money. In a second letter to Williams which was a masterpiece of diplomacy, he managed to get the work stopped without hurting the General's feelings.

He also took special pains to assure the Duke that the apparent lack of response in Lower Canada to the call for volunteers for the Militia did not arise from any reluctance to serve. The reverse was the case; and although the French population refused to adopt the volunteering system, he thought they were quite ready to serve if selected by ballot. He enclosed a copy of a "*Mandement*" (Mandate) issued by the Roman Catholic Bishop who evidently regarded a possible conflict with the United States as a Holy War:

> Nous avons la confiance, nos Très-Chers Frères, que partout l'on empressera de répondre à l'appel du Représentant de notre gracieuse Souveraine . . . Tous nos jeunes gens doivent donc avoir à coeur, en ce moment, de servir une si noble cause . . . Quant même le danger que nous appréhendons viendrait à se dissiper, nous ne pouvons toutefois nous dissimuler que de nouvelles difficultés peuvent surgir, à la première occasion, et nous obliger à prendre les armes.[16]

The surviving letters written by Monck during the crisis known as the "*Trent* affair" are all official ones dealing with military matters and the political and international situation. The personal correspondence of the family has all been lost as has the diary-letter that Elizabeth sent home periodically to her sisters. Consequently we can only imagine the excitement of the children as they watched, fascinated, the drilling of the troops and all the preparations for war and the very different feelings experienced by their mother. With four children, the youngest three-years-old and the eldest a deaf-mute, it was only natural that she should be dismayed by the prospect of imminent invasion, especially with her knowledge of the inadequate defences. As a girl, Elizabeth had been considered rather too daring by some of her sisters; hardy and active, entirely free from the swoons and "vapours" affected by many of her contemporaries. But, as often happens, motherhood brought with it a new vulnerability as if she were conscious of having, indeed, "given hostages to fortune." She to whom "nerves" as such had been unknown, became excessively nervous about her children. Previous deaths of three of her children had increased Elizabeth's anxiety about the safety and well-being of the remaining four. Owing to her ingrained habit of self-control, she was usually able to conceal her fears; but her relief must have been great when the immediate crisis subsided, although it might be no more than a temporary respite. Her husband could not reassure her on that point since his main object was to emphasise the necessity for increased defence. The family was in danger so long as civil war raged on the other side of the border, and it is easy to understand why, in the privacy of the family circle, Elizabeth occasionally expressed the wish that they had never left Ireland.

However every day in old Quebec brought fresh interests. Now settled into the house in the Rue St. Louis, they were looking forward to their first Canadian Christmas, which promised to be gayer and more festive than any they had been accustomed to. But a few days before Christmas, their preparations were halted by a telegram from England announcing the death of the Prince Consort.

Unknown to anyone but himself, Prince Albert had been a sick man when he had redrafted Russell's despatch to Washington a fortnight before. But for his intervention, the original would almost certainly have led to war between England and the United States. After completing the writing of the revised despatch, he had collapsed. His death came as a great shock to the Royal Family as well as to the general public.

Since the Governor General was the Queen's representative, it was necessary for his household to observe court mourning. Consequently, the Moncks' first Christmas in Canada was a quiet one. The children were debarred from attending the annual festivities which included a Rink Ball, when the rink was:

> . . . lit with gas, and decorated with flags and ornaments; there were tables with refreshments on the ice, and the regimental band playing. It looked like a fair in a Dutch picture; most of the girls wore *very short* red petticoats, and grey or black dresses; some wore scarlet and some white feathers in their fur caps, and most of the officers were in their mess uniforms, dancing quadrilles, lancers, or valses.[17]

Carioles (sleighs) were now the only means of transport. The roads were first ploughed, then rolled, and their boundaries marked by small fir-trees stuck in the snow. Even so, there were occasional upsets caused by the frequent holes, *cahots*, in the roads. There was constant traffic on the ice-bridge, the term used to describe the frozen surface of the St. Lawrence. The best routes on this, either up or down the river or across to the opposite shore, were indicated by little fir-trees, as in the roads on the land. Charles Monck wrote home enthusiastic descriptions of the country, its climate, and its winter sports. "Henry has become a first-rate skater," he wrote to his Wicklow neighbour, Sir George Hodson:

> It has been a great amusement to him all this winter. It is carried on here in a large wooden building like a riding house, called a rink, as from the quantity of snow the ice out of doors is unpracticable. Sleighing also is a great amusement here in winter, indeed it is more than an amusement as it is the only way we have of going about, as you cannot use wheeled carriages. As long as the snow is deep and the frost hard, it is a very pleasant mode of travelling and you can go along very quickly . . . The scenery about here is most beautiful, and I think your artist's eye would be well rewarded for a trip across the Atlantic by a sight of one of our sunsets. It is scarcely possible to exaggerate the intensity of the colouring on the sky in the west, and the whole country is covered with a pink tinge like the halo one sees in representations of scenes in tropical climates . . . We are suffering the effects of reaction now after the state of intense excitement in which we were kept all the winter. It was not a pleasant inauguration of my official career here.[18]

He was only too glad to exchange the atmosphere of "intense excitement" for the day-to-day routine business of a Governor, at this time punctuated by the problems of diplomacy and security peculiar to a neutral country next to a nation at war. During the two months between the satisfactory conclusion of the "*Trent* crisis" and the state opening of Parliament on March 21, Monck's chief preoccupation was with the work of the Lysons' Commission: the raising and training of troops, and the drafting of a Militia Bill by which an adequate defence force would be established by Act of Parliament.

Chapter Five (1862-63)

On March 21, 1862, Charles and Elizabeth Monck were driven to the Parliament House in a "shut sleigh" drawn by four horses. Troops lined the streets and a guard of honour awaited them at the Parliament building. Wearing the Governor General's blue and gold uniform, Monck read his speech from the throne, first in English and then in French.

"I opened the session of the Provincial Parliament yesterday," he wrote on the following day to the Duke of Newcastle. "If they can pass the Militia Bill, I shall be satisfied and, so far as I can learn, I do not think there will be any serious opposition to it." He added that he believed the Cartier-John A. Macdonald administration to be, "barring accidents, safe in its saddle for the continuance of this Parliament"; that he had now had the opportunity of seeing most of the leading politicians of all parties and considered that there was no more "political immorality" among them than existed in the Parliament at Westminster.

In reply to a letter from Arthur Gordon complaining of the low standard of political morality in New Brunswick, Monck wrote that he was "rather agreeably surprized" by what he had found in Canada. "Political men as a class are in a lower grade of society than at home, there is much less of pecuniary independence of office amongst them, but on the whole I find here more knowledge, more ability, and I think quite as much, if not more, tenderness of conscience as amongst the same class in England."[1] Of the "purity" of Canadian elections, he could not yet speak with experience, "but I believe it to be quite equal to that which prevails at home, though I am afraid that is not putting it very high."[2]

His opinion, he admitted, might be due to his own lack of acuteness. He certainly showed his lack of experience in Canadian party politics by his belief that the Opposition would defeat their object through their own tactless behaviour. The informality of the Parliament, amounting to slovenliness and disorder during debates, the members "abusing and contradicting their opponents, and throwing paper pellets at each other"[3] perhaps deceived him into assuming that the Opposition was not sufficiently serious to hinder the passing of the Militia Bill. With determined and rather naive optimism he maintained that "the best feeling appears to prevail on all sides with reference to the Militia Bill" and that he had little doubt of getting a satisfactory measure passed. He was soon to be disillusioned.

During the first fortnight of the session, the debate on his opening address was adjourned seven times. Its main theme, defence in general and the new Militia Bill in particular, was set aside in favour of subjects of internal party politics, principally that of the ever-recurring tussle: representation by population. To the Governor's amazed consternation, acrimonious discussion on that vexatious theme continued until April 7 when Parliament recessed; and the introduction of the all-important Militia Bill was delayed until May 2.

Meanwhile, by every mail, Monck was receiving peremptory letters from the Duke of Newcastle:

> A little bird from across the water has whispered in my ear that your Ministers have resolved that the Militia shall not be called out this year, and that the Bill will be delayed in order to prevent it.
>
> I do trust that this is not so . . . I fear we shall have very great difficulty in maintaining peace, and I am quite sure we shall not maintain it by soft words – bristling bayonets may prove more effectual.

But the bristling bayonets, as represented by the proposed defence scheme, were to cost between four and five hundred thousand pounds in the first year, and from £250,000 to £300,000 in the following year. John A. Macdonald, Special Minister for Militia Affairs, was equally aware of its urgency, but better informed than were Monck and Newcastle on the parlous condition of Canadian finances. He knew, too, that the growing suspicion concerning administration of public funds was not without foundation, and that during recent years there had been gross mismanagement, if not worse. It was a bad time in which to propose such a costly scheme, and his was to be the task of presenting it. Before Parliament reassembled, he had taken refuge in a drinking bout. In addition to this lapse, he was believed to have been genuinely ill, and on May 2, his introduction of the Militia Bill was made in a confused and unconvincing manner. His replies to questions concerning the cost were evasive and contradictory, thus providing an opportunity for the opponents of Militia reform to increase their following.

The Bill should have been read for the second time two weeks later, but by then Macdonald was again incapacitated, and the reading had to be postponed until May 20. "Mr. J. A. Macdonald was prevented from attending in his place in the House during the whole of last week, nominally by illness, but really, as everyone knew, by drunkenness," Monck told Newcastle; and during the interval Finance Minister Galt produced his budget, the contents of which drove the final nail into the coffin of the Militia Bill. Macdonald returned to face an Assembly that was predominantly hostile from the start. If he had been in a normal state of health, the challenge would have acted on him as a stimulant, for he was a gifted and persuasive orator. But his speech on the second reading of the Bill was as unconvincing as his first. The Bill was defeated by a majority of seven, and the Cartier-Macdonald Ministry resigned.

In a letter to the Colonial Secretary, Monck confessed to being "deeply mortified" in having to report this failure. It was the result of want of confidence in the Government rather than of hostility to the Militia Bill. During the preceding week, Galt's budget had brought to light "some very damaging revelations as to the waste of public money. . . . Administrative abuses had risen to a fearful degree. This, coupled with the "very strong feelings" of Lower Canada on representation by population had caused the adverse vote.[4] He had at first resolved to refuse to accept the resignation of the Cartier-Macdonald Government and have them appeal to the country. Upon reconsideration he decided that an election might have the effect of ratifying the vote against the Militia Bill which would entail increased taxation. Instead he adopted what appeared to him to be the only alternative: to let those who voted out the former ministers "try their hands at administering public affairs", with John Sandfield Macdonald as Premier. The depressing news of the defeat of the Bill drew a furious reply from the Duke of Newcastle, who maintained that a measure of such vital importance should not be made "a mere stalking-horse for Party warfare. Everybody in the States will look upon it as little less than an invitation to come and annex it [Canada]. The event will create as much joy in New York as it has caused concern in London."

In asking Sandfield Macdonald to form a government, Monck believed that he was taking the only possible way out of an extremely difficult situation. The government having been defeated, a Governor General had no power to keep them in office. He had to ask a member of the opposition to form a government.

The opposition had voted against the Militia Bill, but J. S. Macdonald was not among those who were prejudiced against it. Monck counted on persuading him to support the Bill, which in fact he was able to do. The new Premier had filled the office of Speaker and had been Attorney General for a short time; but he had never carried much weight, nor was he expected to do so in future. "He will have a difficult task to form an administration, and a still more difficult one to maintain himself in power", Monck wrote to Newcastle. One great point in Sandfield Macdonald's favour was that he was reasonably free from party prejudices. He was therefore, in a sense, neutral ground and the leaders of the late government were prepared to support him. He had begun by pressing for a prorogation of Parliament or, at least, for a long adjournment; but Monck obtained a pledge from him that Parliament should not be prorogued before the subject of defence had been dealt with.

Thus, at last, as the result of constant pressure from the Governor, a Militia Bill was passed in June 1862, but it was a Militia Bill hardly worthy of the name. The original defence scheme had been whittled down till it was barely recognisable. It now consisted only of a considerable development of the volunteer system, to which Parliament voted an increase of $166,000 over the previous year's provision. Monck knew that this was hopelessly inadequate, but it was at least a beginning that could be developed into something stronger at a future date. In fact, a revised and more efficient Militia Bill was to be passed a year later.

Besides his own personal disappointment and sense of failure, the Governor had to face another blast from the Colonial Secretary, who declared that reliance on an improvement of the volunteer system was no better than "a delusion." This was followed by an avalanche of reproachful letters containing abuse of the new Government. Monck could not but agree. He had maintained his good opinion of Cartier, John A. Macdonald, and their associates, but admitted that he was disappointed in Sandfield Macdonald and his colleagues, "... a wretched lot. Not one of them is capable of rising above the level of a parish politician, and they are led away by all the small jealousies and suspicions to which minds of that class are prone." He made the same criticism when writing to Edward Ellice, though he admitted that his present "advisers" were "more anxious to do what is right" than their predecessors whom he described as having been "jobbing and corrupt" with regard to finance. Of the Minister for Finance, however, he wrote: "Galt is an able man and at all events understands what he is about."[5] He believed that the people of Canada were in advance of the Ministry on the subject of Colonial defence, especially those who were of British descent. "Among the French population there is a strong feeling in favour of British connection, but I am afraid that means, in their minds, British protection."

At Monck's request, Newcastle sent a despatch to be read to the ministers. In return, they submitted to him a "Report" they intended to present to the Canadian Parliament. The report implied that the Colonial Secretary sought to "curtail the rights of the people and the Legislature". "All I can say is that it is replete with *bunkum*", exploded the Duke,[6] who had never accustomed himself to Canada being self-governing, and held that the Governor General should be able to coerce his Ministers.

A different tone was adopted in personal letters from those members of the British Government who were Charles Monck's personal friends. Their letters showed how well they understood his difficulties and quoted any words of praise for Monck's "tact and firmness" which they heard in the House of Commons or read in the newspapers. Moreover Charles Adderley (soon to be Under-Secretary for the Colonies) had seen the Duke's despatch on Canadian defence which he described as "petulant". "You have indeed a trial before you", he wrote to Monck, "and so far have proved adequate to it; and Constitutional Government after all requires tact and knowledge of men which I think you have."[7]

A visit to Montreal to review the troops should have made a welcome change from politics. But at a city banquet given in Monck's honour, the Mayor of Montreal began his speech of welcome with some very unfortunate remarks. While the guest of honour listened to a complacent description of Canada as a land "free from taxes, protected at the expense of the Mother Country," he had to concoct an *extempore* speech and present what he considered to be the true state of affairs without seeming to be ungracious to his hosts. He began by declaring that it would be "madness" not to recognise the extent of America's naval and military resources and quoted Lord Palmerston's words: "If you want to preserve your independence, and at the same time your friendship, with a great neighbouring power, you can only accomplish that object by being perfectly prepared to defend yourselves from attack." If Canada should be attacked, Monck continued, the whole forces of the Empire would come to her aid. But, he added:

> ... England cannot, alone, supply men to defend Canada; the strong armies which must be arrayed against the enemy must come from the people of Canada themselves. I am perfectly satisfied from the spirit I have witnessed among the people ... that they will not be found wanting should the day of danger unhappily arise.

It was very plain speaking to come from a Governor General. The press in Canada were somewhat taken aback, though in general they approved of Monck's speech. The incident also gave rise to a good deal of comment in the English press, in which the Mayor's introduction and Monck's reply to it were reported. In a debate in the British House of Commons there was a special mention of the latter, "... which indeed all praised as being very manly and wise, and at the same time moderate," wrote Adderley. "You have indeed been thrown in a difficult and important task. Perhaps the solution of the great problems of our present Colonial Empire."[8]

Monck's Montreal speech was even approved by the Duke of Newcastle who wrote:

> I read it with much interest and satisfaction, because it contains a bold, sensible and manly exposition of the duty of Canada in the present conjuncture, and a clear and complete answer to the miserable half-hearted twaddle with which the Mayor of Montreal introduced your name to the Company.

Monck had spoken bluntly in support of Imperial policy; but his letters to the Colonial Office showed that he was able to understand and sympathise with the Canadian point of view, even if he could not agree with it. The majority of Canadians considered that, in the event of an outbreak of war, the only danger to their country lay in her connection with Great Britain; therefore Great Britain should provide adequate defence. Those who took a longer view were aware of the danger of annexation by the United States and that Canada's independence could be secured only if the country were prepared to defend itself. The present Ministry did not include many far-sighted men, and few – if any – of them were willing to risk losing office by taking an unpopular line.

The various political crises and reactions to his Montreal speech kept Monck on the alert. However, his correspondence with the Colonial Office was not confined to political reports. For example, in August, 1862, he wrote accounts of three "atrocious military murders" that occurred in the garrison within two months. In one case a private soldier "deliberately loaded his carbine and shot his victim (a sergeant) on parade, in the presence of all his comrades." The other murders followed the same pattern, and Monck deplored the fact that under the existing Mutiny Act, Courts Martial had "no power to try for *murder* under any circumstances." To avoid handing them over to the civil authorities, which would keep them waiting for trial till the following January, it would be necessary for the Governor to issue a special Commission. The law officers had advised against this latter course, informing Monck that "the juries here are not to be depended on."

Monck asked the Colonial Secretary to recommend that the Mutiny Act be altered, to enable Courts Martial to try murders committed by a soldier on duty. Within the year, his suggestion was taken up by the War Office and resulted in an amendment of the Mutiny Act. In the meantime the Duke of Newcastle wrote: "I hope the mania for military murders in Canada has now subsided, as it appears to have done here."

The month of August was further enlivened by various minor skirmishes on the United States frontier. A party of Royal Canadian Riflemen while "boating" on the lake near Niagara were fired on from the shore. The American sentries automatically shot at any boat that did not immediately pull to land when hailed by them. From then on, boating on the lakes was forbidden to soldiery, since the avoidance of "collision" was of the first importance. This was becoming increasingly difficult.

The problems of neutrality continued to multiply. A large number of Canadians had been employed in the United States before the civil war broke out. Some of these, returning to Canada, were seized at the frontier by American officers and forced to pay five dollars before they were released. That sum was the "bounty" offered as reward for the capture of deserters from the Federal Army, of which there had been a great many. The seizure and detention of Canadian civilians as "deserters" from the Northern army was easy bounty for the United States officers, but this practice naturally led to "disturbances" along the frontier. On one such occasion, a young Canadian, having learned that his brother was being held prisoner in the State of Vermont, collected a band of his neighbours and planned to cross the border by night and effect a rescue. The plan was discovered and stopped just in time; and the Governor General requested that "steady persons" be sent to the trouble spots on the frontier to rectify matters without provoking an "incident."

The urgent need of railway communication between the port of Halifax and Quebec was illustrated during the previous winter when the British troops had been conveyed across country by means of sleighs. Monck, on behalf of his government, invited the Lieutenant-Governors of Nova Scotia and New Brunswick to visit him to discuss the construction of an intercolonial railway. At the beginning of September, 1862, they arrived in Quebec, with their respective ministers. Monck had written to Arthur Gordon, Lieutenant-Governor of New Brunswick:

> I hope we shall be able to do something effectual about the Railroad and the Trade between the three Provinces. There is a third subject–the Union of the British North American Provinces–which

> is also to be considered on the basis of a resolution passed last year by Mulgrave's Parliament. Which of us is to be the survivor if this measure is to be carried into effect?[9]

A souvenir of the occasion has survived in a photograph of the three bearded Governors, Monck, Mulgrave, and Gordon, posed with their *aides-de-camp* on the citadel at Quebec. Lord Mulgrave, Lieutenant-Governor of Nova Scotia, was soon to retire from his post. He returned to England to look after his estates when Lord Normanby, his father died.

The three-cornered conference proceeded amicably enough, and it was agreed that delegates from all three provinces be sent to London to discuss the construction of an intercolonial railway. The railway was to be subsidised by a loan offered by the British Government, and Monck wrote to Newcastle that there had been prolonged discussions on the proportions of the debt for which each province should be liable. Eventually it was decided that Canada should pay five-twelfths, the remaining seven-twelfths to be shared between New Brunswick and Nova Scotia.

The three Governors also discussed the possible Union of British North America; but the Colonial Secretary decided that the intercolonial railway must take priority over legislative union. However, no attempt could be made to assess the cost of the proposed railway until a preliminary survey was carried out. This would take place after the delegates returned from London.

Before the delegates sailed for England, the Governor General and his family set out on a month's tour of what was then formally called Canada West. It is hard to believe now that visits to Niagara Falls, Kingston, Toronto, Woodstock, London, Sarnia, Guelph, and Goderich could have been considered a tour of western Canada. Their party included the Prime Minister, John Sandfield Macdonald, other Ministers, and General Napier, the Assistant Adjutant-General. Monck had tried to persuade Arthur Gordon to accompany them, but the invitation was not accepted.

Leaving Quebec on September 16, the party travelled by steamer and railway to Niagara Falls. From there, the party travelled by special train to Hamilton and were met by a guard of honour from the Rifle Brigade. The procession ended at the Mechanics' Hall where Monck received addresses from, and replied to the Mayor and Corporation, the Board of Trade, and the Mechanics' Institute (which he praised for their help to industry and education). After a reception at the Royal Hotel, the Moncks were entertained by the Hon. Isaac Buchanan, M.P.P., at Auchman House.

The *Globe* said of the visit, "Our new Governor possesses the happy knack of placing those who meet him quite at their ease . . . His manners are very gracious and tactful . . . He does not notice mistakes." As an illustration of that "happy knack," the same correspondent noted that Monck "even made Buchanan laugh at Auchman House," that prominent local worthy being notable for his somewhat forbidding manner.

To mark the occasion, there was a great military parade: the Militia, the First and Second Wentworth Cavalry, the First and Second Volunteer Rifles, the Highland Rifles, and the Volunteer Battery of Artillery. At a review of the Volunteers, Elizabeth presented colours to the "Royals".

In spite of being a civilian, Monck took a deep personal interest in the Canadian Militia and Volunteers. Ever since he arrived in Canada, he had thrown himself wholeheartedly into the work of developing Canada's military strength; Monck now had an opportunity to inspect the results of his efforts. During his tour, most of his addresses contained references to defence, praising what had been done and urging them on to still greater efforts. Not only in the large towns, but also at small stations at which his train halted, the local corps would be drawn up to receive him. "Monck, in almost every instance, contrived with rare adroitness to learn conditions."[10]

After visits to Woodstock, London, and Dundas, they went on to Toronto to witness the usual Guard of Honour and military display, presentations, and receptions. Wearing his blue and gold Governor General's uniform, Monck held a levée at the City Hall, which was said to be "the most brilliant affair ever held in Toronto" and a great improvement on the one held for the Prince of Wales, in 1860.

After a troop review on Spadina Avenue, the Governor, Prime Minister, and party, visited the Deaf and Dumb Institute, in which the Moncks had a special interest; the University of Toronto, the Normal School, the Horticultural Gardens, the Mechanics' Institute, the Roman Catholic House of Providence, and the Provincial Agricultural Exhibition.

Throughout this tour, Monck displayed particular interest in agricultural development. "I have been both surprized and delighted with what I have seen," he wrote to Edward Ellice. "The grandeur and natural beauty of the country are most striking, and the advances which have been made in settlement and in the general appearance of farming are very remarkable." He noted that the stock shown at the Toronto Cattle Show compared "not disadvantageously" with Royal Shows at home. "I say this with some authority, as I have all my life been a practical farmer myself, and been very much engaged in cattle shows at home." "Whenever the occasion arose on his tour, Monck described himself as "a practical farmer", which may have surprised those who had heard of him as connected only with politics.

There was an even greater surprise in store. At Osgoode Hall, he was admitted to the bar by inferment of an honorary degree. During the ceremony he was asked: "What is the highest estate known to the law of the land?" and promptly replied: "A fee simple." Few of those present knew that he had been a barrister.

During the formal part of the tour, Elizabeth had accompanied her husband; but at the end of September she and the children returned to Niagara Falls and remained at Clifton House while Monck "took French leave" across the border for a few days' shooting in Illinois. He reported his impressions of the effect of the American civil war on the people. Because of the depreciated currency and "the drain on the population", the ordinary rate of wages had risen within the past year by 35 to 40 per cent, and during the harvest farmers were paying labourers two-and-a-half dollars a day, one dollar a day having previously been the normal rate of pay.

After his return to Quebec, Monck wrote an account of his tour to his old friend, Edward Ellice. Ellice now lived in England, but was still Deputy Governor of the Hudson's Bay Company and was always eager to hear first-hand news of Canada's affairs. Monck declared his conviction that, on questions of defence, the people were in advance of their political leaders in their readiness –

> to submit to any sacrifice, either personal or pecuniary, which they may be called on to make in order to fulfil their obligations as British subjects. I wish I had it in my power to infuse a small amount of public spirit into the said leaders, or to supersede them altogether in their functions for a few years. The feeling of the people is most excellent, both positively and negatively; positively as regards loyalty to the Queen and attachment to British connection – and negatively as abhorring anything approaching Yankee annexation.

A certain number of Canadians were in favour of annexation by the United States, but exaggerated accounts of this sentiment had reached England. In his correspondence with members of the Imperial Government, Monck was always careful to stress any signs he had seen of "attachment to British connection".

The plan for an intercolonial railway had been approved by the Executive Council in Canada and by the Colonial Office in England. It remained for the delegates from Canada, Nova Scotia, and New Brunswick to go to England and settle final details with the Colonial Secretary. However, in the meantime, the Canadian government prepared a memorandum insisting on the following conditions: that their contribution towards the cost of the railway should be counted as part of their contribution towards defence; and that the proposed railway should be transcontinental. From a Canadian point of view the latter condition was a reasonable one. While the maritime provinces were chiefly concerned in cementing their connection with Great Britain, the majority of Canadians were looking to the future development of the west where agricultural and mineral potential remained untapped for want of communications. They were not prepared to contribute to a railway without a firm guarantee that its ultimate goal was to be the Pacific coast.

Though he hoped a measure to construct the railway would pass through the Canadian Parliament during the next session, Monck warned the Colonial Secretary that there were great difficulties to overcome first. Those members of Parliament who considered the defence of Canada the concern of the Imperial Government felt the same about communications between the port of Halifax and Quebec. Monck himself admitted to the Duke that he "trembled" at the thought of the expenditure involved. "I must in justice say that Mr. [J. S.] Macdonald has behaved with more pluck and firmness in this matter than I gave him credit for possessing. He has had a strong fight with two of his own colleagues and I am not yet sure that they will not resign." He explained that he was anxious that the Duke should be made aware of the difficulties involved before his meeting with the Canadian delegates.

The delegates from Canada had been instructed to enter into no agreement that did not include the two proposals of the Canadian Executive Council. But in spite of Monck's explanation, the Duke of Newcastle was unable or unwilling to look at the matter from a Canadian angle. He considered the Canadian Government's provision for defence inadequate enough without sharing its cost with that of the railway; and since Canada was still relying on Imperial troops to defend her territory, Newcastle refused to look beyond the means of assuring a safe passage for the troops to reach Quebec.

Newcastle's obduracy was a setback for the Canadian delegates, who would have to explain their failure to their own Government. Their hopes were now pinned on the terms of the promised loan; if these were sufficiently generous and elastic, with repayment deferred to some unspecified date in the vague and distant future, it might go far towards appeasing their colleagues. This pipe-dream was shattered when they came face-to-face with the stern and meticulous Chancellor of the Exchequer. There was nothing vague about William Ewart Gladstone, at least where public expenditure was concerned. Neither was there anything unspecified or left to chance in connection with the loan. It was to be paid through a sinking fund invested in British, not colonial, securities. By this method, part of each year's revenues would be set aside and invested in British securities until the loan had been repaid.

This sudden blow took all the delegates by surprise. Tilley and Howe, from the maritime provinces, agreed to it reluctantly; the Canadian delegates gave the appearance of doing so. They neither contested the point nor asked for time, probably because they realised the uselessness of doing so. But they also knew that it would be equally useless to expect their Government to agree to the sinking fund. Without any further palaver, they set out on a pre-arranged tour of the continent. The Colonial Secretary heard no more of them until he received their letter refusing the terms offered and withdrawing from the agreement.

Clearly, there could be no intercolonial railway if one end of the line refused to play. Not unnaturally, the maritimers felt badly let down by the faithless and deceitful Canadians, and Arthur Gordon in particular had a great deal to say on the subject.

The Duke of Newcastle wrote a succession of furious letters to the Governor General, accusing the Canadian delegates of "treason", "treachery", and – worst of all – "ungentlemanly behaviour". "The fact is your Government – afraid of losing their seats – only wish to get rid of every question which entails trouble and difficulty. In course of conversation Mr. Sicotte told me that J. A. Macdonald had lately in a public speech characterized the Railroad an 'insane project' – evidently intending to vote next Session against a measure which originated in his Government. Cannot this be stopped? If he is sober when the Bill is introduced his opposition would probably be fatal." There was a great deal more in the same vein. The Canadians and their Governor General were in disgrace and remained so until the following May brought the usual ministerial crisis.

The Moncks had their own reasons for regretting the absence of winter communications between Quebec and the port of Halifax. Henry was to go to Eton in January (1863) and would have to sail from a port in the United States. At this critical juncture of Canadian affairs, Charles could not ask for leave of absence and it was arranged that Mr. Wilkinson, the tutor, would take the boy to New York and sail with him on the *Scotia* at the end of December. An *aide-de-camp*, Captain Pemberton, travelled with them as far as Montreal, and Sergeant Lambkin, the orderly, escorted them to New York. Henry's dog "Nora" completed the party. Henry's parents waited anxiously for news of his journey through a hostile country in which the civil war was at its height. The party was stopped at the frontier by the American "look-out man," but fortunately, Sergeant Lambkin had procured a pass in Montreal, and the rest of the journey passed without incident.

In Henry's first letter to his parents, he wrote of the great kindness he had received in Montreal from Sir Fenwick Williams. Monck had already received a letter from the General that had contained some tactful remarks about Henry. In writing to thank him Monck said: "I have given your messages to Lady M. You always held a high place in her favour, but what you have said about our boy has *crowned* you . . . "– using an idiom which was, and still is, common in Ireland.

They sailed on December 31 and arrived in time to allow Henry to spend a few blissful days at Charleville with his old nurse, Mrs. Hogan (Agga), and the keeper, Tom Quin. Mr. Wilkinson wrote to the Moncks of Henry's safe arrival at Eton, ending his letter by saying: "I feel somewhat like a fish out of the water. Henry has been my constant companion for so long that I quite miss him now. With kind regards to all friends at Govt House, and many thanks to Lady Monck and yourself for your constant kindness to me."

Henry found his cousin, George Brooke, at Eton, as well as several boys from Woodcote, his preparatory school. During his first week he wrote of the "great deal of work" that he was expected to do at Eton and declared that the place was colder than Canada. In March he described the "great doings" celebrating the marriage of the Prince of Wales and Princess Alexandra. Mr. Wilkinson again took charge of him during the Easter holidays, which began with a visit to Paris ostensibly to see "Aunts"–his father's two unmarried sisters who had a flat in the Champs-Elysées. The rest of the holidays were spent at Charleville of which his father demanded a detailed account, especially of the mares and foals.

In Canada the Moncks were preparing to move; the Rue St. Louis home had not proved to be an ideal situation for children, especially in the intense heat of a Canadian summer. Spencer Wood, a pleasant country house a short distance from Quebec, had for several years been the property of the Canadian Government. Ten years previously, a great many additions and improvements had been made to it with a view to its becoming the residence of the Governor General. It was now in process of being rebuilt after having burned to the ground in 1859. Standing high above the river and enclosed in large private grounds, it would be the perfect answer for a couple with a young family. Charles would still have his offices in the Rue St. Louis, and the state apartments in the Parliament Buildings could be used for viceregal "Drawing Rooms" and strictly official functions; but the rooms in the new Spencer Wood could accommodate quite large receptions, dinner parties, and balls, which could there have the intimate and informal character which the Moncks preferred. It was necessary to redecorate the rooms before they could move in and, more important from Charles's point of view, alterations and repairs must be made to the stables.

Elizabeth was delighted with Spencer Wood and impatient to get there, though it would entail moving house for the second time since their arrival in Quebec. And now they no longer had Brock to supervise the packing and removal of their household goods; after becoming increasingly "difficult," he had left them and taken a post in Montreal. Elizabeth neither liked nor trusted Esden, the new butler. When Henry had broken his journey to New York at Montreal, Brock came to see him on purpose to say how "very sorry" he was to have left the family and asking to be taken back. "I wish you would," Henry wrote to his father, and his letter was followed by a contrite one from Brock himself. "Papa heard from Brock and he hopes soon to come," Elizabeth wrote to Henry in January; and in March a letter from Charles reported that "Brock has come back, and is reinstated just as before, with a most tremendous beard."

They did not wait for his arrival before getting rid of the unsatisfactory Esden. "Captain Retallack has taken up all the plate, etc., from Esden, and he is gone, I am happy to say, and Sergeant Lambkin is taking care of everything, and now all seems quiet," wrote Elizabeth to Henry. "It is a blessing to get rid of such a man as Esden, and I am sure he was always a thief, only not discovered. God always brings sin to light ... If you ever get into any difficulty of any sort, *write at once to Dick*.[12] He will always give you good and kind advice and help you in every way. If you find your money not enough for *reasonable* and rational demands, tell Papa, but *do not borrow*."

Elizabeth's letters to Henry are, in the main, disappointing, being mere covering notes to her "journal" – a circular letter containing a diary of events such as the formal receptions she held every Saturday evening and descriptions of the people she had met. Henry had to forward it promptly to his aunt Fanny Cole, after which it was circulated among all Elizabeth's sisters and sisters-in-law. Then, it was forwarded to "Aunt I" and "Aunt E" in Paris. Two or three fragments that Henry managed to recover are all that have survived of the journal. Therefore, her personal notes to Henry contained little in the way of news – "You will read it all in my journal." They were usually dashed off in a hurry in time to catch the outgoing mail, but they made up in spontaneity what they sometimes lacked in coherence. As in the foregoing letter, her infrequent comments on people or events were interspersed by loving and anxious little homilies making it difficult for

Henry to decide whether or not the subjects were connected. Brief references to Quebec balls and sleigh expeditions with her neighbours and officers from the garrison would be followed by a lecture on punctuality:

> *Never keep people waiting*. Do break that bad habit . . . . it is not right . . . I like so much writing to you on Sunday. I well remember that lovely Chapel, and it was most interesting to see the statue of old Dr. Heath of whom I had so often heard my dear Father speak – headmaster in his time . . . . I was much pleased at yr *accounts*. Sardines are very good things to buy but, as you say, to sit and *munch* at a Confectioners (Laytons I suppose?) is neither good for mind or body. Papa and I shd like you to have a bath, so you can ask for it from us.

She was relieved when "Papa" bought Captain Retallack's pony carriage for Puss and Fan to drive. "It made me sick to see Puss driving a great waggon." Sixteen-year-old Louise ("Puss") was fearless and energetic, but a temporary stop was put to her driving of either waggon or pony carriage by a "sad accident" while skating. "Your letter reached us . . . while I was holding her poor *broken arm* to be set. I hope you think of *Lent*, my dearest Child," Elizabeth added in a postscript.

Since Monck, too, wrote to his son every week, we have regular reports on their family life as well as occasional remarks on the political affairs of Canada. "All the world" called on him on New Year's Day, as was the custom in Canada. In February, their friend Bishop Mountain died and the Synod elected Dr. Williams of Lennoxville to succeed him, to the disappointment of those who, like Elizabeth had hoped that the late Bishop's son would be chosen. He wrote of the smart appearance of the Volunteers, "especially the cavalry," at the opening of Parliament on February 14th; and described a tremendous snowstorm – "drifts 12 feet high . . . opposite my office," and the narrow escape of some people crossing the ice-bridge on the river:

> A couple of days since, Mama and I were looking at the bridge from the Governor's Garden; there were a number of people on foot and three or four sleighs on it, when suddenly the ice parted right across the river and began moving up with the tide. Fortunately there were canoes near, and they took off the people at once, and the sleighs and horses after some little trouble.

The family letters during March, 1863, were full of the approaching move to Spencer Wood, and this finally took place at the end of that month. Charles Monck wrote enthusiastically of the comfortable rooms, of the conservatory – a "must" at that time – which had been built on to the end of the house, and of the "very fair" cricket ground.

First built during the latter part of the eighteenth century, the new Spencer Wood has been described as "a very long house, only two stories high . . . in a lovely spot just over the river. There are thirty windows in each side of the house, and the rooms are, some of them, large. The servants' rooms, kitchen, etc., form a sort of wing."[13] One of the most pleasant features was the deep verandah running the whole length of the house on the side overlooking the river. There the family had breakfast and tea in fine weather; they could watch the ships plying up and down the river below and look across at Point Levis on the opposite shore, with the magnificent view beyond. Since they were surrounded by a menagerie of animals wherever they went, it is not surprising that the Moncks preferred a home in the country. The "improved" stables contained horses for each member of the family to ride, as well as the carriage horses and a pony for Stanley. And there were fifteen dogs and seven cats in the house. At least one of the dogs was the property of Captain Pemberton, the A.D.C., who also kept his birds in the new conservatory. These were soon joined by a tame owl that he had bought in the Quebec market. Another of the dogs belonged to Sergeant Lambkin, the orderly. It was taken so much for granted that each member of the household should be allowed to indulge his own particular taste in pets that Brock's performing fleas were never commented on in family correspondence. It was left to George Augustus Sala to describe them after he had visited Quebec in 1864 and been "hospitably entertained at viceregal dinners" at Spencer Wood. "Lord Monck's butler," he wrote, "was the proprietor of the original Industrial Fleas; and his talented troupe included the flea that drew the cannon, the flea, that rode in the sedan-chair, and the flea that impersonated Napoleon Bonaparte's charger 'Marengo'."[14]

Lord Frederick Paulet, a member of Sir Fenwick Williams's staff, was one of the first to stay at Spencer Wood when he came from Montreal to inspect the troops at Quebec. During his visit, the Moncks made up large parties for excursions to the Montmorency Falls, where they showed him the "natural steps" (a rock-form like a staircase beside the Falls); and to the ruins of Charlebourg, a country house that had belonged to the French Governors of Canada.

Charles wrote to Henry of "a day of alarms" during one of their dinner parties:

> When they arrived they found the fire engine out and the soldiers all ready to put out the "fire" . . . which turned out to be a large log of wood smouldering in a stove the pipe of which ran into my chimney, and this produced the smoke! We went to dinner and all went well until the party were just breaking up when Retallack [Military Secretary] came into the room and told me that Mr. [John

> A.] Macdonald and an American gentleman, who had been dining with me, had been upset in a calèche and were very much hurt. I ran out and found the Yankee lying on the ground and very much stunned. We got him into the house and put him to bed and sent for the doctor, who said he would be all right next morning. He was able to depart after breakfast.

Captain Retallack had reported the casualties as being in the plural yet there is nothing in Monck's letter about the treatment of Mr. Macdonald's injuries, if indeed he had any. The silence on the subject might be thought to imply that Monck blamed him for the accident; but it is more likely that special attention was given to the concussed American for diplomatic reasons, Monck having received emphatic instructions from the Colonial Office to lose no opportunity for keeping on friendly terms with "the Northern Federation".

Chapter Six (1863)

The condition of Canadian politics gave the Governor little time for his new home. He had not expected the Sandfield Macdonald-Sicotte Ministry to last long, and all too soon its instability became apparent. On May 1, 1863, John A. Macdonald moved a vote of no confidence in the Government. This was carried, but contrary to usual procedure the Governor General acceded to Sandfield Macdonald's request for an immediate dissolution of Parliament. A dissolution of parliament, which entails a general election, gives the defeated government a chance to learn the wishes of the country as a whole. The alternative and more usual procedure is to accept the former Prime Minister's resignation and ask a member of the opposition to form a government. In this case it would have meant reinstating those who had been defeated a year earlier. Monck decided that J. S. Macdonald, after only a year in power, had a right to "go to the country", that is, appeal to the electors. There were strong conflicting reactions to this decision, both in Canada and at home.

"Within twelve months the House had expressed its want of confidence in the leaders on both sides," Monck confided to his old friend, John Delane. He went on to explain how the events of 1858 had borne on his decision. In the present case the Duke of Newcastle made no secret of his displeasure with Monck for such an "unconstitutional and irregular" act; but his views were not shared by other members of the British Government, still less by Monck's friends. Among these was Charles Adderley, who wrote to tell Monck that Edward Ellice[1] thoroughly approved of his decision and had written to John Rose[2] to tell him so. Adderley's letter was followed by one from Ellice himself. Monck wrote to thank him for the "kind expressions" he had used and to say how greatly he valued the approval of one who knew so much about Canadian politics. "The party now in power have never had the advantage of a dissolution," he told Ellice. "There was a strong – though I am far from saying *just* – feeling that they had not been fairly treated when that step was refused to them in 1858." Monck was referring to the short-lived Ministry led by George Brown that had hardly been formed when the defeated Ministers proposed and carried a vote of no confidence. Brown then had asked for a dissolution, which was refused by Sir Edmund Head, the Governor General.

Monck told Ellice he believed Sandfield Macdonald to be entitled to a dissolution and was determined that "no technicalities should stand in the way of its being granted. I know . . . that Rose was disposed *personally* to act with forbearance, but he is a party man and you and I both know the power which party ties sometimes exercise over conduct in opposition to personal conviction." There had been resignations from the Cabinet, but Monck believed the new Ministers had "sounder views on the financial requirements of the Province, than either their opponents or those whose places in the Ministry they have succeeded."[3]

"Bob" Lowe also commended Monck's decision[4]:

> Ellice and I had a good deal of conversation about you and Canada . . . and I entirely agreed with him in thinking that you had acted perfectly right and in a manner in every way worthy of you: the Assembly had censured both sides, and of course therefore it must be dissolved. If so, the dissolution was the right of the existing Ministry; it would have been an act of gross partiality to have turned them out in order to give the advantage of the dissolution to their antagonists, merely because the Assembly had withdrawn its confidence from them first. The late Canadian ministry seemed to me the impersonation of evil . . . I am glad they are out, and I think you deserve the highest credit for departing from the precedent of your predecessors and acting with complete impartiality. I am afraid, however, these are not the sentiments of the Colonial office. The Duke of Newcastle is a man of sympathies and antipathies. But out of the Colonial Office I have met with no man acquainted with the subject who does not think you perfectly right.[5]

Monck frequently sought and acted on advice from Downing Street but owing to the time-lag in communications he was often forced to act on his own initiative. Weeks later he would receive the conflicting comments of those who were wise after the event, and here his habit of objectivity stood him in good stead. He could be pleased and touched when those he respected commended him but he did not allow himself to be either unduly elated by applause or too much discouraged by adverse criticisms, accepting both attitudes philosophically as part of the day's work.

Meanwhile, discussions were taking place that would lay the foundations for future events. Monck had private talks with those Canadian politicians who were prepared to sink personal or party differences to build a workable coalition. These men recognised that constitutional reform was needed if petty sectional squabbles were to be no longer allowed to take precedence over such vital measures as military defence and intercolonial communications.

Realizing that no question of principle divided Canadian politicians, Monck sent for past Prime Minister George Brown, leader of the Reformers and editor of *The Globe*. Sandfield Macdonald had already consulted Brown in connection with the reconstruction of the Ministry, and Brown had agreed to help though he refused to enter the Ministry himself. "During an interview of over two hours," Brown reported, the Governor General had been,

> . . . amazingly frank, straightforward and kind in all that passed. He admitted the evils I complained of, felt strongly the necessity of remedying them, and put the question direct: "Mr. Brown, could you repeat what you did in 1858? Would Mr. Dorion go with you to the extent he then did?"[6]

Brown declined to form a Ministry with himself at the head; but he took part in meetings and discussions that preceded the May 16 construction of a new cabinet. Sandfield Macdonald was again Prime Minister and Dorion was leader of Lower Canada. Newcastle warned Monck that the result would be the encumbrance of "a weak Government for a lengthened period," and his prophecy proved to be correct.

During that summer, however, Canadian policy was affected by events in the American civil war. There was a succession of Federal (United States) victories; a final defeat of the Southerners would free the Northern armies to turn their attention to British North America. This alarming probability awakened the government to renewed consideration of the defence question.

With this already in mind, Monck had written to Lyons[7] in April, "I am in hopes of getting something respectable in the shape of a Militia Bill here this year, but I have a very ricketty Ministry in Office at present." The Governor's efforts and unrelenting pressure had been supported by John A. Macdonald's call for a vote of no confidence in the late Government. The turn of the tide of the American civil war added impetus. As a result, the new government passed a new and far more effective Militia Act in August, 1863. It also passed a revised Volunteer Bill that strengthened that force.

These measures marked a definite step forward in the progress of Canadian defence, which continued to develop, slowly but steadily, during the ensuing years.[8]

With the Militia question settled as satisfactorily as could be expected for the time being, the Government now could turn its attention to two other important matters closely connected with defence and development: renewal of the plan first brought forward by Alexander Galt in 1858 for a federation of British North America; and a reopening of the subject of an intercolonial railway. Newcastle had advised that construction of the railway should precede the consideration of political union. If there was no adequate means of intercomunication for the greater part of the year, how could the provinces unite? But the Colonial Secretary failed to realise that construction of the railway depended on friendly collaboration between the provinces. In 1863, this seemed to be further off than ever. During that summer, the Canadian Government offered to vote $10,000 towards the cost of making a survey of the route. With the approval of the Colonial Office Sandford Fleming was appointed as surveyor. However, the Governments of New Brunswick and Nova Scotia expected Canada to abide by the agreement of the previous autumn. Under these terms Canada would pay five-twelfths of the cost of the railroad. The Canadian Government declared that agreement void because the subsequent delegates' conference in London had proved a failure. This caused a storm to break over the heads of the Canadians, the feeling of the maritime provinces being expressed most forcibly in despatches and private letters to the Governor General from Arthur Gordon.

"Thy Servant Arthur" had become increasingly dissatisfied with his post. Earlier in the year he had written to the Colonial Office requesting a transfer. The Colonial Secretary promised to bear the matter in mind; Gordon was due for leave in the autumn, and before that time, it was not impossible that a suitable vacancy might occur. But now Gordon became obsessed with the idea (not a new one) of a maritime legislative union under the British Crown – a union of New Brunswick, Nova Scotia, and Prince Edward Island with himself at the head of it. "This move," he wrote to the Duke of Newcastle, "rather changes my wishes for my own removal for I should certainly like to carry through the measure after having set it going." Later he wrote:

> I have given up the idea of coming home this autumn. The union scheme, if it is to come to anything, will require much management, and I cannot risk failure by my absence. You may think I have written too much as if I were the Governor of the new Province. Of course, as, if effected, it will be very much my work, I should not think it an unnatural appointment.[9]

The proposed intercolonial railway was an integral part of Gordon's scheme for Maritime Union so it was with a sense of personal injury that he learned of the Canadians' repudiation of the original agreement. His indignant despatches were interspersed with long private letters to "My dear Monck," as abusive as they were ungrammatical. "There was a book published some years ago entitled *The Annals of Impudence*," he wrote on October 7. "I confess I think the minute of your Council enclosed in your last despatch merits a distinguished place in that collection."[10] His numerous personal letters to Monck all began by saying that he did not intend to re-open the discussion and that it was not his place to interfere with or comment on Canadian politics. He then proceeded to write several pages abusing the Canadian Government, re-opening the subject again and yet again. He had sent a copy of one of his despatches to General Sir Hastings Doyle, then Administrator of Nova Scotia, Lord Mulgrave, the Lieutenant-Governor, having gone to England on the death of his father whom he now succeeded as Earl of Normanby. General Doyle, who had served in Ireland, was an old friend of the Moncks and always a welcome guest at Spencer Wood. He wrote to Monck –

> Gordon forwarded me officially a copy of that remarkably *pleasant* despatch on the subject of the intercolonial railway ... I do not know in what light *you* have viewed tht document, but, in my opinion, a more self-sufficient and impertinent one was never penned! In one part it seems to me he accuses *you* of want of Courtesy! I only hope you have treated him as I should have done by giving him a stronger "Roland" for his too strong Oliver! I have *twice* been obliged to do so with reference to certain military questions connected with the misconduct of certain officers who were stationed in N.B.
>
> He is, I understand, quite *prepared* to undertake the reins of Government as soon as these Maritime Provinces are united, a question, by the bye, which is being very much canvassed and which finds favour with very large portions of the Community of each Province, and which I cannot help thinking will, ere long, be mooted by them in an official shape with the Imperial Government.
>
> Gordon, I understand, says that Normanby is now out of the betting, Dundas's time nearly expired, and *he must* therefore be *the* man. The *Colonial* papers have named him as Normanby's successor. I do not believe a word of it, and can only say God forbid![11]

The Duke of Newcastle thought Gordon's despatch "very regrettable,"[12] but Charles Monck did not adopt Doyle's recommendation in his reply to it or to Gordon's personal letters.

Throughout the ensuing correspondence Monck's attitude was that of a good-humoured mastiff towards a cross little terrier:

> I believe I am not by nature very thin-skinned, and I do not there-

fore experience any irritation at the tone either of your letter or despatch. If I did entertain any such feeling I hope I have sufficient common sense, independent of higher motives, to prevent me from either resenting or retorting.[13]

He took the trouble to put Gordon "in the picture" with regard to the difficulties of the Canadian Government. "I believe the Govt. here are acting bona fide," he wrote on July 18, 1863.

They have great difficulties to contend with in the condition of public feeling respecting the railway. I warned the Duke of N. of these obstacles last Autumn and I know that if a Bill for the construction of a line had been brought in last session it would have been thrown out by a large majority. The fault committed by Sicotte and Howland in England was that they did not frankly state to the Duke what their difficulties really were, but carried on the negotiation in a very captious spirit, as if the question depended on the terms made with the Imperial Govt, whereas I don't believe that any terms, however favourable, would have enabled them to pass their Bill last session. I think the measure may ultimately be carried, but it must be done by quiet management and nothing, in my judgement, will tend so much towards failure as any attempt to *force* the proposal upon the Canadian Parliament. Let us first get a trustworthy survey as a basis for estimate of the expense, and when we have an estimate which can be relied on, the connection, which the Duke has established between this undertaking and the opening of the North West, may conciliate Canadian public opinion to the former proposal.

In one of his most heated letters, Gordon had declared that Monck was "very generally known" to have said there would never be another Governor General of Canada. Further, he claimed that Monck's private secretary, Denis Godley, had declared it would be "a good thing for England to get rid of the Colonies." Monck flatly denied having said any such thing and assured Gordon that he had never held that opinion.[14] "And I *know* you do Godley great injustice in imputing to him any such opinions," he added.

The dignified mildness of his replies made even Gordon feel slightly ashamed of himself. In writing to thank Monck for the "friendly tone" of his last reply, he added:

I should have been very sorry, indeed, if the late difference of opinion had led to any coolness, or to a withdrawal on your part of that freedom of intercourse which should subsist between the Governor General and his subordinate Lieutenant-Governors. ... Will you kindly exercise a discretion as to showing Mr. Macdonald my P.S. about himself? If you think he had better *not* see it, pray tear off that half sheet.[15]

Monck took Gordon into his confidence as if to prove that he harboured no resentment. "I am ready at once to admit that nothing could have been more unfortunate than the selection of Mr. Sicotte as the delegate from Canada last year, nor more unsuitable than his *mode* of conducting the negotiation in London."[16]

Arthur Gordon's irritation was partly caused by frustrations in connection with the scheme for Maritime Union. While on a private visit to Prince Edward Island, he discussed the matter with Mr. Dundas. His plan was to preside over a meeting of the three Prime Ministers and work out the preliminaries. The scheme would then be presented to the respective Governments as a *fait accompli*. Charles Tupper, Premier of Nova Scotia, not unnaturally objected to such undemocratic procedure and proposed a conference attended by delegates representing all three Governments. Tupper, destined to become one of the "Fathers of Confederation", was a vigorous and forceful personality. He was the last man likely to permit a Lieutenant-Governor to ride roughshod over Provincial Assemblies. His own Governor, Lord Mulgrave, later wrote of him to Monck. "You will find him a clever and presentable man. Between ourselves I think him an unscrupulous blackguard."[17]

Judging by his subsequent letters, Tupper was always on cordial terms with Monck. It seemed to Monck the height of hypocrisy to support the theory of self-government in a province, while reserving the right to dictate its policy. While he often disagreed with the methods of the Canadian Ministers, he was becoming increasingly sympathetic to their point of view. He could appreciate that Canada's future lay in improved communications with the North-West, rather than with Great Britain by way of the maritime provinces. The latter would be vital to the defence of Canada should war break out; but even so, it was useless to expect Canadians to contribute towards a railroad that was not to be transcontinental.

Expansion to the West was never far from Canadian thoughts. During the summer of 1863, the Duke of Newcastle had written to Monck:

> You will be surprised to hear that the Hudson's Bay Company no longer exists. All their property and rights have been bought by a Body of Capitalists who will undertake to make fur-trading subordinate to the settlement of the country, which will be commenced by a formation of a Postal and Telegraphic route across the continent. Mr. Watkin, who will be one of the new Council, goes out by

this mail, and he will explain to you more than I have time to write.[18] You may assure your Ministers, if you like, that the degree of liberality with which Canada will be treated in the district in dispute between the Colony and the H.B. Co. will depend upon the manner with which they fulfil or repudiate their engagements in the East. If they break faith with the Lower Provinces and oppose all Imperial measures for their own Party objects, I shall insist upon extreme rights belonging to England and the new Company in the West. I will not allow that district to be jobbed away for the interests of any Individuals or any Party. They must keep faith as to measures of defence and as to their promises to N.S. and N.B., unless they mean to dispense with all advantages which they cannot get without the aid of England.

The Duke of Newcastle's allusion to "breaking faith with the Maritime Provinces" referred to the railway controversy, which dragged on throughout the autumn and winter of 1863-64. Finally even the Duke was forced to agree that the question be shelved until a political union of some kind had been achieved.[19]

The Duke of Newcastle disapproved of the Governor General's tendency to "think Canadian," but Monck had sympathisers in the United Kingdom. Adderley wrote: "I really quite agree with you in your last remarks on Canadian leading strings having so lately been broken. That is your best defence of your subjects, and if Ministers at home will only stand out of their way in learning to walk, I shall be satisfied." Wise influence and prudent management were essential to maintaining the British connection; and Adderley complimented Monck for maintaining a balance between responsibility to the independent Canadian Parliament and to the Home Government.[20]

"Of your personal success I hear on all sides and with the greatest pleasure," wrote Robert Lowe:

> You seem to enjoy the very highest popularity and that in a land where it is not easy for anyone to be popular much or long . . . Still, though I am sure you will get through your Government with great and well-merited credit, I fear you can do little for a country that has jobbed away its revenues and can now plead with some truth its poverty as a dispensation from the charge of the most absolute duties . . . Our politics here are very simple. As long as Lord Palmerston [Prime Minister] lives and abstains from any conspicuous folly the Government is likely to last. As Palmerston himself says – we lose seats but not votes. The Tory party are so disorganised that two thirds of them like him better than their own leaders.[21]

During the late summer and early autumn of 1863, Monck was not so exclusively preoccupied with matters of state as his letters of that period might imply. Henry had crossed the Atlantic to spend the long summer vacation in Canada with his parents, so there were no personal letters for the next eight weeks.

The Monck's anticipation of his visit was mixed with fear that increased each time they heard news of another wreck. There had already been two that year. Off Cape Race, 200 lives had been lost. Monck's confidence in the Canadian line had been shaken and, to avoid the dangers of the Gulf of St. Lawrence, he arranged for Henry to come by way of Boston in the United States.

Henry duly arrived in the last week of July, with his tutor, Mr. Wilkinson. The ten days at sea had been delightful to the fourteen-year-old boy while few, if any, of his school friends had such a glorious prospect awaiting them. It was his first introduction to Spencer Wood with its stables and cricket ground. Judging by Monck's letters, one of the chief occupations of the *aide-de-camp*, Captain Pemberton, was to improve the cricket-ground and keep it in order; the weekly letter to Henry nearly always contained news of its progress. For all his mature judgement and steadiness of character, Monck was very much of a boy at heart, and a great deal of the pleasure Henry derived from outdoor pursuits arose from the fact that his father enjoyed them every bit as much as he did. One of the horses was Henry's special property, and they went on riding expeditions together. Both father and son were keen fishermen, and in Canada, this sport could be enjoyed on a scale they had never known in Ireland. A steamship, the property of the Canadian Government, was at the disposal of the Governor General, and one of the most exciting events in the holidays was a cruise down the St. Lawrence to its tributary, the Saguenay. Since such a cruise might last for several days, they (the whole Monck family with some of their servants, a dog or two, and any friends who cared to join them) would sleep on board.

From the deck of the steamer they admired the mountain scenery and the wonder of the Montmorency Falls; but the object of the expedition was the excellent trout fishing in the wild and beautiful Saguenay River. At some points the party left the steamer and went in rowing-boats and canoes to the best places for fishing. Henry would have preferred to fish all the time; but for the benefit of any guests on board who had only lately arrived in Canada, the steamer continued down the river and the party went ashore from time to time to see places of historical interest such as Indian settlements.

Henry left Canada at the end of September, and at the same time Lord Lyons returned to Washington at the end of his first visit to Spencer Wood.

Chapter Seven (1863-64)

The British Minister kept Monck informed of the ebb and flow of anti-British feeling in the United States, his frequent confidential letters usually being delivered by special messenger. American threats to abrogate the Reciprocity Treaty[1] kept the Canadians on tenterhooks. Due to expire in 1865, the treaty must be renewed by mutual agreement if it were to continue. For that reason, Lyons privately advised Monck that "the less public opinion is drawn to the Treaty at this moment the better." The reason was the United States' "exasperation" against England as the result of the proceedings of the *Alabama* – a British-built cruiser purchased and armed by the Confederates (Southerners), which had inflicted much damage on Federal (Northern) ships. The British Government, still maintaining neutrality, had expressed its intention to try and stop any more vessels from reaching Confederate service. This, Lord Lyons said, had "calmed . . . the ebullitions of anger here, which break forth in a moment and subside in a moment." Seward had assured him that "the question of issuing Letters of Marque is at rest for the present."[2] The Minister admitted that he was even more afraid of consequences of "the dangerous state of feeling in England" following the Northerners' seizure of the British ships *Peterhof* and *Dolphin* and "attempts to stop our lawful trade with Matamaros by a vexatious exercise of Belligerent Rights." He was doing his utmost to curb the aggressive impulses of both sides and to calm "public irritation".[3]

The exchange of confidential letters between Washington and Quebec had lasted for eighteen months before Lord Lyons' summer, 1863 visit to Spencer Wood. The house, with its children and numerous pets, was not an ideal setting for a bachelor's rest-cure. If the present-day idea of a typical Victorian parent is founded on fact, then

Charles and Elizabeth were very far from conforming to type. Their children had never been confined to a remote wing of the house; nor did they visit their parents for an hour each evening. One is tempted to wonder how the Monck's nurses, governesses, and tutor managed to maintain their authority when their charges were constantly with the parents; or how visitors to the house relished the frequent presence of Stanley, already, at five years old, an incipient *enfant terrible*. Unlike one other guest, Lyons did not actually discover a cat having kittens in his bedroom; but he later confided to Monck's sister-in-law that, on his first morning at Spencer Wood, a dog had jumped on his back while he was kneeling at family prayers. Monck was aware that his guest might need to escape from such concentrated family life; he arranged for him to have the use of one of the Government steamers so that he could visit places of interest at his leisure.

During Lord Lyons's absence from Washington, his First Secretary, Mr. Stuart, corresponded with Monck on a confidential report from the British Consul at Baltimore. The Consul had discovered a Confederate plot to raid United States' towns from a base in Canadian territory. "Chicago would be the place attacked. The plan is to send cannon to some island from whence the vessels of the expedition could embark them." Mr. Stuart suggested that "the object would, of course, be rather to involve us in War, than to inflict injury on towns belonging to the United States. It would, however, be full of danger to our Relations with this Country."[4] A fortnight later, Stuart wrote again to thank Monck for the "judicious steps" he had taken to prevent the proposed raids and for doing so in such a way as to avoid publicity, "which would endanger the position of the Consul, in addition to fermenting anti-British feeling."

This abortive plan was the forerunner of other attempts by the Confederates to violate the neutrality of British North America. The next "incident" took place the following December when Southern raiders (believed to have been assisted by British North Americans) seized the United States coasting vessel, *Chesapeake*. It was recaptured by Federal warships in Nova Scotian waters. This mutual infringement of neutrality did not improve the already strained relations between the United States and British North America. In January (1864) Monck wrote to Lord Lyons:

> I had yesterday from Doyle[5] a regular budget of correspondence about the *Chesapeake* affair. If he is as lavish of blood, when in command of an army, as he is of ink in his correspondence, he would be a most sanguinary general. He is a great friend of mine and I hope you are satisfied with what he has done.[6]

On October 23 the news had reached Spencer Wood that Henry and Mr. Wilkinson had landed in Ireland. His parents were now able to relax and they both wrote to him of the excitement caused by the arrival in Quebec of Barnum's troupe of midgets – " 'General Tom Thumb', with his diminutive wife and sister-in-law, and 'Commodore Nutt'." When Elizabeth took her two daughters and Stanley to see the show, the famous midgets were presented to her. She invited all four to lunch at Spencer Wood, to which they drove out in their miniature carriage-and-four.

At Spencer Wood entertaining was continuous and varied. Charles Monck gave a large Parliamentary Dinner, for men only, each Saturday; besides which Canadian ministers and other dignitaries would be invited, with their wives, to smaller dinner-parties at which the presence of a few senior officers from the garrison would ensure the unofficial nature of the gathering. Clergy and judges with their families, old Mr. Adamson, Librarian of the Legislative Council and his wife, as well as a miscellaneous collection of neighbours within visiting distance, were regularly invited to luncheon, tea or dinner at Government House. A dinner party would often be followed by an impromptu dance, to the delight of M. Cartier who was an energetic performer.

On October 10, John A. Macdonald dined with the Moncks. It was the first time they had seen him since, thanks to his efforts, the revised Militia Act was passed in August, and Elizabeth reported to Henry that he was "in great spirits" as the result. The dinner-party had included several officers who were full of the latest gossip concerning a certain Captain Herbert of the Grenadiers. As the consequence of having married a Canadian, he was to sell out, Elizabeth told Henry, "*and his Father will not let him come home*." She made no comment on this shattering statement; but less than four months later, the lady in question was already being referred to as "the runaway wife of Captain Herbert of the Guards". At a ball in Quebec, "she danced the fast dances with a rose in her mouth," wrote Elizabeth, "and then leaped a kind of *hurdle race* over the seats, with an officer."

Regimental cricket matches continued throughout October, as did the garrison races on the Plains of Abraham. As with those described in Thackeray's novels, only two horses were entered for each race, officers from the different regiments racing against each other. Elizabeth took a keen interest in the races, writing out all the results for Henry, while explaining that she had said nothing about them in her journal – which was sent round the whole family – because "Aunts do not think it right to go to races. Stanley was charmed, and said it was *si amusant*." At five years old he still spoke French more readily than English, a sure passport to popularity with the French-Canadians, though in fact it was merely the result of his having always had a French nurse.

The growing nationalistic feeling among French-Canadians caused anxiety lest there should be demonstrations at public events and Charles, who with Elizabeth had attended the inauguration of the St. Foy statue, wrote to Henry of his relief that the great function had passed off quietly though attended by immense crowds. There had been some foundation for the previous anxiety lest the ceremony should give rise to a clash between different factions; the statue was a symbol of French nationalism since it commemorated the defeat in battle of the English by the French in 1760.

The Moncks had invited some of the officers to spend Christmas at Spencer Wood. As that season approached, they received the usual spate of letters from friends and relations offering to have their elder son to stay in the holidays. Young Henry was in a predicament familiar to any orphaned, or temporarily orphaned, boy with many kind relatives. He grudged any time spent away from Charleville, but Charles insisted that he accept, for the first time, the invitation which kind Mr. Adderley gave before each holidays to stay at Ham, near Birmingham. His mother's four sisters at Barbavilla had to be fitted in somehow, also his father's two sisters in Paris; while plaintive letters from his aunt Georgina Croker urged Henry to spend at least part of his holidays with her and her ten children at Ballynagarde.

By mid-January, Henry's letters from Ireland had arrived. His father wrote to thank him for telling him "all the sort of things I wanted to know about Charleville". The most important bit of news was left to the end: "Please God, it will seem a very short time until you will be coming back to us again, and then I think Mama will go home with you."

In later years, Canadian writers referred to Elizabeth's return to Ireland in September, 1864, as neglect of her duties as Governor's wife, and as a slight to Canada. At the time her reasons for leaving were perfectly well understood, at least by all those who knew the Moncks personally. To begin with, she was merely going on ahead of her husband who had been in Canada for nearly three years and had as yet had no leave. He could not reconcile himself to being an absentee landlord, and if unable to go home himself, Elizabeth must deputise for him.

Also for nearly three years Fan had been without the specialised tuition supplied by the Institute for the Deaf in Paris. The plan under discussion was that Elizabeth should return to Ireland with Henry at the end of his summer holidays, taking the two girls and Stanley. She would rent a house in Paris for the winter, where the girls were to attend classes and, in the case of Puss, music lessons, and go back to Charleville in May when Charles expected to go home on leave, for which he was long overdue.

A fragment from Elizabeth's "journal" describes sleigh-accidents, visits to sick neighbours, dinner-parties, a snowshoe race, and then a charity concert in Quebec.

"The roads are passable again, and so Papa can have his great sleigh to open Parliament. I *believe* I am to receive tomorrow after Papa's Parliamentary dinner," Elizabeth told Henry on February 19. In his letters Monck showed that he sympathised with the French-Canadians' anxiety to conserve their traditions, language and culture; but on this occasion, he wrote to Henry, "they gave me a tremendously long speech to read, and did I not wish '*notre langue*' at the bottom of the sea!"

After telling Henry that eleven men had been killed by an explosion in the laboratory at the Artillery Barracks; that there had been another wreck of a ship of the Canadian Line in which thirty lives were lost; he concluded with a message to his brother Dick, who was shortly to join his staff as military secretary. Richard Monck had married his cousin, "Feo" Cole, who was the daughter of Elizabeth's elder sister. This delightful plan for a family reunion was somewhat marred by the flat refusal of his wife Feo to cross the Atlantic. She hated and dreaded the sea, not only on her own account, but also on that of her baby son, Cecil, from whom she could not bear to be separated. However, neither she nor her husband considered this sufficient reason for disobeying his elder brother's summons, and – "Colonel Monck tells me he is going out alone," Mr. Cardwell wrote to Charles. Feo was not alone in shirking the voyage. When in that same year the delegates from Canada were presented to Queen Victoria, she told them that, much as she longed to visit their country, she would never have the courage to cross the Atlantic.

After Parliament reassembled, there was little in the way of social chit-chat for Elizabeth to write either in her journal or in the covering notes to Henry:

> . . . There is no gaiety going on now, on account of its being Lent. I never was in any place where Lent was so well observed as here.
> . . . I *suppose* it is quite right for boys to learn to box and fight, but to me it is horrid. Like the Roman Gladiators! however I am very glad you were victorious!

This was in reply to Henry's letter, saying he had had a fight with another boy. His father merely remarked that he was "glad you had the best of your fight, but I advise you to have as few 'rattles' as you can."

He too was to have "a rattle", for he was approaching the climax of his career in Canada.

On February 25, 1864, George Brown wrote to his wife of "an awful scene of abuse in the House last night. McGee, O'Halloran, Ferguson and others pitching into each other like fury. The debates so far have not had one hour of practical common sense in them. There ought to be a shake-up and I hope there will be."[7] George Brown owned *The Globe* newspaper and was "the most powerful political figure of Upper Canada."[8] The incident he described was typical of this Parliamentary session. Decisive lines of policy became subordinate to questions of sectional discord; and a state of deadlock was reached, owing to the narrow majority of Sandfield Macdonald and his followers, who were unwilling to risk losing office by introducing any positive measure which could call for a division. On March 18, however, Charles Monck wrote to Henry that:

> Mr. J. S. Macdonald resigned this day week and they have not been able to make a Ministry in the place of his. I think they must have a Coalition of both sides, which would be much the best thing for the country.

Monck has been described as "originator" as well as "advocate and inspirer" of the idea of Coalition.[9] He was firmly convinced that, in Canada, it was the only form of government which could get things done. He approached Fergusson Blair, Alexander Campbell, Cartier, and Dorion, in the hope that one of them would succeed in combining opposing parties to form a strong government. But none were able to surmount the difficulties created by sectional and political rivalries. In a private letter to Chichester Fortescue, he wrote that his late government had been:

> . . . so taken up with their local politicks and the manipulation of their Parliamentary proceedings, that all efforts were unavailing to get them to attend to matters beyond them . . . I hope the present men may be able to maintain themselves, but parties are very evenly divided and I think they have thrown away a great opportunity of forming a strong government by a junction of the best men on both sides.[10]

And to Lord Lyons:

> Your letter has reached me when my hands are full. A "Ministerial Crisis", which has been impending for some time, has just come upon us, and I am, for the moment, without constitutional advisers.
>
> I have tried my hand at an endeavour to reconcile personal

differences – there are really no public questions which ought to keep men apart – but have failed signally, and we are to have a new ministry under the leadership of the opposition chiefs.[11]

The new Ministry was formed with Sir Etienne Taché as Premier and John A. Macdonald again as leader of Upper Canada. Sir Etienne-Pascal Taché, now in his seventieth year, was a member of an old and distinguished French family. He had been a soldier and a doctor, as well as a politician, and was so far above party rivalries and sectional prejudice that he was respected and trusted by all. He was Premier in 1856 and now, in 1864, was in the Legislative Council. Since he had planned to retire, he was reluctant to assume the Premiership but was persuaded by John A. Macdonald, Cartier, and Monck that he was the only man acceptable to all parties. He and the Governor General corresponded bilingually, Monck writing in English, Taché in French, using charming old-world phraseology. One of his letters refers to a "*minute en conseil*" which, owing to an oversight, had been passed by the Legislative Council. No details of it are given except that it concerned some aspect of that inflammatory subject – " . . . *la translation du siège du gouvernement*".[12] Taché had previously discussed the proposal with Monck, and both had decided against it. When it was presented to him for sanction, Monck wrote to Taché querying it; and in his reply the Prime Minister, deeply mortified at having caused "*sensations pénibles*" to the spirit of His Excellency owned that the minute had been passed in haste – "*tandis que mon attention était attirée ailleurs, et sans que j'ai eu le temps de la réflexion*." He begged Monck to withhold his sanction, and ended by assuring him of his profound respect and "*entier dévouement*".[13]

Taché's Ministry was the fourth to be formed within two years. Again, with such a narrow majority, nobody expected it to last long nor regarded it as anything but a desperate expedient to avoid, or at least postpone, dissolution.

Parliament assembled on May 4, 1864. Six weeks later, on June 14, 1864, Dorion and McDougall brought forward a vote of non-confidence in the Government, which was carried by two votes. On the following morning, June 15, Taché tendered his formal advice to the Governor General for the dissolution of Parliament.

During the short time that Parliament had been in session, George Brown had formed a Committee on Constitutional Difficulties "to find some solution for existing problems likely to receive the assent of both sections of the Province."[14] The Committee had produced a positive plan, which could fulfil the Governor General's hope for "a junction of the best men on both sides". To gain time, Monck wrote the following letter to Taché:

Dear Sir Etienne, – I am not yet in a position to give a definite reply to the advice which you tendered me yesterday morning. I must therefore request that you will announce this fact in your house and ask Macdonald to make a similar statement in the Legislative Assembly. You are quite at liberty to say that the cause of the delay is with me *alone*.

I hope to be in Quebec by 10.30 in the morning and expect by that time to give you a final answer.

Truly yours,

Monck.[15]

He then set out his own views in a memorandum, in which he referred to his previous attempt, in March, to form a coalition government:

> ... the time had arrived when an appeal might with propriety be made to the patriotism of gentlemen on both sides of the House to throw aside personal differences, and to unite in forming a Government strong enough to advance the general interests of the country.... The Governor General still adheres to the opinion that such an amalgamation of parties is the course most calculated to confer the largest amount of benefit to the Province, and earnestly hopes that means may be found for effecting such an arrangement without doing violence to the self-respect of any gentleman connected with Canadian Politics.[16]

The delay gave an opportunity for informal negotiations between John A. Macdonald, George Brown, George-Etienne Cartier, and Alexander Galt. Previously Macdonald and Brown had not been on speaking terms with each other, and their private conferences together were a step towards the sinking of "personal differences". The extract quoted above from the *Canadian Historical Review* also states that Monck –

> ... throughout the progress of the negotiations, was busy interviewing now one man and now another, in characteristically genial and energetic fashion exerting his influence to further the harmonising of conflicting views.

The Governor's persistent refusal to "govern by a party" had prevented him from becoming conspicuously popular with any one faction. In a crisis like the present one, men of all parties knew that they could trust him. They had come to know him well from informal visits to his own home. George Brown described him as "frank, straightforward and kind," and his warm, friendly nature made a personal contact of every interview.

The informal discussions resulted in a reconstruction of the Government with Taché still Premier, but with a Cabinet composed of members who had hitherto been in opposite camps. Brown was willing to "sink personal differences" to the extent of motivating the preliminary negotiations; his sphere of influence was wide; and it was he who had introduced, in March 1864, the resolution for coalition in Parliament. For a time, however, he was resolute in his determination not to enter the Cabinet. D'Arcy McGee and others among his associates urged upon him the necessity of his "personal participation"; while the Governor General had several private conversations with him on the subject and finally wrote him the following letter:

> My dear Mr. Brown, – I think the success or failure of the negotiations which have been going on for some days, with a view to the formation of a strong government on a broad basis, depends very much on your consenting to come into the Cabinet.
>
> Under these circumstances I must again take the liberty of pressing upon you, by this note as I have already often done verbally, my opinion of the grave responsibility which you will take upon yourself if you refuse to do so.
>
> Those who have hitherto opposed your views have consented to join with you in good faith for the purpose of extricating the province from what appears to me, a very perilous position. They have frankly offered to take up and endeavour to settle, on principles satisfactory to all, the great constitutional question which you by your energy and ability have made your own.
>
> The details of that settlement must necessarily be the subject of grave debate in the Cabinet, and I confess I cannot see how you can take part in that discussion or how your opinions can be brought to bear on the arrangements of the question unless you occupy a place at the Council table.
>
> I hope I may without impropriety ask you to take these opinions into consideration before you arrive at a final decision as to your own course.
>
> Believe me to be, – Yours very truly, – Monck.[17]

On June 22, Brown told the Ministers that he would enter the cabinet. He admitted afterwards that in making this decision he had been influenced by "private letters from many quarters . . . and the extreme urgency of the Governor General did still more." On June 25 Monck wrote to Lyons:

> . . . I have succeeded, beyond my most sanguine expectation, in my Ministerial arrangements, and I hope I have formed a Government strong enough to lift us out of the condition of chronic crisis in which I have been living since I came to Canada.

Chapter Eight (1864)

It was not correct for a Governor General's wife to meddle in public affairs, but Elizabeth heard all the political gossip from the Ministers and others who attended the frequent unofficial parties at Spencer Wood. Judging by the letters written to her by Hector Langevin, George-Etienne Cartier, and Thomas D'Arcy McGee, she was on friendly and informal terms with some of the ministers. McGee called her "my Governess General." "If you see her, mark her," he wrote to Sir Samuel Ferguson, the poet. "She is one of my best friends." Those who knew her personally were pleasantly surprised by her easy geniality. The upright carriage that gave an impression of "stiffness" was merely an attempt to compensate for her lack of height. The cosily informal nature of her correspondence with old Chief Justice Bowen is characteristic. In replying to one of her letters he concludes by saying:

> ... You were pleased in your Note to compliment me on my handwriting which it does not deserve, it is legible I know, and that for a person well advanced in his eighty-fourth year, and without spectacles, rarely occurs. I have never yet seen such rare and beautiful Lady's writing as your own, notwithstanding "*Pussy on your Lap*."[1]

Since there was then no press coverage for Governors' wives and her journal has been lost, it is only from letters written to her that we can learn how she spent the time which was not occupied by her duties as hostess.

Unlike the wives of future Governors, her activities were confined to a sphere limited by lack of ready railway communications. Within that small radius, she was in close touch with the schools and orphanages (irrespective of their religious denomination), attending prize-givings, and regularly giving school treats at Spencer Wood. She had also established warm relations with some of the less prominent Canadian families, and was on neighbourly terms with those within "calling" distance of Spencer Wood. The son of Bishop Mountain referred to her as "my kindest friend".

Yet, in spite of these and other affectionate tributes to her warm-heartedness and spontaneity, the notion that she was "unpopular" in Canada has persisted to the present day. Although no written evidence has been forthcoming to support the theory, there must be something in it since indirect allusions were made to it as a known fact.

One of the criticisms levelled against her in retrospect is that she was so unappreciative of Canada that she remained there only four years out of the seven during which her husband was Governor. This, however, was not according to plan; Charles Monck had not expected to stay seven years in Canada and certainly did not foresee that circumstances would cause his leave to be postponed again and yet again. When, after nearly three years in Quebec, Elizabeth took her children home, it was in the belief that Charles would join them within a few months. It was in fact a year later that he went home for what the Colonial Secretary called "a little on account" of the period of leave owing to him. Canadian internal affairs made it necessary for him to return to Quebec far sooner than he would normally have gone; and since it was understood that this was merely a brief interruption of his leave, he left his wife and family at home to await his return to Ireland. Recurring political crises, strained relations with the United States, and later, threats of invasion by the Fenians combined to delay his return for a further year. When, after it had at last taken place, he went back to Canada, his wife accompanied him and remained there while his appointment lasted. It would be interesting to check on how many wives of former Governors spent as much time in Canada as she did.

Her prolonged absence had no connection with her feelings, either for or against Canada and Canadians. At the same time, it is impossible to deny that she must have shown those feelings in a way that was neither tactful nor discreet. Having admitted so much, it is only fair to remember that the only thing she complained of – the familiar, informal manners of some of the women of Canada – would have been a great shock to any European woman born, as she was, in 1814, when girls still greeted even their own parents with a curtsey every morning. When she wrote to her son Henry of having attended "one of the nasty Quebec dances", she had intended the letter to be seen by his eyes alone; but it would have been only natural for her to wish her two growing-up daughters to know that she disapproved of the ball at which the coat-tails of her young cousin, Francis Burrowes, were "nearly torn off": "... such drunkenness, pushing, kicking, and tearing he says he never saw; . . . the supper room floor was covered with meat, drink, and broken bottles."[2] The fact that her teenage children welcomed the unaccustomed freedom and informality, would have prejudiced Elizabeth even further against it, at a time when graceful, dignified manners were taken for granted at balls and receptions in London, Dublin, and Paris.

There were, however, many aspects to her life in Canada which she thoroughly enjoyed, and she was becoming as fond of Spencer Wood as she could be of any place that was not Charleville. Yet she was often very homesick, and confided to Henry her longing for Ireland and her wish that they had never left it. This was no reflection on the Canadians; the hardiest mother would have felt uneasy at having brought her young family to a country which might, at any moment, become a battlefield; where, in the event of war with the United States, they would be cut off from Europe for more than half of each year when the St. Lawrence was frozen. The worst fear of all, shared by her husband, was for Henry who came out to Canada every summer to spend his holidays with his family. This was the chief reason why Elizabeth regretted having come to Canada.

All these gloomy feelings were quickly dispelled during the last week of May, 1864, by an unexpected addition to their circle. On Sunday, May 29, the Monck family were roused before breakfast by the arrival, accompanied by peals of merry laughter and little shrieks, of the Governor's cousin – sister-in-law – niece-by-marriage – all combined in one short, plump person encased in an outsize crinoline over a wire "cage"; by the arrival, in fact, of Feo. "Feo and Dick arrived a little after 7 this morning," Elizabeth wrote joyfully to her "dearest Child", Henry.

> . . . I think her looking so nice and well and *how pleasant* it is to have them both . . . Was it not *most extraordinary* Feo taking leave of Dick at Ryde, and Dick embarking at Liverpool, and Feo getting *immediately* so unhappy she made Blayney [Feo's schoolboy brother] take her to Queenstown, and sailed with him. Another passenger got out at Queenstown and forfeited his passage, he was so wretched. She says she would have got out at Queenstown if she had sailed from Liverpool.[3] She told it all out at breakfast, *and there was such a shout*.

Feo, alias Mrs. Richard Monck, was a round-faced, round-bodied, merry little creature. She was of a type that would nowadays be considered a monumental bore, but which was then popular with "the gentlemen". No family excursion or picnic had ever been complete without Feo. She was forever getting herself into the sort of situations that called for the support or protection of a strong, manly arm. The perfect "house-party girl", she was always ready to join in an unsophisticated round game of cards or to delight the company with her singing of simple ballads or comic songs.

Yet there must have been a good deal more to Feo than mere silliness. She had been given a good education, and before her marriage, she had travelled with her parents in Germany, France, Spain, and Belgium. Her mother gave musical parties in their Knightsbridge house, and her father, a close friend of W. E. Gladstone, "collected" writers, artists and actors. Nobody could have guessed, from listening to her frivolous and sometimes futile conversation, that she had been accustomed to intellectual society all her life, nor that she had psychic powers. Her dislike of thunderstorms was not simply girlish panic; she was peculiarly sensitive to natural phenomena, and could "feel" an earthquake or earth tremor in a distant part of the world.

Feo was a shocking snob – "I can't tell you the bliss of seeing a Guardsman in this land," and – "It all seemed so weird and odd (at Spencer Wood) – the Monck liveries, and everything like home, and to think we are across the Atlantic, at the other side of the world, it does not bear thinking of."

But Feo enjoyed every moment of the entertainments given in their honour, at which she met a good cross-section of Quebec society, both social and political. She thought D'Arcy McGee "most quaint-looking. He looks like a wild Indian." After a field day and a series of inspections of garrison troops on the Plains of Abraham, she wrote: "It is pleasant being with the 'swells,' as no-one can get before you." There was a large dinner party after a cricket match one night at which the guests were "mostly ministers. Sir E. Taché (the Premier) took me in . . . He is a nice agreeable little old man. M. Dorion . . . is very agreeable."

She followed her aunt's example in writing her letters home in the form of a "journal," faithfully entering in it her sprightly comments and descriptions every day for a whole year. She described a fourteen-mile drive to Lake Beauport with the Dundases and an excursion to Cap-Rouge:

> . . . Oh! I never could tell you the beauty of the drive through the bush . . . then glimpses of the deep blue St. Lawrence, and the blue hills and green woods; it was all too beautiful.

At the end of June, the Governor and his party embarked on a tour which included Lennoxville College, the Eastern Townships, Montreal, and Ottawa. They were accompanied by two Ministers, Alexander Galt and D'Arcy McGee. They made the first part of the journey by train in a railway carriage consisting of a large sitting-room, two bedrooms, and a smoking room; then they continued their tour in a fleet of open wagons, and were met by a band of musicians as they entered each village. They crossed Lake Memphremagog by steamer and spent the night at a hotel called the Mountain House, re-embarking at 7.30 next morning.

Feo noted that the Governor was received very well at Newport, "though a Yankee town, gay with flags in honour of the 4th of July," rather a tactless date to have chosen for a visit from Queen Victoria's representative. A large coach with six white horses carried them to Stanstead, a border town between Canada and the United States. They lunched at the house of Mr. Knight, Member of Parliament for Stanstead – " . . . so thoroughly Yankee, stiff and unlived in, chairs all round the room, no books, no comfort, only show and stiffness and state. . . . There were some speeches at lunch, and then we had to clear out, as all our servants had to feed in the dining room on what we had left."

Snobbish Feo was more in her element when they arrived at Montreal, where their train was met by General Lindsay, his staff, and a guard of honour of Grenadiers. There were four days of ceremonial functions, including a trooping of the colour on the Champ de Mars and a concert at the Convent school, where Elizabeth "presented prizes most gracefully, and the G.G. made a very good speech." The Governor and his party were invited to stay by Sir Fenwick Williams on his "heavenly island," the Ile d'Orval.

While Charles and Elizabeth went on to Ottawa, Feo and Dick remained in Montreal to attend the parties given for them. They all arrived back at Spencer Wood in the middle of a heat wave, with thunderstorms which sent Feo scuttling to the cellar.

> Mr. Stanley arrived to stay with a letter [of introduction] from his father. He has "strong Northern proclivities", has been travelling all over the North [of the United States], and gave a frightful account of the way the South treat their slaves, and showed a photo. of a slave's back frightfully lacerated. He says he saw some emancipated slaves, some of them *brutish* still, but some happy.

On a later occasion Feo was told:

> . . . how very kind the Southerners are to their slaves; they are just as we are with our servants, and till lately a Northerner would not *speak* to a black. . . . *Uncle Tom's Cabin* has done much mischief. One can't believe what Mrs. B. Stowe says, as she was only a short time in the South.

Feo was favourably impressed by the behaviour of the Roman

Catholic children who came with the Vicaire-Général to a school feast at Spencer Wood: "I never saw so nice and orderly a set. The children were half Irish and half French-Canadians, some of the latter looking like Indians, almost quite black, with round Indian eyes." They were a pleasant contrast to the children from the English-speaking school, who had attended a separate school-treat and shocked Feo by their bad manners.

The entries in her diary are full of anecdotes of "dear old Mr. Price"[4] and his family, who were the Monck's nearest neighbours and with whom they had struck up a pleasantly informal friendship.

Feo's "journal" did not meet the same fate as Elizabeth's, but was treasured by her doting father, Owen Cole, who had ten copies privately printed under the title: *My Canadian Leaves*.[5] Since she entirely ignored the momentous affairs taking place around her (except in so far as they interfered with her social engagements or her physical comfort), it is a purely personal narrative. "A ministerial crisis, so the G.G. [Governor General] can't come," she wrote on June 15 before setting out on a seven-hour expedition, thus lightly dismissing the collapse of the six-weeks-old Taché-Macdonald Ministry.

The series of political crises in June, 1864, had taken place at the same time as the receptions and dinners at Spencer Wood so much enjoyed by Feo. Charles Monck's "delaying action" note to Taché and the subsequent conferences coincided with the Dundas visit; and an eve-of-Waterloo atmosphere had pervaded the reception and ball on June 16, which occured just six days before the formation of what came to be known as the Great Coalition of 1864.

The social activity at Government House had its uses. Ministers and members of the Assembly would meet each other at dinner there and discuss their problems informally. Feo saw no significance in Charles having craftily introduced George Brown to her on June 18 as "one of the new Ministers," showing that he took it for granted that Brown would consent to enter the Coalition Cabinet.

Henry and Mr. Wilkinson arrived in July in time to join his family and their friends in a trip down river in the Government steamship, *Queen Victoria*. Henry was confirmed in Quebec, and soon after Elizabeth and the four children embarked in the *Peruvian*.

Charles, who always hated being separated from his family, tried to speak cheerfully of his impending leave and of how quickly the time would pass until the spring when he was to join them. But, "I am to be alone all the winter," he had written sorrowfully to Lord Lyons when confirming the dates for the Minister's second private visit to Spencer Wood.

*

Throughout the spring and summer of 1864, Monck and Lyons had made frequent use of what the Ambassador called their "secret and rapid" method of communication. Many emigrants from Britain, intending to settle in Canada, had been diverted to New York and forced to remain in the United States. To put a stop to this, the Canadian Government wished to install an immigration agent in New York; but Charles told Lord Lyons that he had vetoed this, for fear of "collision" with the American Government. Both Monck and Lyons were more than usually anxious to avoid any such provocation when the United States might, at any moment, abrogate the Reciprocity Treaty. "I think the wisest plan would be to leave the negotiations to Lyons," Edward Cardwell, the Colonial Secretary, had written on May 13 in a private letter to Monck. The Americans were expected to give notice to terminate the Treaty, thus creating the necessity of negotiating a new one. Cardwell advised the appointment of Commissioners on both sides:

> . . . as the interests of the North American Colonies are not identical, and as more points of difference will certainly arise during the discussion of a new Treaty. . . . The three Americans would fight as one man, our 3 would be divided, and it is not difficult to foresee the result.[6]

On the renewal or revision of the Treaty, Lord Lyons was still strongly in favour of leaving the initiative to the United States. "It is very hard to keep them [the Ministers] quiet on the subject," Monck replied:

> Mr. Holton's proposal is to institute at once negotiations for a modified treaty. . . . My "approval" of a minute of the Executive Council does not necessarily imply personal assent on my part to its contents. I am a constitutional sovereign – bless the mark – administering a system of responsible government, and as long as my advisers can command a majority in the Legislative Assembly I am bound *officially* to approve their policy, whatever may be my private opinion of its merits. In the present case, however, I am at one with my Ministers, and I am afraid I have the misfortune to differ with you. It must be remembered that, even if the notice for abrogating the R. Treaty be not given *this year*, the commercial interests which have grown up under that treaty will hereafter be in a very different condition from that which they have occupied during the ten years which have passed since the treaty was originally concluded . . [7]
>
> I think trade soon accommodates itself to *adverse* conditions, but is paralysed by *uncertain* conditions . . . that it would be much better for our trade that the treaty should be abrogated than that it should be retained only from year to year.[8]

To Cardwell, Monck wrote:

> I do not think that we ought to assume that the people of the U.S. are unanimous in their desire for the abrogation of the present Treaty, or in their grounds of objection to it . .
>
> None of the Colonies, I think, desire the abrogation of the Treaty, and Canadians are, I know, prepared to make concessions in order to extend its operation . .
>
> I have very strong grounds for thinking that the opposition to the Treaty among the people of the U.S. is based on a feeling of political hostility to England quite as much as upon a sense of practical commercial inconvenience.

The United States House of Assembly voted for a postponement till December of the consideration of the abrogation of the Treaty. Monck ended his letter to Cardwell by saying:

> I would strongly urge that the breathing time we have gained by the vote should be turned to account by entrusting to him [Lord Lyons] the discretionary powers which he asked for in his despatch of April 11th.[9]

The "breathing time" proved to be shorter than the Governor had expected; but while it lasted, his attention was absorbed by internal affairs. Brown's Parliamentary Committee had submitted a report to the Government suggesting that a solution to sectional differences lay in "a federative system, applied either to Canada alone or to the whole British North American Provinces."[10] The idea of a union of all the provinces in British North America was not new. It had been mooted before Monck came to Canada, and raised again when, in September, 1862, he invited the Lieutenant-Governors and their advisers to a conference in Quebec. The subject was dropped when the Duke of Newcastle insisted that the intercolonial railway must take precedence over every other scheme.

In April, 1864, a change in the Colonial Office took place that had important results for Canada. Owing to ill health, the Duke of Newcastle resigned his post as Secretary of State for the Colonies. He was succeeded by Charles Monck's friend, Edward Cardwell, a man who was to prove a fervent advocate of British North American union. The new Coalition Government was pledged to forward this cause. Alexander Galt and D'Arcy McGee had long favoured it. On the assumption that any change must be for the better Taché and Cartier were convinced that a federal union of all the provinces would improve the position of Lower Canada, by securing to French-Canadians their rights of nationality. Those ministers like John A. Macdonald, who wanted a legislative union, thought that French rights could be conceded as were those of Scotland within Great Britain.[11] In a federal union, the provinces would be independent states, as in America; in a legislative union, each province would administer its own local affairs while sending representatives to a strong central government. These differences would be discussed later, but all agreed on the necessity for a general union. The maritime provinces were to hold a conference to discuss Maritime Union at the end of the summer; and on June 30, Monck electrified the maritimers by writing on behalf of the Canadian Government to ask permission for a delegation from Canada to attend the conference.

"I feel that your recent change of Government will probably be referred to hereafter as an Era in Canadian history," Cardwell wrote after congratulating Monck on having "a strong Ministry at last.[12] In reply, Monck told him of his proposal to send Canadian delegates to the Maritime Union Conference at Charlottetown. The purpose was to introduce the concept of a Union of all the provinces. The plan took Cardwell by surprise, but he was sympathetic to the proposal:

> The affairs of British North America are always interesting and never more so than at the present time. I was a little startled by the word *Federation*, for Federal Govt has not risen in public estimation recently either in America or in Europe. But if I correctly understand what your advisers are likely to propose, it will not be *Federation* in the real meaning of the word, but *union* of many *municipalities* under one Supreme Legislature. This will exclude altogether the States-rights question which has broken up the U. States, and establish that sort of Legislature which Washington and Hamilton wished for in America. There are so many great questions connected with this, that it is impossible to exaggerate their importance.[13]

Among the advantages of uniting the whole of British North America "in one great and important Province," he mentioned defence; the development of the North-West; and the construction of an Intercolonial Railway.

Arthur Hamilton Gordon had been on leave in England since April, his enthusiasm for Maritime Union having waned after the "management" had been taken over by the politicians. In his absence, Colonel J. A. Cole was Administrator of New Brunswick, and Sir Richard Graves MacDonnell had succeeded Lord Normanby as Lieutenant-Governor of Nova Scotia. Both had agreed to Monck's suggestion that Canadian delegates should sit in on the Conference, though they stipulated that official discussion must be confined to Maritime Union.

When Gordon returned to New Brunswick, the place and date of the Conference, as well as the inclusion of the Canadians were a *fait accompli*. Neither he nor MacDonnell welcomed the introduction of what might prove to be a rival scheme, and both were opposed to the whole idea of a general union of all the Provinces; but it had been difficult to refuse the request of the Governor General. The Canadian delegation consisted of seven cabinet members: John A. Macdonald, Brown, Cartier, Galt, Campbell, McDougall, and McGee.

Although Canadian attendance at the Conference was unofficial, the Maritime Legislative Union between Nova Scotia, New Brunswick, Prince Edward Island, and Newfoundland became so fraught with difficulties that the Conference turned with relief to consider the "informal" proposals of the Canadians.

There would be still greater differences of opinion in the aims of the wider union; but in spite of the hostility of Governors Gordon and MacDonnell, the majority of the assembled delegates were in favour of it. It was agreed to hold an October conference in Quebec to discuss the scheme in detail.

During September and October, the daily entries in Feo's journal carried vague allusions to public events, but only if these happened to encroach on her social life.

Of more immediate concern to her was the renewed threat of war with the United States. Confederate soldiers had captured a Canadian steamship on Lake Erie in an unsuccessful attempt to seize a United States gunboat. Their object was to free Confederate prisoners-of-war from the American prison camp on Johnson Island.

After strengthening border defences, Charles Monck pressed the Colonial Office for permission to put armed vessels on the frontier lakes. This was not the first time he had made the request and again it was refused. "If we are to have British war vessels on the Lakes, we shall also have American; and no one can foresee what may ensue," Cardwell wrote in reply "News of an *émeute* about ships being burnt on Lake Erie," was Feo's entry for September 21st, 1864. "Telegrams coming and going. Lord L. [Lyons] ill with headache."

Lord Lyons and his attachés had arrived at Spencer Wood on the previous day. A peaceful cultured man, he was also a shrewd diplomat. Charles Monck respected his alert intelligence and sound judgement as he steered Anglo-American relations through the stormy years of the American civil war. Relaxing on holiday, the Minister showed a different side of his character, and it is hard to recognise the level-headed diplomat in the portrait of him that emerges from the pages of Feo's journal.

On Lord Lyons' first visit to the Moncks, he and Elizabeth had become very friendly; but his disappointment at having missed her was made up for by the presence of her niece. Feo was the perfect antidote to the strains and stresses imposed on him by his post. She neither knew nor cared anything about politics and was equally indifferent to the causes or the progress of the American Civil War. In many ways, her artless prattle was more soothing to the harassed Minister than Elizabeth's informed sympathy would have been. He excelled at the sort of sprightly badinage in which Feo revelled and after dinner preferred her card-table (where "Old Maid" was succeeded by "Grab") over the whist players. From the first day of his visit, she firmly took him under her wing and was by his side during the many excursions arranged to amuse him. They saw the waterfalls at Chaudière and Shawinigan; visited sawmills at work and watched the timber shooting down slides into the water; boarded the *Queen Victoria* for a St. Lawrence River voyage to St. Anne's: "Lord L. hates ships and water as much as I do . . . He was in bliss at getting out of the ship." Feo was equally terrified when they travelled by road. . . . "on dirt roads, which are no roads," she complained. She squealed and clutched at the reins when the waggons bumped and skidded, and Lord Lyons recited poetry to calm her. He talked to her about books, confessing that he never travelled without a copy of *Cranford*. "He told me a funny story about Mr. Lincoln. He is always running off with the umbrellas of other people, and one day he wanted one, and said to his boy aged about seven, 'Go and get my umbrella from the hall.' The boy returned without one saying, 'Father, I guess the owner's been round.' "

Lord Airlie[14] was also staying at Spencer Wood, and Feo reported a "large dinner party" every night. Monck's weekly Saturday "Parliamentary Dinner" of twenty-four men only took place while Parliament was sitting. Those described in Feo's diary at this time included officers from the garrison and country neighbours, as well as officials and members of the Government.

As with royalty, the procedure was for the Governor General, followed by his house party, to make a stately entrance into the drawing room where the assembled guests awaited. During Lord Lyons' visit, Miss Mountain (presumably a daughter of the late Bishop) attended a party. As usual, she insisted on bringing her dog with her. Just as the Governor made his entrance, the visiting dog was attacked by one of the Spencer Wood cats. A terrible battle ensued. "Guests flew in all directions . . . with difficulty the animals were quieted, and we went into dinner."

Lord Lyons was so delighted with Feo that he invited her and Dick to accompany him to Montreal, the Niagara Falls, and Ottawa, before his return to Washington. "We have great work arranging our long journey," she wrote on October 3, the eve of their departure; "Lord L. leaves it most kindly to Mr. Sheffield [Lyons' attaché] and me to do as we like, and we change our plans every two minutes." Another entry in Feo's diary referred to a dinner party preceding the Quebec Conference:

> ... John A. Macdonald (or J. A. M. as we call him for short) – told me that they are going to give a grand ball here to the Delegates from the Maritime Provinces on Friday, so, having made all our plans, Lord L. offered to undo them so as to let me get back for the ball, which will be an interesting occasion. Is he not kind, and although Mr. S. had telegraphed all the plans to the Legation about letters, now all is undone. The G.G. is going to have a drawing room, which to my great annoyance I shall miss.

Those immediately concerned with the conference bore the responsibility of reducing the many different opinions to a common denominator of agreement. Finally, seventy-two "Quebec Resolutions" were drawn up. But at the time most citizens of Quebec and the numerous visitors were chiefly impressed by the festive aspect of the occasion. "We have had nothing here for the last fortnight but feasting and dancing in honour of the delegates," Charles Monck wrote to Henry on October 28.

After a pause for the observance of Sunday, the round of gaieties and the business for which the delegates were assembled continued. Feo continued to document the festivities:

> Old Coles is I believe a retired butcher, and oh! so vulgar I could not describe him. He is grey-haired and red-faced, and looks as if his legs were fastened on after the rest of his body, to support his fat ...
>
> [John A. Macdonald] is always drunk now, I am sorry to say, and when someone went to his room the other night, they found him in his nightshirt with a railway rug thrown over him, practising Hamlet before a looking-glass. At the drawing room he said to Mrs. G. [Godley] he should like to blow up Sir R. M. with gunpowder; very unfortunate for this week and last, they wanted all Canadians to appear their best before the delegates. I shall not cry when these delegates are gone – it is a bore having to dance with them...

In the atmosphere of political discussion, frivolous Feo was becoming restive. Her boredom was soon to be dispelled, however, by news which was both dramatic and alarming.

Chapter Nine (1864-65)

On October 20 (1864), when the Quebec Conference was at its height, the Governor General received a telegram announcing the most serious threat to British neutrality that had yet taken place. "The G.G. has had a telegram that has fussed him," wrote Feo, "and he has gone on now, the moment after breakfast, to Quebec; it is about Confederates and Yankees I believe." A band of Southern Americans had crossed the border to raid the United States' town of St. Albans. They held up and robbed the bank of $200,000 before retreating across the frontier. Monck immediately ordered out the Militia, who captured fourteen of the raiders and $19,000 of the stolen money. The American papers praised the Governor's prompt action, and United States Secretary of State Seward wrote to thank him for it. "It is so clearly to the interest of the United States to appreciate the fairness of your dealings with them," wrote Cardwell in his reply to Monck's report on the incident.

In spite of this, Seward gave the necessary six months' notice for the abrogation of the 1817 Convention limiting armaments on the Great Lakes and threatened to break off negotiations for the Reciprocity Treaty. At the same time, the United States Commander General Dix issued a proclamation ordering his troops to cross the Canadian frontier in pursuit of marauders.

The Ambassador protested privately to Seward when Dix informed him of the order. "Mr. Seward's answer to Lyons appears to me very uncandid and evasive," Monck wrote to Cardwell:

> I do not believe the order was acted on, nor have I heard that any infringement of our territorial rights (by the United States army) occurred, but I must say it is too bad of Mr. Seward, after having *volunteered* a Despatch thanking me for my conduct in this very

> affair,–to speak in the present note as if no precautionary measures had been adopted by the Canadian Govt. . . .
>
> The examination before the magistrate (in Montreal) respecting the St. Albans people has not yet ended, and no warrant for their extradition can issue until they are committed.[1]

Anglo-American relations had simmered down to their former uneasy but unbroken state, when the Judge at Montreal arbitrarily dismissed the case against the Southern raiders and released them.

M. Cartier brought the news to Spencer Wood. Monck left the dinner table remarking facetiously: "I suppose this is an invasion of the Yankees!" But he soon learned that it was no joking matter. He and Cartier were joined by John A. Macdonald, Langevin, and McDougall. "John A.'s appearance was grotesque," Feo commented, "with his hair flying in all directions, like a Spanish caricature. The fuss was great fun."

She was the only person to be amused by the incident which inflamed anti-British feeling in America even more than the original raid had done. Monck called out 2,000 volunteers and reinforced the policing of the frontier; five of the raiders were re-arrested; and once again, the United States Government was persuaded that the Canadian Government had not been responsible for what had appeared to be a deliberate act of defiance. "My ministers took fright at the possible consequences," Monck wrote to Cardwell, "and at once carried into effect measures of precaution, the necessity of which I had for some time been pressing upon them without any result beyond verbal assent on their part." His letter concludes with a commendation on the "alacrity" with which the volunteers responded to the call. "The conduct of both officers and men has been most creditable, and if you could say something complimentary to the force as well as to the Ministry for enabling me to put it on active duty, I think it would do good here."[2]

The raid that so nearly resulted in war between the United States and Britain had taken place in the middle of the Quebec Conference. Far from hindering the discussions, the incident had given fresh impetus to those delegates who believed the future strength of British North America to lie in a union of all the provinces. Mr. John A. Macdonald, in a clear and brilliant speech, laid the scheme before the assembled delegates, after proposing,

> . . . that the best interests of British North America will be promoted by a Federal Union under the Crown of Great Britain, provided such union can be effected on principles just to the several provinces. . . .

> For the sake of securing peace to ourselves and our posterity, we must make ourselves powerful. The great security for peace is to convince the world of our strength by being united.
>
> In framing the constitution, care should be taken to avoid the mistakes and weaknesses of the United States' system, the primary error of which was the reservation to the different States of all powers not delegated to the General Government. We must reverse this process by establishing a strong central Government, to which shall belong all powers not specially conferred on the provinces.

He subsequently explained the reason for the proposal of a federal rather than a legislative union:

> It was found that any proposition which involved the absorption of the individuality of Lower Canada would not be received with favour by her people. We found, too, that there was as great a disinclination on the part of the people of the Maritime Provinces to lose their individuality as separate political organisations.[3]

The proposal was seconded by S. L. Tilley, Prime Minister of New Brunswick, and adopted by the meeting; and the next two weeks were spent in trying to reach an agreement that would meet the demands of the several provinces. The most difficult questions were:

> The apportionment of the financial burdens, the distribution of powers between the federal and local Legislatures, the allotment of representatives in the Lower House, and the constitution of the Upper House.[4]

Monck was in entire agreement with all Macdonald's proposals and with his arguments for them; but one part of the speech made him uneasy. Macdonald had declared that it was to be a federal union; he also insisted that it was necessary to establish a strong central government in which all powers not specially delegated to the several Provinces would lie – in other words, a legislative union.

This appeared to Monck to be a contradiction in terms. He was all for central government in principle, provided it allowed for protection of the rights and traditions of the French-Canadians (who would represent a minority in the proposed Union). Until a few years before, they had greatly outnumbered the English-speaking Canadians but the recent tremendous increase of English-speaking settlers in Upper Canada had reversed the balance.

There was perpetual discord in the existing joint Parliament of Upper and Lower Canada over rights of representation. French Canada's position would be considerably worse if they were not fairly represented in a central government controlling the proposed general union.

The French-speaking community was further weakened by its political divisions, with the *Rouges* or liberals on one side and the *Bleus* or conservatives on the other. Their defensive attitude and their local and parochial disagreements tended to obscure wider issues. Thus, only such leaders as Taché and Cartier, whose attitudes were national rather than parochial, appreciated the advantages of a general union.

Monck knew very well that in a federal union of politically independent states there would be the danger of any one province being dominated by whichever local political party happened to be in power. This danger would be avoided only by having strong central control to act as final court of appeal. Monck's only criticism of Macdonald's speech was that it contained the word "federal" to describe a union that was not intended to be so.

A compromise between a legislative and a federative union was needed; and Monck hoped this would evolve from the resolutions being considered by the Quebec Conference.

The Conference ended on October 27. Sir Etienne Taché, Canadian Premier and chairman of the Conference, presented the seventy-two resolutions to the Governor General. These became known as "The Quebec Scheme" and, with certain modifications, formed the basis of the British North American Act. The scheme would be submitted to the next session of each of the five Provincial Parliaments early in 1865. Then it would have to be approved and passed by the Imperial Government.

In addition to his official report to the Colonial Office on the result of the Quebec Conference, Monck wrote a series of private despatches and personal letters to Cardwell setting out his own views:

> I must in the first place express my regret that the term 'Confederation' was ever used in connection with the proposed Union ... because I think it an entire misapplication of the term, and still more because I think the word calculated to give a false notion of the sort of Union which is desired, I might say which is possible, between these Provinces.[5]

Cardwell had written cheerfully, "I want these Local Legislations to dwindle down to the Municipal as far as possible,"[6] and that: "It signifies very little what name is employed."[7] But Monck had an inconvenient prejudice against anything that savoured of hypocrisy. He was not happy about the name "Confederation" (implying a Union of independent sovereign states) being given to a scheme that was intended to be, in effect, a legislative union with a strong central government. Such a government would be supreme and possess all powers not specifically delegated to the local governments. He told Cardwell that the Conference might have settled for a "complete Legislative consolidation" had it not been for the anxiety of the French-Canadians, "lest their peculiar rights and institutions might be interfered with by the general government." But, he also doubted whether the great extent of territory proposed to be included in the United Province, the scattered character of the population, and the defective means of communication between its component parts might not have made "a complete centralization of all authority, for the present at least, inconvenient in practice."[8]

In a very thorough definition of both federal and legislative unions he made it clear that the proposed Quebec scheme belonged in neither category. "It was a compromise . . . a great undertaking" embarked on by the public men of the provinces with "the most patriotic motives and the most complete honesty and singleness of purpose."[9]

The Colonial Secretary commented on the proposed scheme in frequent private letters to Monck:

> I shall most sincerely rejoice if we are able to bring to a satisfactory conclusion so great a work . . . The rock on which we are most likely to split will be that on which the American Confederacy has gone to pieces . . . In my opinion, *all* depends on central power . . . [with] complete control over the Local powers. If not, anarchy is to be apprehended as the result, sooner or later . . . If the scheme goes well and the Union is satisfactorily effected, your administration of Canada will leave a great mark in history.[10]

He urged that delegates "of some weight and authority . . . with formal power" be sent to London to present the Quebec Resolutions in order to clinch matters on the spot. He added shrewdly: "If the Bill were to be drawn up in British North America, I doubt whether the unanimity which has characterised your proceedings would be sure to continue."Cardwell had written to warn Lieutenant-Governors Gordon and MacDonnell that they would soon receive instructions from the Cabinet, "to promote the Scheme of Union" to the extent of their power.[11]

He told Monck of his conversation with George Brown, who had spoken enthusiastically about the Union in general but feared that the proposal for the appointment of Legislative Councillors would be "stubbornly resisted" by the French-Canadians, including Cartier. Cardwell replied that it was very unlikely the House of Commons at Westminster would pass an unworkable arrangement:

> At the close of a series of very satisfactory interviews with Mr. Brown, he told me one thing still remained. He should not like to

> return to Canada without having seen Lord Palmerston [the octogenerian Prime Minister] and I therefore wrote to Broadlands, and the result was that Mr. Brown, with Mrs. Cardwell and myself, went down there for two nights. I think he was much pleased.[12]

Cardwell confided to Monck that Brown had tried to pump him on the subject of Queen Victoria's "feelings" towards British North America: ". . . [he] went so far as to suggest inviting her to open the new [Parliament] buildings at Ottawa." Prime Minister Palmerston headed him off that malapropism; the mere suggestion was likely to cause a royal explosion. Opening buildings, however important, did not fit in with Victoria's image, nor with the mystique with which she surrounded herself. And in any case, she had already admitted that nothing would induce her to brave the Atlantic crossing.

Since Cardwell was anxious to be kept informed of all the varied opinions on the Confederation scheme Monck sent him a November copy of the Montreal *Telegraph*. It contained a letter from Mr. Dorion to his constituents against the proposed plan of union:

> He represents a not very large or influential party amongst the French Canadians, and will be the leader of the opposition to the scheme. The Priests are *his* deadly enemies and are Cartier's supporters, and that fact deprives Mr. Dorion of all chance of success in his opposition.
>
> In Upper Canada I hear of no opposition, there they seem to have quite made up their minds to accept the plan.[13]

"Your encouraging accounts do not, I am sorry to say, correspond entirely with what I hear from other quarters," replied Cardwell. "The Governors of N. Brunswick, N. Scotia, and P.E.I. [Prince Edward Island] all write as if the reception of the Scheme in the Provinces was not likely to be favourable. However, we shall soon see."[14]

The Lieutenant-Governors had solid grounds for their pessimistic outlook. The majority of delegates at the Quebec Conference represented the political parties then in power, and there were many dissentient voices in the respective oppositions. At the same time, Cardwell and Monck were both well aware that the Governors, at least of New Brunswick and Nova Scotia, were themselves prejudiced against a Federal Union. If they honestly believed the maritimes would not benefit by the Quebec Scheme, they were also influenced by personal motives. Their provinces were little "kingdoms" with independent governments; and although the Lieutenant-Governors were nominally subordinate to the Governor General, each had the power of appeal and direct access to the Colonial Office. The attitude of Gordon and MacDonnell to the proposed "take-over bid" is expressed in their letters to both Monck and Cardwell. Monck concludes a letter to Cardwell by saying:

> I have a letter from A. Gordon in which he says: "Confederation has hardly any friends here [New Brunswick] but it will be carried by large majorities nevertheless!" I don't understand the component parts of this sentence, but I am satisfied with the sentiment contained in the latter member of it.[15]

The "sentiment" in the latter part of Gordon's sentence was the result of some peremptory letters from the Colonial Secretary instructing "Thy Servant Arthur" to forward the cause of Confederation by every means in his power.

Sir Richard MacDonnell made no secret of his attitude to the Quebec Scheme. Feo noted a conversation with John A. Macdonald in her diary:

> John A. made great fun of [Sir R. MacDonnell], he is so against this confederation scheme, because he would be turned away. He said to John A. – 'You shall not make a Mayor of *me*, I can tell you,' meaning a Deputy Governor of a Province, so John A. humbugged Lady [MacDonnell] till she believed that Sir [Richard] would be made Governor General of the Kingdom of Canada after the present G.G.

Monck had criticised the label "Confederation" as misleading; it certainly gave a handle to those in opposition to the scheme. Gordon wrote to Cardwell:

> You may take my word for this: that it *is* a federation, not only in name but in fact, whatever Monck may be led to say to the contrary. . . . You know Monck far better than I do, and even if you did not it is not my business to describe him to you. How, however, he could have written you that you need not expect a Federation to be proposed to you passeth all man's understanding, – at least it passeth mine. You will see that the *small* amount of its interference with local independence is urged as its recommendation, both in Lower Canada, and here![16]

MacDonnell had refused even to meet Dr. Tupper and the other Nova Scotian delegates in Quebec. He wrote a private letter to Monck describing the Confederation scheme as a "complicated abortion. . . . I hope the country at large will unite to 'smite on the hip' any such unworthy project." He doubted whether it would be safe to incorporate Nova Scotia with "the proposed New Development of the West" and suggested that Halifax, at least, be retained by Her Majesty's Government and "be placed like Gibraltar under a Military Governor."

In support of a Legislative rather than a Federal Constitution, MacDonnell wrote:

> Nothing would please me better than to be released from my present profitless responsible position by *worthily* amalgamating it with the duties of a post so well filled by Your Lordship, but I don't quite like being succeeded by Dr. Tupper![17]. . . . I daresay that I look at Confederation from a different point of view from that in which Canadians regard it . . . I am only sorry that Your Lordship was so prompt in giving an unqualified approval.[18]

Undeterred by either gloomy forebodings or personal criticisms, Monck looked forward eagerly to the union of all the North American provinces. On January 20, 1865, he wrote to Henry:

> I opened Parliament yesterday, and I hope most sincerely it is the last *Canadian* Parliament that will ever assemble. I trust next year we shall have the Parliament of the Union. We shall soon know whether we shall be able to carry that measure or not.

A week later he wrote:

> *Mirabile dictu*, the Lower House agreed to the address in *one* night. Don't you remember how they used to take about a fortnight talking of it. They rejected an amendment repudiating the Union by a majority of 64 to 25, so that I think that there is no doubt that we shall carry that measure.

His weekly Parliamentary dinners, attended by twenty-four ministers and members of Parliament, gave Charles plenty of opportunity to learn how affairs were progressing. Expecting the session to be a short one, he foresaw nothing to prevent him from going home in May for several months' leave. Cardwell had written to warn him that owing to the continued strained relations with the United States, his leave might have to be postponed. Monck replied: "I think you overestimate the chance of misunderstanding with the United States, and also the benefit of my presence here should any arise." However, he had had to admit in January that:

> . . . there is a strong feeling in the U.S. that England should be brought to account for the losses to their trade by the *Alabama*. I think it right you should know that people here are *greatly* alarmed at the aspect of affairs. I have never believed that the Washington Govt would be so insane as to engage in a quarrel with us while they had on their hands the war with the South, but there is a general impression here that peace is about to be patched up in some way, and then undoubtedly the danger of an attack on Canada would be greatly increased.[19]

In spite of this, Monck continued to hope for his release. On March 11, the Quebec Resolutions were passed by the Canadian Parliament by a majority of ninety-one to thirty-three, and Cardwell's invitation to send a deputation to England was accepted. There seemed to be a strong possibility that the Governor General would be present during the London discussions. He told Henry that "a deputation from the Canadian Government consisting of Messrs. Cartier, Macdonald, Brown, and Galt are going home in about a fortnight. Fancy meeting little Cartier in the streets of London!"[20] On April 1, Cardwell still expected to have Monck with him during the discussions with the Canadian delegates. He appreciated the fact that the Governor had been at his post uninterruptedly for three-and-a-half years. But a fortnight later, he withdrew the permission he had so nearly given:

> I cannot venture to say "Come", in answer to your expression of your wish to be here. Looking at all that is going on around you, I think your presence at this moment in Canada could not be spared.[21]

Cardwell had more than one reason for cancelling Monck's leave. On Saturday, April 15, Feo noted in her journal:

> The news has just come in of Lincoln's death by stabbing; it took place in the theatre last night. Is it not too horrible? What will happen next? He kept off war with England always. What will become of America?

Early in April, the main army of the American Southern States capitulated. The British had considered President Lincoln the chief advocate of peace between his country and their own. Now, with the Southern army defeated, the Northern army was free to invade Canada if provocation should arise. Meanwhile Lord Lyons had become so seriously ill that he resigned his post at Washington. He was unable even to carry on until his successor, Sir Frederick Bruce, arrived. Feo heard rumours that "the people here are terrified at the idea of the G.G. going home when everything is unsettled, and Lord Lyons gone."

Later in 1865 Cardwell wrote that present relations with the United States might make it "objectionable" that Monck should be absent from Quebec. "It will certainly render it, I think, impossible that you should be absent long." And in the following year Lord Lyons' successor, Sir Frederick Bruce, warned Monck of the danger of assassination saying: "It would be a serious publick calamity were anything to happen to you during this crisis, for I think Seward would do more for you than for most men in your position." In retrospect, C. P. Stacey wrote of Monck: "It is not too much to say that he deserves to be remembered, along with Lord Lyons and Charles Francis Adams United States Ambassador in London ... as having made a great contribution towards preventing what would have been from every point of view a most shocking catastrophe."[22]

It was not only the threat of war which made it necessary for Monck to defer his leave. Cardwell had referred to the bad news from New Brunswick. Gordon, instructed to support the Quebec Scheme, decided instead on a dissolution of Parliament and a general election on the question of Confederation. On March 6, 1865, he wrote to Cardwell:

> The proposed Confederation of the British North American Provinces has met with a most decided rejection in New Brunswick. The elections have resulted in the defeat of every one of the Candidates favourable to Confederation. Mr. Tilley, the leader of the Government, the Postmaster General, the Solicitor General, Mr. Fisher, and Mr. Gray, Delegates to Quebec, have all lost their seats. The Government is practically overthrown, and the scheme of Union virtually defeated.[23]

This news had a disastrous effect on the other maritime provinces. Prince Edward Island and Newfoundland opted out of the scheme, and in Nova Scotia, Joseph Howe, an anti-Unionist, launched a newspaper campaign against what he termed "The Botheration Scheme." His violent prejudice against Confederation was partly because Tupper led the party in favour of it. Howe is reputed to have declared that he would not "play second fiddle to that damned Tupper."[24]

Sir Richard MacDonnell let off steam in almost weekly personal letters to Monck:"Confederation without New Brunswick is of course impossible," he wrote. "I see little prospect of the question being favourably received here." He said he had been zealously and conscientiously helping to carry out Mr. Cardwell's instructions; but in the same letter declared that Confederation was "a selfishly Canadian" measure which could be of no possible benefit to Nova Scotia:

> The incautious admission of Sir Etienne [Taché] that Confederation is a matter of self-preservation for Canada, whilst John A.'s declaration of alarm lest the present scheme be not carried and strong union might be established between the Maritime Provinces, all are adapted to make men here very cautious how they surrender themselves and their revenue to an Ottawa parliament.[25]

In all his immensely long letters, MacDonnell betrayed his disgust, shared by Arthur Gordon, at the prospect of being controlled by a Canadian Parliament, in which their provinces would be represented by those very politicians whom they distrusted and despised. As Lieutenant-Governors, they had been in direct contact with the Imperial Parliament by way of the Colonial Office, and this suited them very well. "The course of post to Quebec is little shorter than from here to London," MacDonnell remarked parenthetically when writing to Monck.

Another sore point was the rumoured exclusion of a definite plan for an intercolonial railway from the proposed Act of Union. Though the Quebec Resolutions stated that construction of this intercolonial railway was to be one of the first enactments of the Confederation Government, it was rumoured that a definite plan for this was excluded from the Act of Union. Nova Scotia, said Sir Richard, "would have liked to ensure its construction and put it beyond the reach of chance in the Ottawa Parliament."[26] He was confident that the Quebec Resolutions would not get past the Imperial Parliament when presented by the Canadian delegates. "The superfluous steam generated by Federal discussions" would be worked off in this safety valve, "an admirable save-all, and *scapegoat*! Here we are quite decided to leave all we can to the Queen's Government *in London*."[27]

As soon as he heard that Confederation had been defeated in New Brunswick, Monck knew he could not accompany the Canadian delegates to London. His leave must be postponed until after the next Parliamentary session at Quebec. He wrote to Henry: "I shall not be able to go home as soon as I expected. It is a great disappointment to me but it cannot be helped, and I am looking forward to spending the summer holidays with you at Charleville."

Everyone else seemed to be going on leave, Arthur Gordon in June, and the Richard Moncks on May 20. Feo was thrown into a state of agitation, uncertain whether to be glad or sorry.

> Of course I am *enchanted* to see you all again . . . but at present I am thinking too much of the horrors of the passage to realize anything else. I said last night at dinner that I hoped it would not be supposed at home that I knew anything about the American war, because I know *nothing*. The G.G. advised me to say – 'The *Times* is wrong,' then people would be shocked for a few minutes at my presumption. Then I am to say – 'I have been in America, and saw it with my own eyes!'

A guest at dinner tried to calm her fears of the voyage by quoting Sir Samuel Cunard, who had said that the reason the ships of his line were so safe was that they were "well prayed over."

When Elizabeth and her children left Canada in September, it was understood that Charles would follow them in the spring. It was the first time in twenty years that he and his wife had been separated for more than a few days. Knowing how disappointed she would be over the postponement of his leave, he was glad to hear that Henry was spending his Easter holidays with her in Paris. Elizabeth had rented a house at Versailles where the girls' education was continued by visiting masters, and Stanley's by Fraülein Denneler. Oblivious of the bad news on the way, Elizabeth had written cheerfully to Henry in March:

> I hope the time will pass quickly until we are all together again. Papa may soon be able to name a time for coming. I trust the federation will be carried, as there seems every prospect of. I have been reading the debate on the defences of Canada.
>
> ... The Canadian Parliament is to be prorogued – 3 of the Ministry to come over to England to confer with Government on the subject – on their return, Parliament is again to be called together – in short, Papa sees no hope of coming over before July, and cannot come to London. He wishes however that we should go there for a while and tells me to stay here till it is too hot, and then go to London. He speaks of getting Dick to meet me there, and be there with me.

In expressing her bitter disappointment in the continued separation from her husband, Elizabeth had dwelt particularly on the fact that he would not be able to "come to London." She was not, as might be supposed, referring to his absence from the Canadian Ministers' negotiations with Cardwell, but to a more personal matter. Having never doubted that Charles would be with them in May, at the latest, it had long been settled that Fan should be presented at the Queen's Drawing Room held during that month. She was in her twentieth year and the ceremony could no longer be delayed, though it would now have to take place without the support of her father.

The Richard Moncks landed at Greencastle, in Ireland, early on the morning of May 30 and were in Dublin by six o'clock that evening. Their little son Cecil was with Feo's mother, Fanny Cole, at her house in Leeson Street. Fanny had also temporarily taken charge of Stanley, while Elizabeth and her daughters were living it up in London. Feo had remained in Dublin with her mother and her child while the obliging Dick hurried on to London to look after Elizabeth who moved soon afterwards into a house in Eaton Square belonging to a distant connection. "I think by all accounts that the girls seem to be amusing themselves very well in London," Charles wrote to Henry. "Mama also tells me that she is now quite well." Short of being present himself, he had done his best to smooth the way for his wife in the matter of presenting their deaf-mute daughter, with the result that, on May 8, the Lord Chamberlain had written a private letter to Elizabeth:

> Dear Lady Monck. – I had the pleasure of receiving a few days since a letter from Lord Monck, and I have the honour to inform you that I have received the Queen's Commands to invite your Ladyship and Miss Monck to a Ball at Buckingham Palace on the 16th Instant, and I would venture to observe that it would of course be convenient that Miss Monck should be presented at the evening Drawingroom of the 18th Inst.
>
> I have also been commanded to send an invitation for Her Majesty's Reception at Buckingham Palace on the 15th Inst.[28]

Fan wrote to her father an account of these functions in which Puss was not included, her own presentation being deferred to the following year, though she joined in many of the gaieties. Henry wrote to Charles that "Mama and Sisters" had been down to Eton for the Fourth of June, the celebrations for which had actually taken place on the 6th, June 4 having fallen on a Sunday that year. It was the first time since he went to Eton that he had had his family with him on the "Fourth", and he may have been over-excited and showing off a little to his older sisters, which would account for the letter Elizabeth wrote him next day:

> My dearest Child. – You are such a good child to me, and such a comfort to me, I want you to do one thing for me –
>
> ... Will you, to please me, not go to the tap ... drinking beer between meals comes to be a *real* bad habit. I remember the present Lord Clonmel, as nice a looking youth as any I saw yesterday – he began by taking glasses of beer between meals – we used to laugh at him – he went from one thing to another, and is now *insane* from drink, taken care of by your grandfather's old servant, *Starr*.
>
> Another thing I ask from you, is not to get into the habit of betting. No words could express the misery-that I have known result from that habit.
>
> Knowing that there is nothing I would not *do* or *give up* for *you*, will you do those two things for me.

The awful example of this warning against drinking between meals, was the 3rd Earl of Clonmel who died a few months later. Naturally Elizabeth did not then know that his youngest daughter, Edith Scott, was to become her dearly-loved daughter-in-law. The next Saturday and Sunday were to be one of the occasions on which Henry "managed to run up to London and see Mama" as his father had hoped would be the case.

In all his letters to Henry, Charles showed that he was continually thinking of his wife and children, following their movements with affectionate interest and with a certain degree of anxiety –

> When you see Mama, give her a scolding from me for getting up so early in the morning after having been up late at night . . .
>
> I hope you do not smoke much because you are really too young, and many fellows hurt their health by smoking at an early age. Indeed I should much rather, while you are at Eton, that you did not smoke or do anything against the regulations of the place . . . I hear great accounts from London where Mama and the girls seem to be amusing themselves very well.

The time spent in London was ostensibly for the sake of "amusing" the girls, but there is no doubt that Elizabeth, too, was thoroughly enjoying herself. The rather solemn tone of her notes to Henry, without the accompanying journal, gives a misleading impression; and it is from other sources that one learns that she was at heart a very gregarious person. That section of the community to which she and Charles belonged was a great deal smaller and more closely-knit than it was to become in later years, and the saying that, in it, "everybody knew everybody" was not very far from the truth. Certainly Elizabeth knew a great many people, and some of her mother's relations had houses in London.

During that summer there was a good deal of excitement over the general election in which the Liberal government was returned; added to which, in political circles at least, Canada was "in the news", partly owing to the continuing threat of war with the United States, and partly as the result of the interest aroused by the proposed scheme of Union. Political hostesses vied with each other in entertaining the visiting Canadian Ministers, and Elizabeth received a certain amount of reflected glory as the wife of the Governor General.

"I think Mama intended to leave London about the 22nd [June], but perhaps she may stay a little longer," Charles wrote to Henry, and his forecast was correct. On June 24, Sir Julius Benedict[29] wrote: "Dear Lady Monck, – I shall be very happy to give Miss Monck a lesson on Tuesday next at eleven o'clock if perfectly convenient." Puss could not be allowed to miss the opportunity of being given a singing lesson from a man who was then considered a celebrated musician, and this entailed their remaining in London until after June 27.

By this time poor Dick had been allowed to return to his wife and to the child whom he had scarcely seen. Charles's next commission to him was to buy a horse for Henry whose old pony was now too small for him. Charles had arranged for him to have one of the home-bred colts, but the agent (Henry Sandys) reported that it would not be sufficiently schooled for him to ride during the holidays. Early in July, Elizabeth tore herself and her daughters away from London and crossed to Ireland.

The Canadian Parliament could not re-assemble till the four Ministers returned from England, and Charles would not be able to go home until the session was over. "Until they [the Ministers] come, I can settle nothing," he told Henry. "They have been so fêted and made much of in London that I suppose they are only too glad to make out an excuse for staying there." Towards the end of June he wrote:

> I am greatly afraid that I shall not be able to get home before your holidays begin, as these Ministers have been delayed so long in London, but I hope to get over before you return to Eton and to stay over the Christmas holidays.

Monck was very well aware that it was not only the persuasions of London hostesses that detained the ministers, having received regular reports on Cardwell's discussions with them. In addition to the Confederation scheme, the discussion included the defence of Canada and the distribution of the burden of expense.

> Your Ministers have not come to me *officially* [on May 6]. We have had many unofficial conversations, and they are enjoying a full opportunity of discovering what is the opinion here. I was very anxious that this should be the case, for any proposals founded on such impressions as Messrs. Galt and Cartier seemed to entertain, when they first arrived, would have thrown everything into confusion.

A month later he was able to write: "We have got on better this week," intimating that he had managed to persuade the delegates to adopt a national outlook on Confederation instead of regarding it as the solution to their respective sectional grievances: "Your Ministers are to waive all the works [for Defence] west of Quebec until after Confederation; to train their Militia; and to negotiate for the purchase of the rights of the Hudson's Bay Company, we guaranteeing the purchase money." On June 17, he reported that the delegates were all perfectly satisfied with the result of the discussions. Canada was to be a "quasi-independent country, primarily responsible for its defence, though assured of the powerful support of England" in the event of attack. Macdonald and Cartier were to stay on for a few days, and Cardwell welcomed this opportunity of talking over with them the possibility of putting "pressure" on New Brunswick with regard to Confederation: "I am anxious to turn the screw as hard as will be useful, but not harder."[30]

Cardwell's pressure took the form of a peremptory letter to New Brunswick's Lieutenant-Governor, Arthur Gordon:

> In your high position, your personal sentiments cannot have been a matter of small moment; and if you suppose that the world in general have not been aware of those sentiments, you are entirely mistaken. It is as well known here that the Lt. Governors of Nova Scotia and New Brunswick are adverse to the Confederation, as it is that their names are Gordon and MacDonnell; and though I have never heard any suggestion from any one that they have not loyally obeyed their instructions, since they received them, it is felt that all the might of their personal convictions has been thrown (against their present wishes) into the opposing scale.[31]

Monck took a different line with Gordon, still believing that he could be won over by tactful persuasion. MacDonnell had long been regarded as a joke by the Colonial Office and would be removed from Nova Scotia if he continued to be a nuisance. But Monck regarded Gordon's touchiness and jealousy as a form of protracted adolescence that needed only kindness and patience to effect a cure. With this aim in view, he invited Gordon to come to Spencer Wood for a private visit during the second week in June. He hoped that a friendly and informal talk with "Thy Servant Arthur" might be more profitable than the acrimonious correspondence in which that inveterate letter-writer persisted, both with himself and with Cardwell. Gordon accepted, but at the last moment cancelled his visit. At the same time he accused Monck of blaming him (in letters to the Colonial Office) for the failure of Confederation in New Brunswick. Monck replied in his usual pacific vein:

> . . . in truth I have never written a word to Cardwell respecting the exercise of your influence on the Elections one way or the other. I know that a Governor can exercise very little if any influence on the returns . . . I do think however that a Governor may exercise a very considerable moral influence during the discussion of any measure in the Legislature by private intercourse with the members.[32]

His letter included a detailed account of all he had ever written to Cardwell on the subject of New Brunswick. He sent a copy of this letter to Cardwell, who replied: "I am very glad that with your accustomed frankness and sincerity you have told him the truth, as I have done."

The problem presented by the two Lieutenant-Governors could best be solved by relieving them of their posts. Cardwell wished to do this tactfully, making it look more like promotion than recall; and Gordon's periodical requests for transfer gave him the required opening. "I have submitted Gordon's name to the Queen for Hong Kong, which is vacant," wrote Cardwell. "I do not doubt he will accept it, and my intention is to leave N.B. in the hands of Doyle at present."[33] However, Gordon kept changing his mind:

> I cannot make out from his numerous letters to me whether he wishes to go to Hongkong or to stay in N.B. Yet I understand he is coming over here, and I hope, in friendly conversation, to overcome the difficulties which in correspondence are not easily surmounted. Meanwhile in Doyle you have an old friend, with whom you will be on perfectly easy terms, of whose cordial cooperation you can be sure.
>
> Since writing this, I have received yours suggesting Sir F. Williams [General Sir Fenwick Williams]. But you will observe that *as at present advised*, I do not wish to appoint any permanent Governor. However, I will bear your suggestion in mind, in case of further contingencies.[34]

Charles Monck's letter to Henry of June 30 contained good news:

> I am sure you will be rejoiced to hear that some of the Ministers have actually arrived in Canada from England and the remainder are on their way, so that I hope by next week's letter I shall be able to tell you the day when I hope to leave Quebec for England. It has been a great bore having been kept so long in doubt about the time but it could not be helped, and I hope I shall be able to get good long leave when I do go home.
>
> I think the Canadians will be pleased with the arrangements that have been made in England, and that we shall have a short session of Parliament.

But "next week's letter" (July 7) announced further delay:

> Mr. Macdonald has not yet arrived from England, and until he comes I cannot fix anything for certain about setting out for home. I am afraid I shall miss a good deal of your holidays, but that I cannot help . . . Old Cartier is in the greatest delight at the manner in which he was received in London. He said to me–"I did not dine at home more than twice the whole time I was in London . . . Lady Monck is furious with me, she says I stayed amusing myself in London and left Lord Monck in Quebec!"

That grand old statesman, Sir Etienne-Paschal Taché, died on July 30 (1865), a little more than a year after he had made Coalition Government possible by sacrificing his wish for retirement and accepting the Premiership. Four days after his death, Monck invited Sir John A. Macdonald to breakfast at Spencer Wood and asked him to form a Government with himself as the head. Macdonald agreed. Having been

Premier in 1857 he was the obvious person to succeed Taché.

Monck's next ordeal was to break the news to George Brown, leader of the Reformers, and far too valuable a member of the Government to lose. Monck knew only too well that Brown had made a great concession by sinking his personal feelings and serving alongside Macdonald and Cartier – but under Taché as Prime Minister. Now he was to be asked to stretch unselfish patriotism still further and serve under his old enemy with whom he had been forced to associate for the past year. Propinquity had not made him love Macdonald more, but rather the reverse. When invited to Spencer Wood for a private interview, he stood his ground and flatly refused to join any Government led by either Macdonald or Cartier. When Monck pressed the point, he threatened to resign.

Monck refused to go back on his arrangement with Macdonald. But Macdonald himself stood down and proposed that if a suitable Premier-figure could be found to replace Taché, he, Cartier, and Brown should carry on as before, on an equal basis. "Under these circumstances," he wrote to Brown:

> and to prevent the possibility of the scheme for the Confederation of British North America receiving any injury from the appearance of disunion among those who coalesced for the purpose of carrying it into effect, Mr. Cartier and I have agreed to propose that Sir Narcisse Belleau[35] shall assume the position of First Minister.[36]

In his biography of Alexander Galt, Skelton[37] describes Belleau as "a somewhat pompous mediocrity". Nevertheless, he had been speaker of the Legislative Council since 1857[38] and was to become Lieutenant-Governor of Quebec after the forming of the Dominion of Canada.

During the week Macdonald sailed from England, Cardwell received a delegation of Ministers from Nova Scotia and New Brunswick, the latter being anti-Confederation. He wrote Monck on July 15:

> I have got here Smith [Premier] and Allen from New Brunswick, Tupper [Premier] and Henry from Nova Scotia. Tilley [past Premier of New Brunswick] we hear is coming. I am sanguine that in one way or another we shall accomplish our object.
>
> Gordon has been very troublesome, and after much see-saw has declined Hongkong . . . I have to tell you that MacDonnell goes to Hongkong. Gordon I expect is coming home on leave. I have some thought of trying whether Fenwick Williams would go to New Brunswick for a temporary purpose, and letting Doyle administer Nova Scotia. You must not mention this, however, as I am not certain ...
>
> I have seen the Ministers of Nova Scotia and of New Brunswick.

I have told both that I shall endeavour to bring them to this point: that they shall return to communicate in a friendly way with your Govt, in order if possible to obtain such assurances as may enable them to go with a prospect of success to their own Legislatures, and then come over here next year to carry Confederation . . . Speaking generally, I learn from both that there is great jealousy of Canada, and that while Imperial influence may be pressed, Canadian predominance must be *sup*-pressed.[39]

The "jealousy" of the politicians from the maritime provinces was shared by their Lieutenant-Governors. In one of his letters to Monck, MacDonnell had alluded to the disparity of their respective salaries:

I do not really see any or scarcely any difference in my expenditure here and your own at Quebec, or at all events no difference to compensate for that of our respective salaries – of £2,750 – and £7,000.[40]

Before leaving London, Prime Minister Smith of New Brunswick had an interview with Lord Derby. Cardwell wrote the following report to Monck:

Lord Derby said, in reply to Smith's statement that he objected to Confederation but would favour a Legislative Union, – "that they were moving in a wrong direction; that Legislative Union was out of the question, for the Lower Canadians are already swamped by the Upper Canadians, and would be still more so if the New Brunswickers and Nova Scotians were added to an assembly." I suspect that Smith feels very much the pressure of public opinion here, and does not like the responsibility of opposing all England and the great majority of British North America . . . but he has not committed himself to me, and I can only give this as an impression I have formed.[41]

The Ministers had raised again the Maritime Union, so much favoured by their respective Lieutenant-Governors. But Cardwell had refused to ask the Imperial Parliament's sanction of any scheme that would not unite all British North America in one Government. "Tupper," he wrote, "seems confident that he can carry it in Nova Scotia." He ended his letter with formal permission for Monck's leave.

Cardwell's optimism was shaken when he received "a somewhat uncivil Minute from New Brunswick" in reply to his communication urging the claims for Confederation. He hinted to Monck that it might be wise to offer the New Brunswickers a variation of the scheme as they would "dislike it less" if it provided for stronger central power. But he left it to Monck and his Ministers to keep the balance between the maritime claims and the very different ones of Lower Canada.

> I have a letter from Gordon saying he will be here immediately. It is unfortunate that he has not acquired more experience from the rubs and kicks which we usually acquire either at public schools or in fighting our way up in early life. He dwells in an atmosphere of his own; and I could not please him, unless I acted as if the Colonies were made for Governors, not Governors for the Colonies.[42]

A week later Cardwell wrote a warning that Monck's leave might again be revoked. The American Secretary of State refused to negotiate for renewal of the Reciprocity Treaty, and it would be unwise for the Governor General to be absent from Canada at this time, especially since MacDonnell was about to be transferred to another post and Arthur Gordon was on his way home.

"Gordon, whose movements and non-movements are a difficulty to me, now sends me an official Letter asking for *two months* leave, and a private notification that he is coming by next mail." For once, the thorn in the side of the Colonial Office did what he had said he would do. "A. Gordon has landed," Cardwell reported in his next letter:

> He has written to me requesting that, if H. Kong is still vacant, he may know before it is disposed of. But I believe MacDonnell goes there. However I presume this shows that A. Gordon begins to open his eyes to the real nature of his position in N.B. He is gone to his lady love, and after the useful influence of Sir J. Lefevre's household has had two or three days time to operate on him, I shall see him, when I will write to you more fully what I am going to do.

Lefevre and his household did their work well. When Gordon went to Cardwell, he had become a convert to Confederation and undertook to carry it in New Brunswick.

> Gordon . . . will not only see from his relations with me what he must, and what he must not, do: but Lefevre and all his friends will impress him with the same conviction. I am satisfied that it will be better to send him back a convert, than to replace him. His successor, sent expressly to carry Confederation, would be in too direct an antagonism to the N.B. Ministry and Parliament. . . .
>
> After some coquetting, MacDonnell goes to Hong Kong, and will arrive in England at about the same time with yourself."[43]

Monck was to leave for London in early October since Cardwell wished to see him before Gordon's return to New Brunswick.

Early in September Monck presided at the Confederate Council on Commercial Treaties, attended by representatives from all the provinces. The Reciprocity Treaty was the main subject for discussion, but the Council also discussed alternative outlets for trade. Finally on September 15 came Monck's triumphant announcement to Henry:

> I have made all my arrangements to sail from this on the 26th [September] in the *Himalaya*. Lethbridge, her Captain, is a very nice fellow, and when he was here a short time since, he begged me to go home with him . . . Last, but not least, I shall not have to pay for my passage . . . We may expect to get to Portsmouth about the 9th or 10th October. I will telegraph to you on landing and I suppose you will have no difficulty in getting leave to come up and meet me in London. I shall be in too great a hurry to get home to allow of my going down to Eton, as I shall be busy with Cardwell, etc., all the time I stay in London. I shall go to Thomas's Hotel in Berkeley Square.

His "hurry to get home" was even greater since Cardwell had written again to say that the leave of absence must be very short, instead of the several months for which he had hoped. He had not seen his wife and children for over a year, and he had been away from home for exactly four years.

Chapter Ten (1865-66)

British Prime Minister Lord Palmerston died on October 18, 1865, and Charles Monck arrived in London in time to attend the funeral. He got through his business with the Colonial Office as quickly as possible and at last returned to Charleville. He had three months' leave, not long to catch up on four years' arrears of estate business and to see his numerous friends and relations. The family was at Charleville for Henry's holidays and for the "Christmas together at home" to which they had looked forward so long.

Cardwell had arranged with Monck that the three months were to be considered a little on account towards the far longer period of leave owed to him. When he left Ireland in January (1866), it was understood that he would be back again before the summer. Therefore he decided against taking his wife and daughters with him for such a short time. Only his brother Dick joined him on the *Australasia*. Before going on board at Queenstown, Charles wrote a farewell letter to his "dearest Fan and Puss": "God bless and keep you both, my own precious children, and make you a comfort to Mama while I am away from her." They landed at New York on February 9, and Charles wrote to Henry:

> We had a very good passage, though rather slow in consequence of head winds. The *Australasia* is a very fine ship and is the most comfortable passenger ship I have ever been in. I never missed a meal the whole voyage, and had my tub every morning as regularly as if I were on shore. We had only one very cold day, but that day all the rigging was covered with ice and the sea *smoking* from the cold. Dick was a very bad sailor on the voyage, but is quite well now. Judging from its present appearance, New York is not a very inviting place. The streets are full of snow half-melted so that it is bad

both for wheels and runners. I mean to remain at Montreal till the time for the meeting of Parliament.

Meanwhile in the maritime Parliaments, the fate of the Confederation scheme "seesawed" (to use Cardwell's expression) between those who were for and those who were against it. General Sir Fenwick Williams had replaced "Governor MacPotato" (his nickname for Sir Richard MacDonnell) as Lieutenant-Governor of Nova Scotia. In New Brunswick, Arthur Gordon was under strict orders from the Colonial Secretary to make it his business to see that Confederation was carried – as though "responsible government" had never been heard of. Because there were anti-unionists in both political parties, changes in the government merely delayed matters and confused the issue.

Confederation was still hanging fire in New Brunswick when the time came for General Sir Fenwick Williams to deliver his Speech from the Throne at the opening of the Nova Scotian Parliament. He had expected to follow the lead of New Brunswick and was taken aback to discover that he himself was expected to take the lead. Being unprepared, he played safe and delivered his Speech without any mention of Confederation. Arthur Gordon, who had run into a ministerial crisis as the result of obeying orders, rather naturally felt let down by the Nova Scotian Lieutenant-Governor.

Monck telegraphed Williams and advised him to rectify matters with a "message" to Parliament. At the same time, he wrote in a letter to Williams:

> Gordon's ministers may with some fairness object to having a paragraph in his speech recommending Union *thrust down their throats*, on the ground that he [Gordon] had been desired to bring the subject forward by the Secretary of State, if they see a similar instruction given to you not complied with in *any form*.

This, though politely worded, amounted to a rebuke. As if to point out the contrast, Monck then went on to praise Gordon's perseverance and resolution:

> I am quite sure that Gordon is working well and judiciously, he has great difficulties to contend with from many causes and my desire is that we should all act so as to strengthen his hands as much as possible. . . . I think he deserves *great* credit for the amount of success he has obtained up to this time."[1]

None of those who had hammered out the Quebec Scheme expected all seventy-two of its Resolutions to meet with universal approval; even those maritimers who supported it in general hoped that certain amendments would be made. The Lieutenant-Governors and pro-union Ministers appealed to the Governor General, pointing out that they would stand a better chance of winning over opponents to the scheme if certain clauses in it could be changed. But Monck was adamant that all discussion and criticism must be postponed till the scheme could be laid before the Imperial Government. He knew only too well that, even in Canada, the French-Canadians and many other parties wished to propose amendments. If the matter were once again thrown open to discussion on this side of the Atlantic, they would be back where they started.

In February, Monck wrote to Henry that everything was going satisfactorily –

> . . . and I think it is nearly certain that I shall get home again in the summer. It all depends on the Union succeeding in New Brunswick, and *that* is now almost quite sure.

In April, he wrote less confidently:

> The Union has been carried in Nova Scotia, and by the Upper House in New Brunswick, but Mr. Gordon has quarrelled with his Ministers and they have resigned, and I am afraid this will occasion a good deal of delay, and prevent me from getting home as soon as I had hoped.

He had written to Cardwell of the "very annoying delay" caused by the New Brunswick crisis, adding: "I do not wish, however, to be understood as finding fault with Gordon who has, I think, done very well."[2]

A week later, he wrote to Henry:

> Mr. Gordon telegraphs me that he is *certain* to carry the Union in New Brunswick, and I don't think he would speak so confidently if he had not good grounds for it.
>
> I go to Ottawa *D.V.* on Wednesday next, and I think I shall probably call our Parliament together about the second week in May, so that if they are successful in New Brunswick, I may hope to get home towards the end of June. In any case I shall try to get home to spend your summer holidays with you.

Another disappointment came on May 2 when he heard that "they are obliged to dissolve Parliament in New Brunswick and that will delay my coming home." Gordon had asked Monck not to call the Canadian Parliament till after the New Brunswick elections; but "I have determined to summon my Parliament for June 8th," Monck wrote to Cardwell, "by which time the elections in New Brunswick will be pretty well decided. We cannot wait any longer, as our financial year ends on June 30th."[3]

The session was to take place in the new Houses of Parliament in Ottawa. They had been built in imitation of those at Westminster, and there had been widespread discontent with regard to the expense which had exceeded by far the original sum granted. Charles Monck described them as "truly magnificent . . . to my thinking in every respect infinitely superior to those at Westminster."

The choice of Ottawa as the seat of Government was unpopular with the majority of parliamentarians. The decision had been made as a compromise between the claims of Upper and Lower Canada, and a great deal had been said and written about the choice. Trollope,[4] visiting Canada in 1861, described Ottawa as "a town still to be built on the river of that name," and in 1864, George Brown wrote scathing criticisms of the site in general and of Rideau Hall, the future Government House, in particular: "The Governor General's residence is a miserable little house ... To patch up that building will cost more than a new one."[5]

Feo Monck and her husband had visited Ottawa in 1864 while on tour as the guests of Lord Lyons and his staff. "We were disgusted by the squalid look of Ottawa, though we only saw it by lamplight which was scarcely any light, such *wretched* gas. The streets were so rough, like dirt roads. I went on wondering how we could ever live there, when the seat of Government is moved there," she wrote; she later added, as a footnote to her published diary: "I little knew how happy I should be there, after all."[6]

Nevertheless, the Government decided to patch up, or rather, make an extensive addition to the existing "miserable little house," and the work was in full swing when Monck and his staff moved into the original Rideau Hall on May 2, 1866. "We were all agreeably surprised by this house," he wrote from Ottawa on the day after he moved in to Rideau Hall:

> It is small as far as the number of rooms is concerned, but the rooms are all good and they have been papered and painted and furnished, so that everything is clean and comfortable . . . .
>
> They gave us a great reception here last night. I think nearly every man, woman and child in the place must have been out, and there appeared to be 'great enthusiasm.'[7]

Every week he wrote of the good progress the workmen were making with the new building and what an "excellent house" it was going to be. "It requires a good deal done to it, and I mean to set them to work at once so as to have it *decent* before I bring Mama here." He was anxious that "Mama" should form a favourable impression, knowing that his family had heard continual grumbles from their political friends in Quebec about the move to Ottawa. "I think you will like Ottawa pretty well," he told Henry, "as there is very good boating on the river." He wrote frequently of the splendid rides that could be had in the surrounding country, which was "very well cleared and settled." Far from complaining of the "dirt roads", he mentioned them as a particular advantage for horsemen since "none of them have been macadamized and you can go as fast as you like."

Extra land had been added to the grounds of Government House to give access to the river. Dick and Captain Pemberton had both acquired boats and Charles went to Ottawa each morning "in a six-oar police-boat ... the crew all dressed man-of-war fashion ... in regular sailors' shirts and white hats, and they look very smart. We have an awning to the boat which makes it very comfortable in the sun. It is a great luxury, as we can land close to the public buildings and it saves us the dusty road in hot weather." He admitted that the flies and mosquitoes seemed more numerous than at Spencer Wood but was confident that mosquito-netting over the blinds would defeat them. His philosophic outlook set the tone for his staff, and Captain Pemberton obligingly gave up his bedroom and slept in a tent when Admiral Sir James Hope spent a night at Rideau Hall "and there was not a single spare room in which to put him."

In his letter to Cardwell, Monck had praised the new Houses of Parliament, but added:

> There is only one fault I can see about them, and that is the locale. It seems like an act of insanity to have fixed the capital of this great country away from the civilization, intelligence and commercial enterprise of the Province . . . where the political section will live in a position of isolation and removed from the action of any public opinion. My confident belief is that, notwithstanding the vast expense which has been incurred here in public buildings, Ottawa will not be the capital four years hence.[8]

Monck was not alone in this belief, nor in his views. "All the members are dead tired of this place already, it certainly is not lively," he wrote to Henry in June after Parliament recessed. He confessed he was glad to be back at Spencer Wood after the cramped conditions he and his staff had endured at Rideau Hall. "However, the new house, when it is finished, will be very comfortable," he reiterated.[9]

The New Brunswick elections had resulted in a triumph for those in favour of Confederation. A resolution in favour of a union had already been carried in Nova Scotia. This would have caused great rejoicing in Canada had the news not been overshadowed by the very event that helped to tip the balance in favour of Confederation. It was the threat of invasion that finally convinced many anti-

Confederationists of the necessity of British North American Union.

All through February and March, Sir Frederick Bruce, the British Minister at Washington, warned Monck of possible invasion by members of the Fenian Brotherhood in America. This was a secret society of Irish-Americans whose parents had emigrated during and after the Great Famine in Ireland. In the American Civil War they had formed a considerable part of the Northern army and were experienced well-trained soldiers. The situation was summed up in one of their marching songs:

"Many a battle has been fought
"Along with the boys in blue,
"So we'll go and conquer Canada
"For we've nothing else to do."[10]

But this was only one side of the story. These Irish Americans had been brought up on their parents' bitter memories of the ill-treatment of Ireland by the English. The Fenian Brotherhood was an underground movement in Ireland, which looked to America to help them fight on Irish soil for political independence. It was only certain Fenian leaders in the United States who were in favour of attacking the British through Canada. Since their intentions were known to the United States Government, that government was in a difficult position.

> The assurances I receive of the Government to suppress any overt act of the Fenians, are positive enough, [Bruce wrote in a confidential letter to Monck] but . . . there is great unwillingness to take any publick step which would show the Irish that they must not count on American support. [Owing to] the weakness of the Administration, and the necessity they are therefore under of trying to form a new party, they are very loth to quarrel with any section of the voters . . . I strongly urge you to show a determined front during the crisis which is apparently approaching.[11]

Bruce also kept Monck informed of the Fenians' movements and plans that had been discovered. He described "a Torpedo which the Fenians are treating for, . . . Professor Foy's machine . . . constituted something on the principle of an alarm clock, being used for exploding torpedoes."Charles Monck sympathised strongly with Irish resentment of the misgovernment which had caused so much suffering in Ireland, and Sir Frederick Bruce expressed his views too when he wrote:

> I hope to God Parliament will be able to devise some measure to allay discontent in Ireland. Everyone concedes that the law of Landlord and Tenant requires amendment, and nobody seems to appreciate the advantage of taking a step in the right direction.[12]

The Minister at Washington and the Governor General of Canada agreed that the root of the evil and its remedy lay on the other side of the Atlantic, not in the action or inaction of the United States Government. But for the present, Monck's duty was to Canada, and he felt nothing but anger towards the "Americanised Irish" by whom she was threatened. He was in close correspondence with Admiral Sir James Hope who had stationed himself in the St. Lawrence and at Halifax, ready to "extemporise some defence on the Lakes." Like Bruce, the Admiral urged Monck to prepare for invasion and wrote privately that he had recommended that the Admiralty send two or more ironclads to Halifax–"ostensibly for the Fenians, but in reality as a quiet hint to our American friends who fancy nobody has ironclads but themselves." He believed that the Fenian leaders would feel bound to take some action to justify having "talked so much and extorted so much money."[13] Funds were raised by subscriptions from the hard-working and often poor American-Irish. Described as "a movement . . . backed by washerwomen's pennies,"[14] Fenianism in America was also supported by the issue of "Irish bonds."

Bruce suggested that invasion through the Upper Lakes might be "among the possible plans of Sweeney [American Fenian General] and Co.". He concluded:

> Pray take care of your own personal safety. Assassination to produce confusion is a means to which these people would resort. It would be a serious publick calamity were anything to happen to you during this crisis, for I think Seward would do more for you than for most men in your position.[15]

Henry also expressed fears for his father's personal safety. He had been "very much frightened" by rumours published in English newspapers. Monck replied reassuringly, emphasising the thorough preparations being made against an attack he did not believe would come. "There are to be three ships of war in the St. Lawrence to protect us from the Fenians!"

In April, according to reports, the Fenians were on the wane.[16] Therefore, when "a force of between 800 and nine hundred Fenians crossed the Frontier from Buffalo to Fort Erie on the morning of June 1st,"[17] they outnumbered the Volunteers who attacked them at Limestone Ridge. The Volunteers were forced to fall back "under heavy fire".[18] Reinforcements of regular troops were rushed to the spot, but the Fenians had retreated across the border leaving sixty-five prisoners in the hands of the Volunteers. This enterprise had been intended to spearhead a larger scale invasion. There were reports that forces amounting to 10,000 Fenians (veterans of the Civil War), with arms and ammunition, were assembling at different points on the American side of the frontier. Although Monck did not doubt that a large-scale attack had been planned, he believed this to be an exaggeration – 5,000 would be nearer the mark.

"The American Government behaved very well about the Fenians," he told Henry:

> They stopped the men coming, seized their arms and arrested their bodies. At the same time we had a large force waiting for them . . . I think we should have beaten them easily enough even if the U.S. people had not interfered, but then it would have cost much money and probably bloodshed too.

In the "Battle of Limestone Ridge," six Volunteers were killed and thirty-one wounded. Monck praised highly the spirit and discipline displayed by the Volunteer force. He also paid tribute to the prompt action of the officers and men of the Canadian Militia generally, of the regular troops, and of the officers of the Royal Navy "for the rapidity with which they extemporized gunboats for the defence of the St. Lawrence and the Lakes."[19]

At the end of a telegram despatched on June 7 to Cardwell, announcing that the "invasion crisis" was over, Charles added: "Please send a copy of this to Lady Monck, Charleville."[20] "I don't think Mama had heard of the Fenians when she wrote," Charles told Henry in his letter of June 22. "I am very glad of it, as she would probably hear at the same time of the attack and its failure." Others were concerned for Elizabeth's feelings. At the end of a very long letter to her, D'Arcy McGee wrote from Montreal:

> You must not be too anxious if this present mail does not tell you that the crisis is past, and the invader crushed or repelled. Another week, or at the outside another fortnight, *must* finish the Fenians. Our population are up and united as one man . . . we shall have this week 12 to 15,000 regulars. We have improvised *six* gunboats, with fighting crews supplied by Admiral Hope . . . I am here for one day, returning to Ottawa in the morning. Lord Monck whom I saw on Sunday is in excellent health and spirits. He is worked very hard, gets little or no sleep, but keeps up his hearty look, and has the same zest for a joke, as if the seventh part of a continent was not entrusted to his charge. Ottawa, you may depend on it, the filibusters will never see. The railroad can in an hour be rendered impracticable and the highroad, nearly 60 miles or three days' march, leads through woods and marshes and over so many 'creeks' – that a

single Company of Artillery could defend, that there is no possible danger of the new Capital.[21]

The Atlantic cable was not completed until two months after these events took place, and all Charles's considerate precautions could not prevent his wife and children from reading the first newspaper reports of the invasion before they received his own messages. The account in the *Evening Standard* of June 13 had greatly alarmed Henry. "I really hope you are in no danger," he wrote to his father. "*Do* write as you get this and tell me all about it." "Thank God everything went so well," Elizabeth wrote to Henry after the excitement had died down; and she admitted that she, too, had been in "a great fuss".

Chapter Eleven (1866)

On June 30, 1866, Elizabeth received a letter from Cardwell.

> My dear Lady Monck,–I have Lord Russell's authority for saying to Monck that the Queen has signified her pleasure that he shall be made an English Peer. Lord R. says "I have said 'Baron Monck' ". Do you know whether he would prefer any other Title? If you have anything to say on the subject, pray let me know *forthwith*. Of course we are right in believing that he wishes to be an English Peer? Pray accept my sincere congratulations and Believe me, always truly yours, Edward Cardwell.[1]

There is no means of knowing how Elizabeth replied to the embarrassing question as to whether her husband would prefer "any other Title." But it may be presumed that she intimated an English Barony would do very nicely for the present since this honour was duly conferred on him. The announcement was not altogether a surprise because there had been premature rumours in the English press two months earlier. "I saw that paragraph you speak of about my getting an English peerage," Charles wrote to Henry on May 3, "but I have heard nothing about it myself."

"*The Times* of this morning praises you very much," Henry wrote to his father. The Prime Minister had recommended other people for peerages, but the Queen had refused her consent to all of them except "Lord Monck, who has well deserved the distinction by his administration of Canada."[2]

The precarious state of the Government at Westminster increased Monck's desire to go home, and he hoped to end the Canadian Parliamentary session as early as possible. "I hope most sincerely that the Government at home will not be beaten on their Reform Bill", he had written to Henry on June 14. "I want to get the Act for the Union of the Provinces passed by Mr. Cardwell, and besides I should be sorry on political grounds that they were put in a minority."

The possible change of Government in England had been the fear underlying Monck's impatience over the delays caused by New Brunswick. The Confederation scheme had now been approved, in principle, there and in Nova Scotia, but there were still large factions of opposition. Given time, these factions might yet gain the ascendancy. Even if Russell's Ministry remained in power, it was essential that the Act of Union be presented to and carried by the Imperial Parliament before it recessed. The alternative was to wait until Parliament reassembled, and by that time the whole plan might have fallen apart.

In Canada, there remained the delicate matter of adjusting final details of the Local Legislatures to satisfy both Upper and Lower Canadians. Knowing the critical state of affairs at Westminster, Monck was frustrated by the "inaction" of the Ottawa Parliament. On June 21 he wrote a brusque letter to John Macdonald:

> I cannot help thinking that valuable time is being lost, and a great opportunity in the disposition and temper of the House is thrown away by the adoption of this scheme of delay . . . It is not merely that no step has been taken . . . for the arrangement of the plan of Local Governments, but the subject of education in Lower Canada, which ought to have been settled before the passing of the Union Act, appears to have also dropped out of sight[3] . . . If this session is allowed to pass without the completion of our portion of the Union scheme, my sense of duty to the people of Canada and to myself would leave me no alternative but to ask for my recall.

He explained that he did not intend to over-estimate his own influence nor use his resignation as a threat. He merely wished to inform Macdonald of his intentions in advance, "in view of the frank and friendly spirit which has always marked our intercourse with each other."[4] Macdonald's reply explained the various causes of delay, adding, "I must ask Your Excellency to leave somewhat to my Canadian Parliamentary experience."[5] Macdonald had previously received urgent warnings from the Nova Scotian Ministers, who, like Monck, thought that delay at this point might prove fatal. Five days after that letter, Tupper and Archibald arrived in Ottawa and did not leave before they had obtained agreement that the Canadian delegation would sail for England on July 21.

On July 10, the news Monck had been dreading reached Ottawa. The Reform Bill had indeed been defeated. Lord Russell had resigned on June 26, the day before the Nova Scotians visited Ottawa. Monck immediately telegraphed to the Lieutenant-Governors of New Brunswick and Nova Scotia advising them to postpone the departure of their delegates. Tupper telegraphed back to Macdonald that they were leaving on July 19. Monck telegraphed again to Sir Fenwick Williams:

> In the present condition of political affairs in England, it is simply absurd to send delegates home until we have some communication with the new Secretary of State. I have a letter from England to say that the general impression is that the session will be immediately wound up whatever Ministry is in office. Please keep your people quiet if you can, and all will be right.[6]

The letter Monck referred to was from Cardwell himself. There was no chance of a Bill being passed during that session. Since he could not know whom the Derby-Disraeli Ministry might appoint to that office, Monck had no alternative but to wait for instructions from the new Colonial Secretary.

In defiance of letters and telegrams from Ottawa, the delegates from the two maritime provinces sailed for England. On their arrival, they learned that the new Colonial Secretary, Lord Carnarvon, was as ardent a supporter of Confederation as Cardwell. Monck received letters confirming this, and on August 2 he wrote to Henry:

> Though I am very sorry my own friends did not remain in to do it, I think I am very fortunate in getting Lord C. and Mr. Adderley at the Colonial Office. Fancy, I got a telegram *yesterday* from Lord Carnarvon dated *July 30th*.

This was the first message he received by the new Atlantic Cable, which had at last been successfully completed. The message had taken two days because of a breakdown in the cable between Newfoundland and New Brunswick. "When that is repaired, I suppose it will take as many hours. They charge £20 for a message of 20 words."

Lord Carnarvon expressed his willingness to receive all the delegates and to make at least an attempt to pass the British North American Act before the Imperial Parliament rose. However, he thought it was almost impossible to do so and subsequently owned that he was relieved that Monck and the Canadian delegates had postponed their trip to England. It was not until he had seen the maritime delegates that he learnt of the disparities between their views and those of the delegates from Canada. In a personal letter, Monck summed up the situation:

> The Canadian Legislature last year adopted a definite plan of Union, known as the Quebec scheme. This year the Nova Scotian

> and New Brunswick Legislatures adopted resolutions in favour of Union but without indicating any specific plan for its accomplishment, empowering however the Lt. Governors to appoint delegates to proceed to England armed with full authority to arrange with H.M. Govt and the representatives of the other Provinces the terms of Union. . . . My advice would be that your Lordship should instruct the delegates from all the Provinces to repair to London about the month of November, so as to afford ample time for the meeting of Parlt in spring. I may add that I think there are strong reasons for not allowing any long period to elapse between the time when the measure shall have been finally agreed upon and its introduction to the Imperial Parlt.[7]

Monck did not detail the differences likely to arise. The maritime delegates had been appointed by their Lieutenant-Governors both of whom had stated their wish for a stronger central government than that provided for in the Quebec Scheme, thereby curtailing the powers and responsibilities of the local governments. Two years previously Monck had told Cardwell of his own doubt that "complete centralisation" would be practicable. He agreed with Macdonald and Cartier that it would be unacceptable in French Canada. The maritimers distrusted the independent spirit of Canada, and saw great advantages to their provinces in retaining what Monck had called "the leading-strings" of the Imperial Government. They now relied on the support of that Government in their repudiation of those articles in the Quebec Scheme to which they objected. Meanwhile –

> The Delegates now in England come here uninvited, [Carnarvon wrote on August 10] but it would be obviously impossible to send them away and ask them to return later . . . I believe that the best course will probably be a middle one – that your Lordship and the Canadian delegates should be in England not later than the end of September . . . I hope therefore that you will consider yourself free to take your leave of absence as soon as you find yourself able to do so . . . Your presence I need scarcely say will be most valuable, indeed I should be very sorry to conclude the negotiations without you unless some Fenian or U.S. difficulty intervene.[8]

On the very day on which Carnarvon's letter was written, Monck wrote to him that "We have reports from many quarters all pointing to a renewal of the Fenian attack."[9] Almost daily he received private letters from the British Minister in Washington and from Archibald, the British Consul at New York, reporting on the movements of Fenian troops. Monck had already requested a supply of breechloaders for the Volunteers to replace the outmoded Enfield rifles.

> A very great feeling of alarm has sprung up within the last 10 days and can only be allayed by increased preparations for defence [he wrote to Carnarvon two weeks later]. I am to see Sir J. Michel[10] tomorrow. I think it probable that the result of our consultation will be an application for a considerable reinforcement to our garrison of regular troop which I hope will not be refused to us. I think October will be the time when danger is most likely to threaten us, and it is very likely that the arrival of reinforcements from England and the provision of breechloaders for the Volunteers might have the effect of averting it.[11]

After consultation with General Sir John Michel, Monck sent a cable to the Colonial Office asking that three battalions of infantry and one of cavalry with an appropriate supply of arms and ammunition be shipped to Canada at the earliest possible date. Monck's refusal to panic was so well known that an urgent appeal by him for reinforcements would not be treated as the unnecessary request of an alarmist – certainly not by the Colonial Secretary, nicknamed "Twitters" Carnarvon because of his nervous temperament. Monck's cable reached him while he was in the country enjoying a rest from the pressures of office. He hurried back to London and demanded that four battalions be sent to Canada with all possible speed. "Your telegram brought me up to London and I have been here since then, making the necessary arrangements for the despatch of troops," Carnarvon wrote on August 31.[12] Monck had followed his cable by a letter stating that while he doubted there would be a large-scale invasion,

> . . . the state of feeling here will interfere with our going home on Union business at an early day. As far as I am *myself* concerned, I should be quite satisfied *at any time* to leave affairs in the hands of Sir J. Michel, but the real difficulty is about those of the Administration who must accompany me. The persons who *must* form the delegation will be the leading members of the govt . . . My personal inclinations would all lead me to obey your directions by hurrying home, as Lady Monck and all my family are on your side of the Atlantic, and with the exception of about three months last winter I have been separated from them for the last two years.[13]

His letter crossed with Carnarvon's, urging him not to leave Canada:

> A Fenian raid may be crushed down now as it was crushed before by the military force under the directions of military officers, but in the very doubtful state of affairs in the U.S. it is impossible to guess what difficulties and delicate questions may not arise between us. It is, I assure you, a very great cause of regret to me that I am likely to be deprived of your assistance in dealing with the difficult question

> of Confederation . . . It is of great consequence that some of them [the Canadian delegates] should come soon. The N.B. and N.S. delegates came on their own responsibility and at their own risk; but they are here, and I can see that a feeling of considerable irritation is springing up at the delay . . . They said that their own situation is an embarrassing one and all the more from the appearance of neglect and slight to which they may seem to be exposed in their own Colonies. It would greatly strengthen their hands, in their view, and remove this appearance if any one of the Canadian delegates could come and keep them company till the arrival of the others. Of course no business could be transacted, but appearances would be saved.[14]

The maritime delegates in England felt once again that they were being "let down" by the unreliable Canadians, who had, a short time previously, been urging haste. John A. Macdonald did his best to smooth ruffled feelings on both sides of the Atlantic and sent Monck a copy (in his own hand) of a letter he had written to Tilley. He enclosed it in a private note:

> My dear Lord Monck, – Tilley in one of his letters to Galt assumed a tone which provoked the latter to write him a sharp reply. He sent it to me, but I withheld it at the time. I have however thought it well to write Tilley this morning on the whole subject, in view of our speedily meeting in England. It is as well that they should be fully informed of our position *before* we meet. I enclose a copy of my letter as you may perhaps like to see exactly the ground I take with Tilley. I have marked it Private, so that it can do no harm.[15]

Macdonald pointed out to Tilley that Canada had accepted the Quebec Scheme in its entirety and had sent a delegation to London to present it to the Colonial Office in 1865. Further, he stated that the Canadians would have been in London for the final conference before the change in the British Government had they not been asked to wait until after the New Brunswick elections.

> Lord Monck received letters from Mr. Cardwell stating that there was no chance of the Bill being passed in the then session of the Imperial Parliament. Lord Monck felt that he ought to wait for instructions from the new Colonial Secretary, and lost no time in informing Mr. Gordon and Sir Fenwick Williams that Canada could not send a delegation on the 21st [July] . . . The delegations from New Brunswick and Nova Scotia therefore went at their own risk, and after full notice that they would not be joined by a deputation from Canada. Since our Legislature rose, . . . again and again have

the Fenians made preparations and combinations for attacks on Canada. Lord Monck, under the circumstances, would not have been justified in abandoning his post or allowing his principal advisers to leave Canada. . . . We think it of great consequence that Lord Monck should be in England during our deliberations. Canada is bound by the address to the Queen praying her to submit a measure to Parliament based on the Quebec resolutions. Nova Scotia and New Brunswick require modifications of that scheme. How are we to arrive at a satisfactory solution of the difficulty? Only, I think, through Lord Monck. He thoroughly understands the question, has been completely behind the scenes, and knows and appreciates the points of difference between the several provinces.[16]

Macdonald knew very well that without the Governor General, the delegates would soon be at loggerheads with each other. At such a time, they would trust him when they would not trust one another. Monck had written to Macdonald, "I have received in the past, and am likely to receive in the future, much more credit for the business [Confederation] than – I say it unaffectedly – I have a right to claim."[17] Yet Macdonald, in his letter to Tilley, justified Monck's painstaking study of Canada's general problems, his refusal to court popularity, his sympathy with Canadian interests at the risk of censure from his masters at Westminster, and the trouble he had taken to get acquainted with his Ministers.

Carnarvon suggested that some of the Canadian delegates proceed at once to England "to keep them" (the maritimers) "company". But Monck was unable to persuade any to go in advance of the others:

> There are two parties in Upper and two in Lower Canada which must be represented in order to do business. The leading members of the Ministry are very averse to leaving before the closing of the navigation shall have rendered Fenian attack almost impossible.

On the necessity of his own presence at the London Conference, Monck now wrote to Carnarvon:

> I am very unwilling to say much on this point as it looks as if I placed a high estimate on my own knowledge or influence, but the truth is that the plan of Union was passed here without opposition from some very influential men who disapproved of some of its details, mainly on the ground that the decision here was not final and that I would have an opportunity of urging my opinion before the scheme was irrevocably fixed, and I feel myself in a great degree personally bound to these gentlemen . . . I will say nothing

about my going home myself. At present I *would* not leave, nor should I feel justified in doing so as long as there was any probability of a renewal of Fenian troubles.[18]

In all his letters reporting threats of invasion, he reiterated his belief that no attack would actually take place once it became known that reinforcements had arrived, even if such an attack had ever been seriously intended. Nevertheless, Carnarvon, Macdonald, and the Minister at Washington all agreed that Monck should remain in Canada until the Fenian danger had passed. Bruce wrote on September 26, "I am in good hopes that the Fenian business is dwindling, still we are not entirely safe on that score, and in the still delicate question of the prisoners, and generally in our relations (with America) . . . [He wrote of] the good will felt towards you by Seward, and your experience and popularity in Canada, the deprivation of which I confess I look to with some dismay."[19]

The "delicate question of the prisoners" was a complication that made it very undesirable for the Governor General and his "chief advisers" to leave Canada. The Fenian prisoners, captured during the June invasion, fell into two categories. Some were American citizens of Irish birth or descent. Others were Irishmen who had not yet become naturalized Americans. The former were "foreigners" and could be tried and convicted for felony; the latter were technically British subjects and liable to be tried and executed for treason. The Fenians regarded their captured comrades as prisoners of war and demanded that they be treated as such. The United States authorities were finding it difficult enough to control the Irish section of their population as it was, without the demonstrations that would certainly ensue if any of the prisoners in Canada were executed. Between the fury of the Canadian population demanding revenge for casualties inflicted on their Volunteers, and the unofficial appeals for mercy for individual prisoners from America, Monck was snowed under with correspondence on the subject. To Seward's original tactlessly-worded note,[20] he had replied that the course of justice could not be interfered with at the "dictation of a foreign Power." But Monck had approved of the recent legislation passed during the Canadian Parliamentary Session that brought the law against "hostile invasion" in Lower Canada into line with that of Upper Canada. Previously it had differed: under the old law, the prerogative lay with the Crown; but once Imperial sanction was given to the new Act, capital punishment levied on prisoners convicted of treason could be commuted to a term of imprisonment as a felony. The Fenian trial was postponed pending the Imperial sanction. This in turn was delayed because Lord Carnarvon had "misapprehended the scope and nature of the Act." Macdonald replied that Carnarvon's course was "extremely unfortunate and embarrassing" as "we are by it driven to try the Prisoners before a Court Martial." Monck, who had himself had legal training, had complete faith in Macdonald in all matters concerning litigation, and during this period, letters passed between them nearly every day. Macdonald quoted the exact wording of the clause in the Act which, in the event of hostile invasion put subjects and aliens on the same footing. That is, all would be tried for felony and not for treason. "It is important," he added, "that the trials should proceed while you are in Canada, as the question of punishment may otherwise arise in your absence. I must say that I would not like to be absent when that question is considered, for I fear that great pressure will be brought to bear by public opinion in favour of severity."[21]

Monck relayed the substance of Macdonald's very clear exposition to the Colonial Office and eventually sanction for the Act was obtained. In the meantime, British representatives in New York were under constant pressure from the anxious Americans. Pierrepont Edwards, Archibald's successor as British Consul at New York, sent Monck an extract from a newspaper describing a "Great War Meeting of Fenians," with the sub-heading: "A New Advance upon Canada Imminent." The meeting had passed a resolution to avenge the death sentence (given by a British Court in Canada) on Lynch, McMahon, and others "engaged in lawful warfare for the purpose of freeing their native land." One speaker declared: "It depends upon you whether these men shall die. . . . There are enough Irishmen in the City of New York to drive the British rule off the continent of America." "Every redcoat sent out [to Canada] makes the power of England in Ireland become less. We want her to send all her soldiers to Canada. Let them come. We will be able to kill them all." The guest of honour, General Spears, informed the meeting that:

> . . . the old Springfield and Enfield rifles, seized by the United States Government, are being returned and being converted into breechloaders. There were five batteries of light artillery being organised within 300 miles of New York. Three months since, affairs looked a little blue, but now matters were looking brighter than ever. They had no less than 3,000,000 rounds of cartridges. Men were plenty, but money was wanted. Every penny received into the treasury was capable of being accounted for . . . not a penny would by any possibility be misapplied.

These and similar communications reached Charles Monck in August, the time when he had expected to be on his way home.

On October 19 (1866), a great fire at Quebec destroyed more than two thousand houses. Most of them had been built of wood "and burned like tinder." Monck privately asked Lord Carnarvon to initiate a subscription to help those whose homes had been destroyed, and suggested that his despatch be published to that effect. This was done, and a "considerable sum" was raised.[22]

The *Orontes* had docked at Halifax, bringing the final consignment of troops from England. The same ship brought a letter from the Horse Guards to Sir John Michel warning him that the regiment, the "61st", was mainly Irish with strong Fenian sympathies. Should a "favourable change in Canadian prospects" have taken place, the letter suggested that the regiment not be allowed to disembark, but be sent on to the West Indies. A succession of private letters from Michel to the Governor General urged him to make an immediate decision on this point. The Admiral informed Michel that the *Orontes* would not be available, and pending their transference to another ship, the men must land and go into temporary encampment:

> Unfortunately the weather will *soon* be so cold that I cannot encamp them for any length of time . . . and I should have to clothe them at large expense in winter clothing. I am quite aware that, without strong and definite knowledge, you cannot decide.[23]

By mid-October, Monck had received "definite knowledge" that the danger of invasion was on the wane, if not entirely over, and the suspected troops were shipped to Bermuda where the need for "winter clothing" would not arise. After reporting the incident to Carnarvon, Monck added: "Why they ever sent them here when their fidelity was suspected is a mystery to me, unless it was supposed that the Canadians were too strong and it was intended to handicap them in their contest with the Fenians."[24] In November, New York Consul Edwards wrote that though reports "seem to indicate intended action against Canada, I think the present agitation is to be looked on as an expiring effort, due entirely to the immediate question of the day, and that it is likely to die out with its cause."[25]

The immediate question was the trial of Fenian prisoners. The date had been fixed for December 13. On November 16, Lord Derby, the Prime Minister, wrote to Queen Victoria:

> Lord Monck has telegraphed to Lord Carnarvon pressing for remission of the capital sentence [of Fenian prisoners], and suggesting a commutation for a term of imprisonment which appeared much too short to meet the justice of the case. Lord Carnarvon telegraphed his answer, approving of the prisoners' lives being

spared, but desiring that the term of commutation should not be decided until he should receive full instructions, which have not yet been sent out.[26]

While Monck waited for permission to commute the sentence and then for permission to publish the commutation, various reprisals were planned for the supposed intention to execute the more notable of the prisoners. The inhabitants of Fort Erie and the neighbouring district demanded special protection, following Fenian threats to abduct them as hostages for the prisoners. During September Bruce wrote of a plot to blow up "the public buildings of Ottawa," enclosed a letter from one of his secret agents with details of the plan, and suggested that appropriate precautions be taken.[27] "They have all the ammunition they require for the destruction of the Parlt Buildings", the agent wrote; "1,000 lbs. powder, 50 10-inch shells, and 6 torpedoes each capable of containing 200 lbs. powder, which are to be placed in the air ventilators or conductors leading from the banks of the Ottawa river under ground and under the buildings for the purpose of airing the Halls of Assembly." This was not the first attempt to destroy the Canadian seat of government. On August 12, before Charles Monck left Ottawa, he had written to Henry: "The last news is that a lot of gunpowder was found under the Houses of Parliament as if they meant to have another Guy Fawkes plot."

Late in October it was decided that the Canadian delegates need no longer delay their departure for England. Consternation was caused by Galt's refusal to accompany them. He had resigned from the Government during the last session, after the defeat of the Separate Schools Bill.[28] While resigning from the Ministry, Galt, as the former Finance Minister, had agreed to take part in the delegation, but on October 20 Macdonald wrote to Monck:

> We are still in trouble about the Education question. Galt is quite reasonable, but my R. C. colleagues ask similar provisions for their U.C. co-religionists. The questions, in fact, which caused Galt's resignation are revised in another form. I very much fear it will end in Galt's not going to England, a result the consequence of which I do not like to contemplate.[29]

Monck was already aware of the trouble and had received more than one letter from Galt on the subject.

> Nothing would have given me personally more gratification than to have accepted such an honourable mission, [Galt had replied] but no action having been taken by the Government towards reassuring the Protestants of Lower Canada on the Education question, I find

> myself precisely in the same position as caused my resignation, and I do not feel justified in taking a further active part in consummating a measure which was suggested by myself and friends in the full assurance that certain guarantees would be afforded to our people, but which have not yet been granted. I am therefore obliged most respectfully to decline acting as a Delegate.

Later, he wrote, "I expect to see Mr. Cartier tomorrow in Montreal, when I hope something may be settled."[30] His hope was realised, and he wrote on October 23 that he had

> .... great pleasure in stating that a satisfactory solution has arisen out of the difficulties with the Lower Canada Education question, and I am therefore in a position to accept the appointment of Delegate to England. I beg therefore, with Your Excellency's permission to withdraw the expression of my disinclination to go and to repeat my acknowledgement of the very gracious and kind words in which you informed me of Your Lordship's concurrence in my nomination.[31]

> The Education schism is healed [wrote Macdonald] and I think in a very satisfactory way. At the last moment I made a new proposition which was ultimately accepted. Galt is coming up here in a day or two, and I am sure that I shall make it all right with him. I find that I can always influence him when we talk matters over, but he is very impulsive and apt to act hastily. Cartier writes that his explanation with him was satisfactory.[32]

On November 7, two of the delegates sailed for England and the others followed a week later. Monck had stayed on in Canada, very much against his own personal wishes, owing to his anxiety that justice should be done in the case of the Fenian prisoners. His legal experience stood him in good stead in Canada, because in those days judges were often unreliable and juries not immune from corruption. To him nothing was too much trouble in order to ensure fair trial to a prisoner, however obvious his guilt.

Yet at this very time, when conscientiousness over a legal matter kept him from going to London, when he desperately wanted to be present for the discussions and visits with his family, he slipped up on a legal point.

The Lamirande Case, *l'Affaire Lamirande* concerned a French cashier in the Poitiers branch of the Bank of France. By making false entries, he defrauded the bank of 700,000 francs. To escape arrest he fled to New York where the French authorities caught up with him; he escaped and crossed the border into Lower Canada. The French Consul General applied to Monck for a warrant for an *arrêt de renvoi* – arrest with a view to extradition. While the case was tried by a Montreal magistrate, Monck left for Quebec on what he had hoped would be the first step of his journey home. On the morning after he reached Spencer Wood, M. Hector-Louis Langevin, Solicitor General for Lower Canada, brought him a warrant for the extradition of Lamirande. Forty-eight hours had elapsed since the magistrate committed Lamirande for extradition; there would be between eight and ten more hours before the warrant, with the Governor General's signature, could reach Montreal. Langevin, to avoid a second journey to Quebec, advised Monck to sign the warrant. After the Solicitor General assured him that if a writ of *habeas corpus* were in the meantime applied for and allowed, the warrant would not prevent the prisoner from obtaining the benefit of the writ, Monck signed the warrant.

Monck relied on the word of a senior law officer and signed the warrant prematurely. There is no denying that Monck was taking a chance. All might still have been well, however, had there not then occurred one of those hopeless muddles involving Canadians, Americans, and French, to which Monck must have become well accustomed, and against which he should have guarded. First, Lamirande's counsel waited for two days after the judgement was given before petitioning the judge for the writ of *habeas corpus*. Secondly, the counsel who had represented the prisoner in New York gained possession of the extradition warrant issued there and refused to surrender it. This caused a great deal of confusion and was probably the reason for the delay in applying for *habeas corpus*. Thirdly, the judge at Montreal ruled that *habeas corpus* be allowed but deferred the actual issue of the writ until the following day. By that time the new warrant for extradition had been received. It was acted upon with suspicious promptness by those who, it was believed, had an interest in appeasing the French Consul. That very night Lamirande was "surreptitously" removed from prison and taken on board a ship under orders to sail to Europe. His counsels lodged a protest, sent an account of the case to the Colonial Office in London, and interviewed the Governor General, who admitted that their protests were justified.

Opinions on the affair were aired in the press of both Canada and London. In London, Monck was blamed for what amounted to a miscarriage of justice. The Canadian press, whose editors were better informed, exonerated Monck and had a great deal to say about the "conspiracy" that involved Cartier, Attorney-General for Lower Canada, as well as Langevin and his subordinates.

Meanwhile, British Government officials tried to intercept

Lamirande when his ship docked at Liverpool, but his French escorts eluded them and he was taken on to France. There he was convicted, although Lord Carnarvon, through Lord Stanley, officially had requested the French Government to delay all proceedings against the prisoner until a full report could be received from Canada. The ultimate fate of Lamirande has not been recorded; the affair died down as quickly as it had blown up and is only relevant to this narrative in that it affected Charles Monck's future relationships with Langevin, Cartier, and Galt, all of whom represented Lower Canada in the delegation going to England. It also drew the first and only official "rocket" that Monck was ever to receive. The stormy outbursts from the Duke of Newcastle had not been intended for Monck personally and could be discounted; but the official despatch of November 24 from Lord Carnarvon stated that he was "obliged with whatever reluctance to express my decided disapproval of the course which your Lordship was induced to adopt." The principle of British justice had been violated. The British Government could not allow it to be thought that they condoned "an insult . . . passed upon the dignity of the law."

By the same mail, Carnarvon sent a personal letter to tell Monck how greatly he regretted having had to write the despatch, while knowing that Monck was taking the blame for what was actually the fault of his "Law Officers".

Naturally Monck was appalled that such a miscarriage of justice had been perpetrated (some people in Canada thought deliberately) by those under his authority; and though officially he took the blame on himself and did his best to defend his law officers, the least he could do was to reprimand them severely. There is no record of what he said to them; but it is known that the incident cost him the friendships of Langevin, Cartier, and Galt, who were all prominent members of the Westminster Conference on Confederation, and whose resentment was not diminished by finding the atmosphere rather strained when they reached London.

In one of his earlier private letters to Monck, Carnarvon had said: "I am sorry to see my old friend Cartier's name mixed up with the [Lamirande] transaction in a somewhat unsatisfactory manner."[33] Later, in his formal despatch, he pointed out: "the fact that the partner of the Attorney General [Cartier] conducted these proceedings on the part of the French Government has naturally given rise to suspicions, and that the conduct of the Solicitor General [Langevin] in obtaining the warrant while the case was actually under hearing by the judge, has not yet been by any means satisfactorily explained."[34] "The two delegates, Mr. McDougall and M. Langevin called on me last Monday," he wrote in a private letter to Monck. "It was so far as the latter gentleman was concerned a restrained and uncomfortable interview, for the part which he played in the Lamirande affair was I think in his mind as it certainly was in mine."[35]

Apparently no such awkwardnesses clouded the Colonial Secretary's exchanges with "beautiful, calm-faced McDougall," as Feo described him; but Alexander Galt was in a disgruntled frame of mind and from this time adopted an acid tone in all references to the Governor General. "I tell you as a State secret that it is most improbable Lord Monck will ever return to Canada," he wrote to his wife from London. "I am much grieved to say that such a view is taken of his conduct in the celebrated Lamirande case by the Govt here, as will I think induce him to resign."[36] Even "little Cartier," as Monck called him, is said to have been less cordial after the Lamirande episode, though his resilient spirit was able to ride any disapproval shown by British Ministers, and he was soon living it up in London society as vigorously as during the previous year. "Our friend Cartier devotes so much time to society that we do not get much work out of him,"[37] Galt commented sourly. There seems to have been a tendency on the part of the Lower Canadians to be a trifle waspish about their fellow delegates. Langevin described John A. Macdonald as "a sharp fox ... very well informed ... ingratiating, clever and very popular. He is *the man* of the conference ... Galt is a clever financier, but too headstrong and too yielding. He is not stable. ... McDougall is capable ... frankly lazy, possessed with great ambition and little frankness. Mr. Tupper of Nova Scotia, is capable but too incisive; he makes many bitter enemies for himself; he is ambitious and a gambler."[38]

These letters were written before Monck arrived in England. "I am writing to ask Lord Carnarvon to allow me to go home on the 12th December in the *Scotia* which sails on that day," he wrote to Henry. "Things are very quiet here now and I don't think there is much chance of any disturbance during the winter. I think there is no doubt that he will allow me to go." He had suggested leaving a month later than the delegates because of the Fenian trials:

> I hear Lynch and MacMahon mean to move for new trials, in which case it would not be right to commute their sentence until after their appeals have been heard and decided. I don't think I should like to leave until the excitement caused by these trials has completely died out ... Independently of any assistance which your Lordship might think I should be able to afford you, there are reasons connected with my private affairs which render me very anxious to go home this winter. I shall be glad to have your answer as soon as convenient.[39]

On November 16 the Cunard mail brought him Lord Carnarvon's official permission for leave in time for him to be home for Christmas.

Chapter Twelve (1866-67)

Monck was determined to spend Christmas at Charleville; but immediately afterwards he intended to go to London and stay there until the Confederation Act had been passed. With this in view, he had asked Elizabeth to find a suitable London house to rent for that period. He was also preoccupied with Henry's progress at school. The boy's new tutor, Mr. Thackeray, had considered that he was not yet ready for Oxford, and should have another year at Eton. Monck had given in, though unwillingly, and nearly all his weekly letters to his son contained injunctions to work hard and not to yield to the temptation to spend the extra year at school in idleness. "I am glad you are reading Sir W. Scott's novels," he had written in the spring, "but I advise you to make a rule with regard to them, as well as all books of *light* reading, not to take them up until you have finished all your serious work for the day. When I was your age, and indeed still, I act upon this rule myself and I think it very good as keeping the *fresh* part of the day for actual work and also as a good discipline of the mind." The Moncks were patient with Henry but found it hard to understand his lackadaisical attitude to life.

A further family problem arose when Charles's sister Isabella died in Paris. Charles and Dick were in Canada at the time. Young Henry had cut short his visit to the Fifes at Mar Lodge and gone over to Paris to his father's other sister, "Aunt E.". Now she was in Ireland, staying alternately at Charleville and with her niece at Summerton; but it was necessary that one of her brothers come home to advise her on her financial affairs. As a "charge" on the Charleville estate, quarterly payments were paid into her account by Flood, the family solicitor, whose records show that she invariably asked for her money in advance.

At Charleville, preparations for Christmas always began early in the autumn. There were presents for everyone on the place, warm petticoats for some of the old women and "frieze coats" for the men, and a Christmas Tree Party in the house for the tenants' and employees' children. Elizabeth's happiness at her husband's return for Christmas was mingled with fear for his safety. On November 15, Consul Edwards wrote from New York:

> I trust that Your Lordship will not consider it impertinent if I offer a suggestion which has occurred to me in reference to your proposed going to New York en route for England. In the present state of feeling among the Irish population it seems to me – if you have decided to come this way – that Your Lordship's stay in the States should not be prolonged beyond what is necessary, and that undue publicity ought not to be given to the fact. Although it might seem preposterous to credit the possibility of anything like personal annoyance being offered, yet knowing the class of men we have to deal with, I hope you will not consider me to be wholly unwarranted in offering this suggestion.[1]

In Ireland, alarming rumours were being circulated. It was said that "almost every ship that crossed the Atlantic brought to Ireland men of military experience, the motive of whose coming was scarcely concealed."[2] At the end of November, Elizabeth wrote to Henry:

> My dearest Child, – I fear that you will be vexed at the contents of this letter, but I cannot but feel that you will think me right. Your Papa told me if I heard of a good house in London within his terms to take it from January 1. I have almost concluded for one in Hill St. Berkeley Square. He speaks of all being quiet in Canada as far as the Fenians are concerned, but the accounts in Ireland are fearful, there is no doubt a rising is at hand. *He* is a marked man on account of his proceedings against them in Canada. You know how rash he is, that no one could prevent his being on the roads after dark. The country is becoming *full* of suspicious looking Americans, and I feel terrified as to what *may* occur, if he land in Ireland at this time. I have therefore almost decided, if I can get the house on the 19th of Dec., to go over *then*, and I am saying to him today (my last letter!) not to be surprised if he finds a letter from me at Cork telling him not to land, but to go on to Liverpool . . . I do not feel that I could bear the terror, and it is *only* a few days' difference.

Monck did not pay the smallest attention to any of these suggested precautions for his safety. He had said he would arrive at Charleville in time for dinner on December 21; and it was from Charleville that he wrote to the Colonial Secretary on December 22 to report that he had arrived there on the evening before. He wrote again on December 27 to thank Lord Carnarvon for his kind invitation to stay with him at Highclere, near Newbury "to talk over N. American affairs, perhaps with more leisure than is possible in Downing St."[3] but explained that he would like to have a little time at home before going over to London. On January 7 (1867), he and his family moved into 24 Hill Street in London, which remained his base until the passing of the British North America Act.

Alexander Galt and his colleagues, who in their letters home had repeated backstairs gossip of ill-informed nonentities about Monck and the Lamirande case, must have been surprised to discover the esteem in which their Governor General was held by Cabinet Ministers and other prominent statesmen. Poor Lord Carnarvon found himself in Queen Victoria's black books for not having "announced Lord Monck's arrival in England."[4]

Because the preliminary discussions took place in the Westminster Palace Hotel, it became known as the Westminster Palace Conference and is commemorated by a "conversation piece" painted by J. D. Kelly, in which Charles Monck stands with Lord Carnarvon at the head of a long table round which the delegates are informally grouped.

Henry came up from school to attend the opening of Parliament on February 5 and Elizabeth and her daughters went back to Ireland to be near Charles's sister Henrietta. Her husband, Francis Brooke,[5] was seriously ill.

Of the disturbances in Ireland at that time, Charles wrote to Henry on February 15: "You will have seen in the papers that there has been a sort of rising in Kerry." But every day brought news of risings in different parts of the country, and in March there was a "skirmish" at Tallaght – only a few miles from Charleville. "The K[ilmaines] are gone to London. Lord K[ilmaine] is so afraid of the Fenians," Elizabeth wrote to Henry. "I am so afraid of the Fenians, that I have Tom Quin and his gun to sleep in the house. Naturally, he comes just in time for supper. I have the back door locked, so he has to come thro' the hall, when we are at tea and that amuses Fan."

On February 19, Monck, now a peer of the United Kingdom, made a short speech in the House of Lords following Lord Carnarvon's introduction of the Confederation Bill. Hansard's report quoted him as saying that:

> . . . these colonies had so much increased in trade, in wealth, and in commerce that, taking into consideration also their peculiar geographical position, they had interests connected with questions of foreign policy, he would not say antagonistic to, but at all events,

> distinct from those of the mother country. We had, and he thought very wisely, conceded to these Provinces the management of their own affairs, and it would not be politically wise or just to dispose of every matter connected with the foreign relations of these Provinces without consulting the people interested.

Those who knew him intimately would have detected an echo of the "leading strings" motif, when he hinted in his speech that self-government should be conceded to Canada in fact and not only in name.

Before he left Canada, Charles Monck had written to Carnarvon:

> There exists in Canada a very strong desire that Her Majesty would be graciously pleased to designate the Union a "Kingdom," and so give to her representative the title of "Viceroy." The wish is based on . . . the natural yearning of a growing people to emerge . . . from the provincial phase of existence.[6]

The Colonial and Foreign Offices did not submit this request to the Queen because it would appear as a provocative gesture to the American Republic. John A. Macdonald appears not to have known that the Governor General had recommended the title of "Kingdom." In a letter written two years before his death, he blames Monck and the Duke of Buckingham for the substitution of the title "Dominion." "Both good men," added Macdonald, "but quite unable, from the constitution of their minds, to rise to the occasion."[7]

Sir Frederick Bruce, the British Minister in Washington, had reported to the British Foreign Office that the title "Kingdom of Canada" had "aroused much remark of an unfriendly nature in the United States of America."[8] Dr. C. P. Stacey, in an article, "Lord Monck and the Canadian Nation" in *The Dalhousie Review*, points out some inaccuracies in Macdonald's letter, including the references to Monck and the Duke of Buckingham. The article quotes in full Monck's confidential despatch to Lord Carnarvon of September 7, 1866, in which he urged that the union of British North America should be designated a Kingdom. In his letter, Macdonald deplored the fact that when the Confederation Act passed, the Duke of Buckingham was Colonial Secretary in place of Lord Carnarvon, who, declared Macdonald, would have sympathised with Canada's views. In fact, Carnarvon held office until after the Act passed.

It was therefore as "The Dominion of Canada" that the Act, finally passed on March 8, united the Provinces of Upper and Lower Canada (now renamed Ontario and Quebec), New Brunswick, and Nova Scotia. The Act provided for the entry of Newfoundland and Prince Edward

Island into the Union if and when they desired, also for the inclusion of British Columbia, the North West, and Rupert's Land.

The British North American Act received the Royal Assent on March 29, and the Canadian and maritime delegates recrossed the Atlantic.

Monck was at last free to go home for the remainder of his leave. He was again in London on May 24 when he wrote to ask John A. Macdonald to form a government with himself as Prime Minister – the first Prime Minister of the Dominion. "My purpose is to sail on the 14th of June, direct to Quebec," he said at the end of his letter. "I shall go in the first instance to Spencer Wood, but I can, of course, come to Ottawa whenever it is necessary." He had been commissioned as the first Governor General of the new Dominion. Some writers of Canadian history have stressed the fact that this was the result of his own expressed wish. In fact the "expressed wish" came from the Colonial Office, after the Duke of Buckingham succeeded Lord Carnarvon as Secretary of State for the Colonies.[9] While Monck was the obvious person to perform the ceremony of inauguration, it is clear from his private correspondence that his chief motive in returning to Canada was that which had made him anxious to take part in the Westminster Palace Conference. In stating the case for Monck's presence in London during the "deliberations" before passing the Confederation Act, Macdonald had pointed out that "Lord Monck thoroughly . . . knows and appreciates the points of difference between the several provinces." "I feel myself in a great degree personally bound to these gentlemen,"[10] Monck had written to Lord Carnarvon when explaining that the delegates were not entirely at one in their views on Confederation. "These gentlemen" represented the French-Canadians of Lower Canada, the Nova Scotians, and the New Brunswickers, some of whom were still opposed to Confederation as a whole, while many more were uneasy as to how certain clauses of the Act would be interpreted. It was in order that their views should not be lost sight of that Monck felt that it was his duty to be on the spot during the early stages of the new regime. He was well aware that he would thus be exposing himself to the various and conflicting criticisms levelled at the provisions of the Confederation Act by the several provinces.

His term of office had already lasted longer than was usual and, after accomplishing the task of "setting the coach in motion" (as he himself expressed it), he hoped to be replaced as soon as a successor could be appointed. His duties as an Irish landlord and his family commitments all pointed to the necessity of returning home on the earliest possible date. By remaining in Ireland until June 14, he was leaving the barest minimum of time in which to reach Canada for the inauguration ceremony on July 1. Fortunately the *Peruvian* made a reasonably smooth passage, and Monck and his family arrived at Spencer Wood on June 25.

Their voyage was described by Monck as having been "a little rough at first, but afterwards as smooth as a millpond," Elizabeth described it as "tedious, rough, sick, wretched, and *so* slow." To make matters worse, the ship stopped at 2:00 a.m. in mid-ocean, the engine having become overheated with the "continual tossing," and they had to wait four hours for it to cool.

The Captain had given up his "charming" cabin to Elizabeth for a sitting room. After a few days of sea-sickness, she revelled in the sea air and in having plenty of time to read. She and her family made friends with the other passengers and enjoyed the community-singing and the games on deck. When the *Peruvian* docked at Point Levis, Denis Godley and other members of the staff came on board. There was a Guard of Honour to welcome the Moncks. Addresses were presented, guns fired, the band played, and the crowds cheered.

"So lovely this place looks, and feels so still and cool," Elizabeth wrote on arriving at Spencer Wood. On the same evening Puss drove her out in the pony carriage to call on some neighbours, and the whole family went to "early Church" next morning.

From this time the tone of Elizabeth's letters shows that she now shared her husband's love for Canada. Spencer Wood was not Charleville, but they had all grown extremely fond of it. It would not be long, so they thought, before they would all be going home for good; and meanwhile the family were reunited, or would be when the boys joined them. Stanley and Fraülein Denneler had been left behind, but were to follow when the hot weather was over. Henry would come out in the *Peruvian* immediately his holidays began.

Chapter Thirteen (1867-68)

In the new Parliament buildings at Ottawa on July 1, 1867, Monck set his signature to the document inaugurating Confederation and was sworn in as Governor General of the new Dominion. The town was decked with flags, volunteers paraded, guns were fired, and church bells pealed. Among French-Canadians, however, there were still those who considered this birthday of the Dominion a day of "public misfortune;" while in Nova Scotia flags were flown at half-mast and the *Morning Chronicle* displayed a black-edged paragraph announcing: "Died! Last night at twelve o'clock, the free and enlightened Province of Nova Scotia."[1]

In the hope that feelings of hostility would have time to die down during the four months before the opening of the first Parliament of the Dominion, Monck had suggested to Macdonald that all public displays of enthusiasm be reserved for that occasion, and that the inauguration ceremony be performed with the minimum of ostentation. "I hope the people of Ottawa will be satisfied to postpone any *demonstration* until I come to remain at Rideau Hall, as I should like that my present visit should be considered one for business only."[2] Accordingly he was dressed in plain clothes and accompanied only by Denis Godley when he arrived at the Parliament buildings, and he performed the necessary ceremonies in a businesslike way. A Knighthood of the Bath was conferred on John A. Macdonald, and the Order of Commander of the Bath on Cartier, Galt, Tilley, Tupper, Howland, and McDougall. All these had been delegates to the Westminster Conference; George Brown, who had contributed valuable services to the cause of Union, had not consented to join them at the Conference, and his name was not included in the list of Confederation Honours.

In a private letter telling Brown how distressed he was at the omission, Monck implied that the final decision on the distribution of honours had not rested with him. He must have been consulted but he did not have it all his own way. Nevertheless, he was blamed for the "stupid discrimination" of giving Macdonald precedence over Cartier and Galt, and accused of deliberately insulting Lower Canada though in England it had been taken for granted that the man who had been Premier both before and after the Act of Confederation passed should receive the highest honour. In a letter to his wife, Galt commented acidly on his Order – "intended as a distinction;" subsequently, hearing that Cartier was refusing to accept his, Galt refused also, writing again to his wife – "It is an ungracious and most unusual thing to refuse an honour publicly conferred, but if Lord Monck is an ass, I cannot help it."[3]

On November 7, 1867, Monck opened the first Parliament of the Dominion of Canada. In contrast to his sober, businesslike attitude to the inauguration of Confederation, he left nothing undone to mark this day as a splendid and memorable occasion. "My Parliament is to open on the 7th," he wrote to Henry, "and I believe it is to be no end of a function. They are bringing up the Governor General's bodyguard as a Cavalry escort for me," and, four weeks later:

> We have had people staying here for the opening of Parliament all this week. Dinner parties every evening, and tonight Mama is to have an evening party. The weather has become very cold but fortunately very little snow, so we were able to drive in the carriage today to the opening of Parliament . . .
>
> I made all the ladies who came to the body of the House come in evening dress, and there were a great many there and very well got up, and the whole thing looked very pretty . . .

He himself wore court dress, as did the Prime Minister – now Sir John Macdonald, K.C.B.

If Monck's notions of pomp and display fell short of what was required, he was kept up to the mark by Brock, the faithful but exasperating house steward. "Brock has taken it into his head to make the footmen wear powder," he told Henry. "You should see Carbury, who officiates as a footman, in his powder! He is something quite wonderful." The promotion of "Carbury" to footman from whatever his normal duties may have been, was caused by yet another vacancy in Brock's department. Failing to find anyone in Canada to suit her exacting house steward, Elizabeth decided to import a footman from England. She wrote to ask Henry to interview the man, at the same time replying to her son's questions about the High Church practices which were becoming fashionable in Oxford, confusing the two subjects in her usual manner and leaving Henry to sort them out as best he could:

Sunday, Oct. 28. St. Simon & St. Jude - My dearest Child, – Will you look after this footman. Ask him his terms. Get his character from Mr. Hales, make him read this list & say if he would feel equal to the duties. Send the list back to me, & tell me about him as soon as you can . . .

About the vestments. I think every thing should be done to make the worship in the Church whatever seems beautiful and attractive to those who have the arrangement of it. *I* do not admire the coloured vestments, because perhaps that I am old & it is too much of a *novelty*, but I do not the least object to them, nor mind their being *like* Roman Catholics, if we do not share the *errors* of the R.C. Church.

Your fondest Mother, – E. L. M. M.

Tell what he *looks* like.

She and Charles were anxious about their daughter Louise who had been taken seriously ill soon after her arrival in Canada. They thought that she was suffering from sunstroke, but the doctor finally diagnosed tuberculosis and warned her parents that the Canadian winter might be fatal to her. All this had happened before the Moncks left Spencer Wood, and Elizabeth had been torn in two between the claims of her husband and those of her sick child. Eventually it was decided that Henry should escort his sister to Ireland and, before going up for his first term at Oxford, hand her over to one of her aunts, who took her first to Torquay then to Cannes. The family party at Rideau Hall, though reduced by two, was enlivened by the Richard Moncks – Dick and Feo – with their child Cecil. "Feo is expecting a baby any day now, *entre nous*," Fan wrote in one of her delightful letters to her brother Henry. Feo's round face and rotund shape could never have been mistaken for the slim figure of Elizabeth, who was twenty years her senior. Yet, in later accounts of that period, the two have often been confused as in the family group photographed outside Rideau Hall, in which the central and most prominent figure is Feo. Feo, not Elizabeth, was "the soloist at the first concert held at Her Majesty's Theatre at Ottawa in aid of St. Bartholomew's Church."[4] And it was Feo, not Elizabeth, who gave offence by speaking slightingly of the women of Canada.

In all his letters home, Charles Monck emphasised the advantages of Rideau Hall and of the climate there "which seems to suit every member of the family." Elizabeth had convinced him that she was "pleased with the place"; and though on a rainy day just after they arrived, she wrote that "the place is gloomy-looking and the rooms dark," she was soon able to report: "A lovely bright day, the sun shining on the coloured leaves makes them so gorgeous."

The weather may have accounted for the unfortunate impression she made on Lord and Lady Amberley, the son and daughter-in-law of the Duke of Bedford, when they stayed at Rideau Hall during their tour in Canada. Lady Amberley noted in her diary that they arrived in "a tremendous thunderstorm" and drove from the station to Government House through "pitch dark and very rough roads . . . I liked Ld M. and found him very easy and agreeable but Lady M. did nothing but grumble and complain about Canada, Canadians and her life out there and bored A. intensely." It was certainly an unattractive way for the Governor's wife to behave; however, Lady Amberley, mother of the great Bertrand Russell, was herself in a carping mood. Her bedroom, she said, was "very grand and less pleasant than the quiet American houses we had been in." On the whole, their visit was not an unqualified success. Monck usually the most tolerant and charitable of men allowed himself to criticise Lady Amberley's appearance in his letter to Henry. She wore, he said, "a very funny sort of dress which made her look as if she had forgotten to put on all except her first garment."

A. E. Meredith, the diarist, received Elizabeth's "grumbles" in a different spirit. "Lady Monck was most gracious . . . she came up to me in the evening to chat . . . and when I was leaving, thanked me for having made her laugh so much! She promised to send me a card whenever she wished to have a *growl* about Ottawa, putting '*growling*' instead of 'music' or 'dancing' in the corner."[5] According to contemporary reports, there were few who did not "growl" about Ottawa. In the same entry in which she had written so severely about Elizabeth, Lady Amberley added: "Everyone all over Canada complained of it [Ottawa]; as a horrid, out of the way, rough place to live in and quite unfit for the seat of a govt, the streets are unpaved and there are neither houses nor hotels fit to live in." "I know not what is to be done about this place," Elizabeth wrote to Henry in December (1867):

> . . . the members are so angry at being brought here – no wonder. I hate it for Papa. The Lieutenant Governors have *so much* to do, that *he* has much less than he had, so he just goes in for a *little while* to Ottawa most days. Fan drives with Denny for him. I do not like to be out of the way while Dick is in Ottawa, on account of Feo, so I do not drive. Do not either of you remark to *him* on anything I say. If it was a life fit for him, *I* should not mind, but you see it is not.

In 1866, Monck had put forward a suggestion rejected by the Colonial Office that the post of Governor General of the Dominion should be combined with that of Lieutenant-Governor of the Province of Ontario, thereby maintaining in a certain degree personal contact with the people of Canada, and avoiding "rubber stamp status." Elizabeth's letter shows that she guessed that he felt useless in his new isolated position, though his own letters say nothing of it.

His public despatches and private letters to the Colonial Secretary, the Duke of Buckingham, dealt with the proposed inclusion of the North West Territory,[6] in the Confederation the large following gained by Joseph Howe in Nova Scotia for the repeal of the Confederation, and reports that the Fenians were planning another invasion of Canada. After first cabling its contents he forwarded a copy of a letter from a George Kelly, an orderly in the office of a Fenian Commander. He warned that a party of Fenians had embarked from New York intending to land "somewhere in the Bristol Channel" and to assassinate Queen Victoria, the Archbishop of Canterbury, and several prominent members of the British Government. The report could not be ignored at a time when many "outrages" were being committed in England, but it was eventually proved to be without foundation.

Monck was not an alarmist. Although it was his duty to sift any rumours of plots and invasion-scares, and to pass on the more definite reports to the Colonial Office, he usually assured the Duke that he suspected them of being false alarms. When reporting George Kelly's letter, he wrote: "I shall be very glad to bear the ridicule of having been taken in if the story shall prove to be a hoax." There was no question of ridicule. As the result of a series of acts of violence, security officers in England were continually on the alert at that time, and the Colonial Secretary relied on Monck to keep him informed of all assassination rumours, probable or improbable. He in his turn passed to Monck anything heard in London regarding the ever-recurring threats of invasion of Canada. Monck would have been the first to be amused could he have foreseen the comments made, more than a hundred years later, by the author of a book about Queen Victoria: "Where Lord Monck got his information [on the assassination plot] is not clear. What is clear is that His Lordship was recalled from Canada, his career resting under a cloud, before another twelve months were out."[7] So legends are born. Monck "got his information" from Sir John A. Macdonald who had been alerted by Edward Archibald, the British Consul in New York.

Monck did leave Canada eleven months after the above incident, in spite of the urgent entreaties of the Colonial Office that he stay longer. There was no "cloud," unless warm tributes from the Governments in both London and Ottawa as well as from Queen Victoria herself, could be so-called.

Monck and his friend, Charles Adderley, who was Under-Secretary for the Colonies, regularly exchanged private letters. In the course of their correspondence Adderley put out a feeler as to whether Monck would be prepared to stay "over his year." In his reply and in many subsequent letters to the Colonial Office, Monck said that he would like to go home as soon as a successor could be appointed to relieve him. To the best of his ability he had done what he had set out to do. He had "set the coach in motion," and in doing so had become a target for the various criticisms levelled at Confederation by the provinces and sections, each of whom was dissatisfied with some part of it. This was no more than he had expected when he returned to Canada after the passing of the Act; but he felt that it was now high time for a change of Governor General.

Living in daily expectation of his release, his weekly letters to Henry convey a sense of "marking time," while he wrote serenely of such day-to-day events as he thought might amuse or interest his son. An old Indian Chief had attended a Levée – "in *full dress* and with his head all stuck about with feathers"; Elizabeth had held a large evening reception at which the band of the Rifle Brigade played. "They gratified our *ears* very much, but I cannot say much for the effect on our *noses* as the *esprit de corps* was rather strong." Feo had had her baby; Elizabeth and Fan had never been better; while Stanley was actually putting on weight and had taken to skating. "Stanley has put his pony into the red cariole . . . he drives into Ottawa sitting on the knifeboard, with Brock sitting in the body of the sleigh. To my astonishment I saw him yesterday driving Col. Hawley about Ottawa."[8] Of political news, he wrote that Mr. Galt had resigned, and Mr. Rose had succeeded him as Finance Minister; and the Nova Scotians were going to petition for a Repeal of the Union. "I have to go down to the House to give assent to some bills. Don't you remember old Taylor reading out: '*Sanctionne ce bill!*' . . . " At the end of 1867, Fergusson Blair, the President of the Council, died suddenly. "I don't think his loss will cause any embarrassment to the Ministry," Monck wrote to the Duke of Buckingham, "and may be the means of enabling them to reduce the number of the Cabinet wh. I think is at present too large."

In February, 1868, Howe went to England as the representative of the anti-Confederationists in Nova Scotia to petition the Queen for the Repeal of the Union. Adderley had written privately that Sir Fenwick Williams had told him: "Howe carried the elections by United States money, and all goes against him since."[9] And in February he wrote: "Howe is just arriving. He certainly has an awkward case for us to deal with. Dr. Tupper ought to send us ample material for reply . . . We shall simply tell him that it is a *fait accompli*, & cannot be reopened."[10]

During that month, Dr. Tupper wrote two long confidential letters to the Governor General before going to London himself. In them he listed the various causes for complaint:

> ... compulsory taxation to support education, the issuing of fishing rights to America, and the widespread impression among the electors that the rights of the people had been ignored by refusing to submit the question of Confederation to the people at the polls ...
>
> When however the appeal to the Imperial Government is met by the statement that the Imperial Act was passed upon the request and after the approval of two thirds of the Representatives of the people of Nova Scotia; and when it is demonstrated, as it will be twelve months hence, that all the taxation collected under the Dominion Tariff and Legislation will be less than must have been raised in that Province had it been outside the Union, confidence will be destroyed in those who have misled them, and the people will recognize and appreciate the advantages which union will secure to them.[11]

During the course of the conversations between Howe and the Colonial Secretary, the former accepted an invitation to visit the Duke at Stowe. Adderley wrote:

> Nova Scotia is in a fair way, I hope. Benjamin Franklin said to Chatham: "Give me a cellar of good Madeira, and I will settle any Treaty." I think the Stowe wine and the Duke's hand-rolled good cigars have brought things forward. Tupper has also seen Cardwell, who will talk Bright over, and Howe ... will be content with recommending your Parliament to adjust matters of dissatisfaction between the Provinces. Meanwhile I hope you will be getting measures passed of conciliatory tendency.[12]

On the same subject, Adderley wrote to Monck an account of an interview with Gladstone, who had expressed an opinion shared by Goldwin Smith and John Bright:

> Gladstone said to me the other day: "Canada is England's weakness, till the last British soldier is brought away & Canada left on her own legs. We cannot hold our own with the United States, and must put up with constant insolence & plottings, as they know they have the first trick in War." I told him what you said of the Canadian ambition of extension, which he thought showed more vitality & spirit than they had credit for.

That this opinion – that Canada was "England's weakness" – was wrongly attributed to Monck himself may have been partly due to his constant recommendation that Canada should be allowed greater independence, on the premise that the initiative and sense of responsibility of her legislators would increase if they did not have the Imperial Government perpetually breathing down their necks. At the time, it was believed that the indiscreet remarks of "Almighty" Godley led people in Canada to believe that the Governor General was among those who wished England to "get rid of the colonies."

Each time the mail from England arrived, Monck expected to hear of a definite date for his release; but nothing had been settled about his successor when, in February (1868), Lord Derby resigned and Disraeli formed a Conservative Cabinet. Adderley wrote:

> We are all looking up after the blow of Lord D.'s resignation. Dizzy will die hard at all events, but I don't think he will die this year at all.
>
> I have recommended Denis Godley to go out to you again, whether you stay or not . . .
>
> The Duke [of Buckingham] has gone down to Osborne to tell the Queen of the Duke of Edinburgh having been shot, not fatally, by a Fenian in New South Wales.[13] They secured the brute who stated himself a Fenian, Offaly by name, & they were trying him, he setting up a plea for insanity. The Duke was at a picnic, & shot in the back from behind a tree. The ball . . . was easily extracted, and he is on his way home.[14]

Charles Monck had already written to tell Henry that he had been officially informed of the attempted murder "by a telegram that arrived while we were at breakfast". He had also heard that–

> . . . Godley had failed to get any precise information from the C.O. about my being relieved, but I have myself no doubt that I shall be relieved in the course of the summer, though I dare say not until late . . .

While on leave during the winter, Denis Godley had lost one of his eyes as the result of a shooting accident. By the end of February, he was ready to return to duty, but his plans depended on whether or not his employer was coming home.

Monck was relieved to hear that Henry had already decided to spend the Easter vacation at Cannes with his sister. Puss's health had been steadily improving, and her doctor expected her to be able to return to Ireland towards the end of the summer, by which time her parents hoped to have arrived at Charleville. Stanley, too, showed signs of having outgrown his delicacy, and most of his father's letters contained references to his sturdy constitution. "He has been for some days busily engaged in making maple sugar," Charles wrote on April 5, "and he has really succeeded in making a great deal. This is a very good season for it, as the cold nights and warm days make the sap run very fast." Charles also confided to Henry his intention to send Stanley to school after the summer. "Between you and me, I think he is getting a little beyond petticoat government." There was no question as to which preparatory school he would be sent. Mr. Wilkinson's services as holiday tutor to Henry being no longer required, he had started a private school of his own at St. Leonards-on-Sea. His venture was enthusiastically backed by Charles and Elizabeth who never spared themselves in their efforts to help their friends. Neither did they spare other people, and all their acquaintances were urged to send their sons to "Quebec House", as the school was nostalgically named. "Please ask Mr. Wilkinson to send me some more of his cards," wrote Charles, having exhausted the first batch; while Elizabeth never missed an opportunity of canvassing those among her friends who were the mothers of little boys. "My numbers do *not* increase at all in proportion to the accommodation I have provided for them," poor "Wilkie" confessed in a letter to Henry:

> . . . which circumstance sometimes makes me very anxious. I cannot, for the life of me, make out how it is that, with my apparently good connection, no more pupils are sent to me . .
>
> I hope, old fellow, you are really reading hard now, in spite of the little love you seem to have for your subjects. I do want to see you *well* through your college career.

To amuse his father, Henry forwarded to him two letters he had received from the Charleville keeper, Tom Quin:

> Dear Sir, – I write to let you know that their is no sign of the corn been sown for the pheasants yet the time is getting late some time ago hobson [gardener] was talking about sowing buck wheat there is no use to sow buck wheat in Charleville the ground does not answer for it oats or barley is the best – he have cut down all the big lorrels in the garden and pleasure ground the are going to cut the burnt house[15] this season agen everything is going on very well here.
>
> I had a Letter from Mr Stanley asking about his rabbit and pidgeons I was glad to hear that the family is all quite well dont let on to Mr Sandys that I rote about the corn
>
> I am dear Sir your humble and obedient servant
>
> Tom Quin.

The next letter, written later in the season, reported that "the young Phesants is going on verry well so far," and that he had sent three "nicely taned" (tanned) setter puppies to the Clancartys at Garbally. "Norah never proved to be in pup, I think she was to fat when I Brought her to the Dog."

There was great rejoicing when Henry wrote that he had won the

Christ Church two-mile race and had come in third in the mile race; but his next letter brought the unwelcome news that he had failed in "Smalls" – the first of his Oxford examinations. He told his parents that he was deeply sorry to have disappointed them and promised to work harder next term. "Of course I am sorry you did not pass the examination, but I am sure you worked for it, and please God you will have better luck next time," replied his indulgent father. "My principle all through life has been never to spend time 'crying over spilt milk', and I am sure you will work hard next term."

Elizabeth expressed herself more strongly, having perhaps heard something of her own father's inglorious career at Eton – "nearly at the bottom of the school."

> My dearest Child, – *one* great reason that I was so distressed about your not passing was that *whatever* profession you go into, there are *competitive* examinations, and if you cannot pass them, you can go into *none*, & then you will lead an idle life, & that would be misery to yourself & to us *all*. The *great* secret of success in *any* mental undertaking is to acquire the habit of *firmly* fixing your attention on whatever you have to do. You have a bad habit of undervaluing your own powers, of thinking you are not clever, & cannot do things, whereas if you *determine* on any success, & bend your whole mind to it, you will achieve it. Get your mind into a *habit* of hard study. Ask anyone who has achieved success, if I am not right! . . .
>
> A sorrowful Easter this will be to me, still separated, but God knows best.

Family triumphs and failures were eclipsed by a tragedy which took place in Ottawa on April 8, 1868. Rumours of a great Fenian conspiracy culminated in the murder of D'Arcy McGee, who was shot in the back on reaching his home after attending a Parliamentary session. Thomas D'Arcy McGee, poet and historian, had in his early days been an Irish patriot and escaped to America after the rout of the Young Ireland Party in 1848. He subsequently settled in Canada, where he became one of the earliest and most enthusiastic supporters of Confederation. At the time of his death, he was member of Parliament for Montreal West, and Minister for Agriculture and Emigration.[16] His murder was the consequence of his open denunciation of the Fenians. "I cannot doubt that you have heard of the fearful tragedy which has filled us with horror," Elizabeth wrote to Henry on April 9. "Poor Mr. D'Arcy McGee's murder. I send newspapers. Never was there a more *fearful* occurrence, I never was more shocked! As you know, I always liked him *so much*." Ten days later, Charles wrote: "Mr. McGee had a very large public funeral at Montreal on Monday last . . . They actually *cheered* in the Church when the Priest, who was preaching the funeral sermon, denounced the Fenians."

A state of political uncertainty at Westminster delayed still further the appointment of Monck's successor. It had been expected that Disraeli's government would resign after they were defeated on the Irish Church Bill, and the Duke of Buckingham postponed making the appointment until he knew which party would be in power. He was not sorry to have this valid excuse for shelving a difficult decision. Among the few men capable of filling the post of Governor General of Canada, he had not yet found one who was willing to accept it; and it was easier to let things drift, and reply with vague promises to Monck's frequent appeals to be released.

By the end of April, however, it became clear that Disraeli had no intention of resigning. "My letters from London say that they expect that Dizzy will hold on until after the general election, which cannot take place till after the 1st of January," Monck wrote to Henry. Believing the last obstacle to his replacement had been removed, he wrote confidently of being at home in a few weeks. A rumour that Lord Normanton was to be the next Governor General was succeeded by the definite information that the post had been offered to Lord Mayo and that he had accepted it. Monck wrote the news to Henry, in strict confidence – "since it is not yet official, and Lord Mayo might not like it to be talked of," but it could only be a matter of days before the appointment would be officially announced, after which Monck had only to wait until it was known how soon Lord Mayo would be ready to sail.

The Moncks had actually begun preliminary preparations for the journey home, when all their plans were cancelled. A measure was introduced in the Canadian Parliament to cut down the Governor's salary from £10,000 to £6,500, five hundred pounds a year less than the pre-Confederation salary. As soon as this was known in England, Lord Mayo was so annoyed that he threw up the office, "not," as he was careful to explain, "because of the £3,500, but for the lessened prestige and dignity of the appointment."[17] The Colonial Office was now placed in an embarrassing position. It was an awkward moment in which to offer the post to anyone else, and the Duke of Buckingham wrote to ask Monck if he would consider staying on, at least for a few months. Monck sympathised with his predicament and consented to remain until November, on condition that he should not be asked to stay longer.

According to Sir John A. Macdonald, the reduction in the Governor's salary was:

> . . . the only thing that went wrong during the whole session [sum-

mer, 1868] . . . The Government opposed this with all their might, but there was a regular stampede of friends and foes in favour of the reduction. Most of the young members had pledged themselves to vote for a reduction, and they carried out their pledges. There is a great cry for retrenchment just now, which originated principally in the Maritime Provinces . . . It unluckily so happened that the Governor's salary was the only point in the Union Act that could well be objected to, and it was made a handle at all the elections.[18]

Monck had offended some of the members from Upper Canada, now the Province of Ontario, by sympathising to a certain extent with the French-Canadians and with the representatives of the maritime provinces who, in their turn, thought that he did not give sufficient consideration to their claims. Since each faction had a different grouse, the increase of salary was the only point on which they could agree, and Monck was the obvious scapegoat for all the various resentments. Macdonald's private secretary and biographer reports his Chief as having said:

I was a good deal surprised to find that Lord Monck was very unpopular among the members of Parliament. I like him amazingly, and shall be very sorry when he leaves, as he has been a very prudent and efficient administrator of public affairs. Still, he seems not to have the power of making friends, and there is a bitterness of feeling displayed towards him for which I was altogether unprepared . . . I think Lord Monck feels the passage of the Bill a good deal, not that it is of any pecuniary consequence to him.[29]

Joseph Pope was recording from memory a conversation which had taken place many years earlier. It is in complete contradiction to the words Macdonald had actually written to Tilley, assuring him that "only through Lord Monck" could the differing views of the several Provinces be reconciled. If Pope was not mistaken when he quoted as Macdonald's opinion that Monck lacked "the power of making friends," the comment may have been intended to be applied in a political sense. If so, Macdonald was probably correct in thinking that Monck was deficient in a certain brand of slick diplomacy, that he made no "favourites", and did not seek to gain the impassioned support of one particular faction.

It is easy to believe that, at the time, many members of the Confederation Parliament nursed "feelings of bitterness" towards their Governor General, besides those who had been involved in "l'Affaire Lamirande". In drawing up the Confederation Act, it had been impossible to evolve a scheme that would please everybody, and no political party was entirely satisfied with the outcome. That Monck himself regretted some of its resolutions is known by a letter from Lord Carnarvon, in answer to one from himself which unfortunately is not included in the collection of Carnarvon Papers. On January 15, 1868, after ceasing to hold the office of Colonial Secretary, Carnarvon wrote the following in reply to Monck's (untraced) letter of December 28, 1867:

> In Canada you have perhaps more than even your fair share of difficulties to deal with: but in politics the longer I live the more I am convinced of what you say – that real success depends far less upon the nature and precise structure of constitution than upon the moral qualities of the men who have to give effect to them.
>
> I do indeed regret with you the decision that was come to last year in London on some points; but for that decision neither of us are responsible. Anyhow I do not doubt that the new system will have every chance in its favour under the guidance of your experienced hand.[20]

Whether it was discontent with the provisions of the Act of Confederation, the aftermath of the whisperings and intrigues surrounding the Lamirande case, or the annoyance over the distribution of Confederation Honours, there is no doubt that the references made to Monck during his last two years of office were very different from those of the preceding five years. During the earlier period, frequent allusions were made to the fact that he had won "the highest popularity"; "the Governor . . . is very popular with all parties personally." From the end of the year 1866 he was criticised first for one thing, then for another, so that an atmosphere of disapproval was created and when he left, in Lower Canada at least, no tears were shed.

Both past and present Canadian writers have used such contradictory adjectives to describe Charles Monck that a complex personality emerges out of their descriptions which would have greatly surprised the original and his numerous devoted friends. When his appointment to the Governorship was made in 1861, some of the London newspapers had published criticisms of Lord Palmerston for sending to Canada one of his personal friends who was "an unknown man." He was described by Edward Watkin as "a jolly, well-bred Irishman, and nothing else." An article in the *Montreal Herald* opposed these criticisms, saying that –

> What we want is an honest man, who has no whims of his own to serve, and who keeps himself from such personal friendships and antipathies as will influence his conduct – a man, in short, who will act in Canada as Her Majesty acts in England.[21]

The one quality on which all seem to have agreed was his "impartiality." As if the article in the *Montreal Herald* had been prophetic, it was said that he was the first Governor General of Canada to have been strictly impartial. When he left the Dominion finally, *The Ottawa Times* commended him for having –

> ... held the impartial balance between conflicting parties in the most trying times of political excitement, and having never exposed himself to the reproach of having favoured one at the expense of the other.

In all their letters, Charles and Elizabeth wrote of their longing to be at home and their disappointment over the continual delays. Yet, according to contemporary accounts, their guests at Rideau Hall found them as cheerful and good humoured as ever, and with what the late D'Arcy McGee had described as "the same zest for a joke." Just as the weekly "Parliamentary dinners" at Spencer Wood punctuated an almost continuous succession of gay, informal parties, so at Rideau Hall the functions on a grand scale were interspersed with more light-hearted gatherings. There was not always a rigid borderline between the two kinds of entertainment. Accustomed to the traditions of European society, Charles and Elizabeth thought they were paying a far greater compliment to Canadian dignitaries when they invited three or four of them to meet their own relations, their personal friends, and some distinguished visitors from overseas, rather than "lump them together" in a strictly official dinner.

Mr. A. F. Meredith was one who thoroughly enjoyed these intimate parties and wrote descriptions of them in his diary, reporting that Lord Monck had been "most affable" and "Lady Monck very pleasant and agreeable, full of gossip and very confidential." "Lady Monck was most gracious," he wrote on another occasion. He also noted that the Ministers relaxed in the informal atmosphere, and complained openly of the unsuitability of Ottawa as the seat of government, all agreeing that it could not remain so permanently.

But not everybody appreciated the easy and casual atmosphere in which guests were treated as friends, to entertain whom was a pleasure rather than a solemn duty; and while Charles was strict about those points of etiquette which were consistent with good manners, he disappointed some people who would have preferred more gubernatorial bustle. The *Montreal Gazette* accused Monck of "parsimony" for not having entertained more lavishly in the 'splendid mansion" provided for him. In fact, Rideau Hall was not completed until November 1867, a month after this article was published.

No such publicity was given to the complaints made against

Monck's successor, Sir John Young, whose formal dinner-parties were described as "gloomy affairs punctuated by long silences . . . the gas-lights being turned out at the end of a party as a signal for guests to depart."[22] The guests at these sad functions may have thought nostalgically of the Moncks, whose dinners were often followed by dancing and community-singing, and who were more likely to have forgotten the lights and left them burning all night.

As for the much disputed salary, Monck admitted to Henry that, although he had originally accepted the appointment in order to be able to help his family financially, "owing to circumstances", he had not saved a single penny during his seven years in Canada.

Chapter Fourteen (1868)

Passage of a Bill reducing the Governor General's salary was as Macdonald had said, of "no pecuniary consequence" to Monck. But it greatly increased the Colonial Secretary's difficulty in replacing him, and Monck felt bound to help him out by consenting to stay in Canada till November.

His decision threw the family plans into confusion. When Parliament rose in June, he had made the first stage of the journey home by removing the whole of his establishment to Spencer Wood. "We arrived at Ottawa in good time for the Quebec boat," he wrote to Henry on June 12:

> The day was very fine and it was a very pleasant excursion. The place looks very well and we are so far on our way home. I mean to stay here till my successor arrives. I don't know yet for certain who it will be . . . I am glad you are working so well for "smalls," and I do trust that by this time you are all right, but you need not be afraid that I shall be annoyed with you if you do not succeed, as I am sure you are going your best and no man can do more than that.

"I am in such a state about the success of your examination," Elizabeth wrote during the following week:

> I know you have worked as hard as possible & trust all may be right, but it is so trying being so far off. Please God, that will not be for long! It was so pleasant to hear Papa say to Captain Malan, 'We shall be home ourselves in a few weeks,' [and] to hear him talk of the different things he will have to do at home. The *uncertainty* is very trying, but it is so much better to be *here*, & it is like a step towards home, & we feel quite different since we came.

The "uncertainty" concerning Henry ended on June 25 when his letter arrived with the welcome news that he was "well through 'smalls'."

No sooner were his parents relieved from the suspense concerning Henry's examination than it was decided that they were not to go home after all. Poor Elizabeth had good reason to be vexed. Stanley and Fraülein Denneler had already sailed, escorted by Francis Burrowes who was going home on leave. The boy was to spend a few weeks in the "bracing air" of Llandudno, and his parents had expected to be in Ireland when he arrived there. It had been arranged that he should go to Mr. Wilkinson's school in September, but this must now be postponed until after Christmas.

Also Puss (Louise) was due to arrive home from Switzerland where her doctor had ordered her to "drink the waters" at Bex. Her parents had not seen her since the previous autumn when she had developed a patch on her lung; and though, after spending the winter and spring at Cannes, the cure was nearly complete, they had counted on being at Charleville to look after her when she returned. Charles wrote imploring her not to overtax her strength. "Don't think I am preaching to you, my pet child, but I know that excitement and high spirits may carry you beyond the bounds of prudence." He seemed almost equally anxious lest she should override her horse.

While Henry went to stay with the Fifes in Scotland for grouse-shooting and the Braemar Gathering, Puss paid a visit to her mother's sisters at Barbavilla. Her parents approved of this plan, knowing that she would be in good hands. Elizabeth might be Lady Monck and the mistress of Charleville, but she still regarded her beloved elder sister Anne as "Mother Superior" in the Monck sisterhood. Puss would go back to Charleville in time to welcome Stanley and "Denny" when they came there from Llandudno. But instead of the news of their safe arrival, the next mail to reach Spencer Wood brought a letter from Fraülein Denneler to say that Stanley had "the whooping cough," the one illness which Elizabeth dreaded above all others. At least one member of the family had died of that illness. "You may suppose that Mama was at first rather uneasy and had made up her mind to go home next week," Charles wrote with his usual mastery of understatement. "But today brought us so good an account that she has quite given that up, and is reconciled to remaining until I am relieved." He was soon able to write "The accounts of Stanley are very good. He appears to have the whooping cough very lightly, and it is a good thing for him to get it over before he goes to school."

At the end of September, letters from home reported that Puss was able to lead a perfectly normal life and that Stanley had arrived at Charleville with his cough "nearly quite gone." Charles and Elizabeth had become as serene as was possible while the Atlantic divided them from three of their four children, when the peace of Spencer Wood was shattered by startling news from Henry. During his visit to the Fifes at Mar Lodge in Scotland, he had fallen in love and returned to Charleville an engaged man. He realised, or perhaps Puss reminded him, that at the age of nineteen he must first gain his parents' permission before being officially engaged or even making a formal proposal. This permission he now asked in letters he afterwards discreetly destroyed. Later, Charles referred to the object of Henry's devotion as "Lady Alexina"; and as she was aged seventeen, she can have been none other than the Fifes' youngest daughter, whose brother Macduff had been Henry's great friend both at Woodcote and Eton.

More than thirty years earlier, Louisa Monck had written of Elizabeth that "Love, Lovers and Lizzy seemed to belong to each other"; a romantic love affair was to her as the smell of battle to a war-horse. Never was there a more sympathetic "confidante". "Captain Webber comes here almost every day to talk to Mama about his bride!" Fan had written to Henry from Spencer Wood. Now that her own darling son was in the toils, Elizabeth's letters were all passionate interest and sympathy. They were sorrowful, too, for of course she supposed that Charles was right in saying that Henry and Alexina were both too young to bind themselves; that Henry had only completed one year at Oxford; and that he had not yet decided on a career. She also knew that the family finances were in an unsatisfactory state, and that the greater part of the debts left by her own father were still unpaid.

Charles wrote wise counsel, imploring his son to:

> . . . resist the temptation to act with haste and want of due consideration; to think over the very great objection – even if the objection on the score of fortune were removed – to *either* of you *engaging* yourselves to the other at your ages. If either you or Lady Alexina, while such an engagement existed, discovered that you had made a mistake in entering into it, your duty would be to break it off. But, you may depend on it, that is more easily said than done. If you saw that she was deeply attached to you, or she saw the same thing in you, an unwillingness to give present pain and the dread of appearing to act dishonourably, might induce either of you to fulfil an engagement, the performance of which under such conditions could be attended with nothing but unhappiness for the rest of life. Of course I am most interested in *your* happiness, but believe me hers is as much consulted by the advice I give you. If she cares enough about you to make you a good wife, she will not be induced to marry any other man; and if her feeling towards you is only a

girlish fancy, you may trust me that you would not be doing well by *her* in asking her, at the age of seventeen, to bind herself to you. If, as I told you in my former letter, after two or three years you both continue of the same mind, I will do all I can to enable you to marry, though it is only fair to tell you that even then it may not be possible for me to give you a sufficient provision.

He went on to explain that his "principal object" in accepting salaried appointments had been that "money obstacles" should not prevent Henry from marrying; but that owing to "various causes" he was returning from Canada no richer than when he left England. He hoped, however, to get employment in England, in which case "one of the greatest gratifications will be that it will enable me to do what you wish."

There is a fragment of a note from Elizabeth:

> You *well* know how very near my heart is in *all* connected with *you*. I am sure Puss has been a great comfort. She feels it all so deeply herself. Dear Georgy & Hen, *indeed* they will never tell. They are *so* tender & sweet.

The rest of her letter is missing, or perhaps Henry destroyed it; but her reference to Georgina Croker and Henrietta Brooke implies that Henry's two aunts had known of and perhaps encouraged his attachment. Letters came and went by every mail, but never are Alexina's parents mentioned, and one wonders what they could have been about to have allowed matters to progress so far. It was still an event to be photographed, but Henry was able to send a photograph of Alexina to Canada, as well as some new ones of himself.

> My dearest Child. – I return the sweet innocent-looking nice-looking photo: without loss of time. She must indeed be just what you describe her. I feel it all more than I can say, & pray that God may make us all satisfied with whatever is HIS will, in *this* & in all else!
>
> My child, I do not like yours *at all*, it quite distresses me even to *look* at them. I do not *at all* like a beard on you & I do not like the way your hair is settled in these photos. I used *so much* to like the *Eton way* in which you used to have it, very short & divided down the middle. These do not bring *you* at all to my mind, but something *so* different.

Elizabeth must indeed have felt that it was high time she went home, as much to deal with her son's altered appearance as with his lovesick condition.

"Henry is never out of my thoughts," she wrote in a letter to Puss, saying again how charmed she had been by Alexina's photograph. She seldom if ever disputed Charles's judgement; but had it been left to her, it is possible that she might have seen no reason why her "dearest child" should not be allowed to marry his first love and live in a corner of Charleville – as two of her sisters and their husbands had done, and as – many years later – Puss was to do. After the first week in November there were no more letters about Alexina – or, if there were, Henry did not keep them. He fell in with his father's suggestion that all "further discussion" be postponed until they were able to meet; but there is no record of what then took place, nor of how long Henry remained inconsolable after the faithless Alexina married Henry Coventry during the summer of 1870.

The next mail brought good news from the Colonial Office. Sir John Young,[1] lately Governor of New South Wales, had definitely accepted the Governor Generalship of Canada. It also brought permission for Charles to sail on November 14, whether or not Sir John had arrived. Meanwhile, Sir Charles Windham, K.C.B., Commander of Her Majesty's Forces in British North America, was to act as Administrator.

The next weeks were a whirl of farewell parties given by and for the Moncks. "We are just beginning the bore of packing up," wrote Charles, adding that Fan was driving herself about with a pair of ponies in the pony-carriage, paying last visits to their neighbours. She had also attended a luncheon-party on board ship and the Burstals' dance. She had greatly enjoyed all the dances in Quebec, and this was the last she would ever attend. Though devoted to Charleville, she had developed a great love for Canada where she had been treated with so much kindness and consideration. Besides the parties given to and by their friends, there were many formal dinners and other functions; also an official farewell to the Canadian Volunteers for whom Charles Monck felt so much pride and affection.

Shortly before he sailed, Monck received an official despatch from the Duke of Buckingham:

> The Queen desires me to convey to you Her approval of the manner in which you have discharged the duties which have been confided to you. The period of your administration has not been uneventful. The relations between Canada and the United States, before and after the termination of the civil war . . . have presented questions of much moment and delicacy and it has been your fortune to bear a distinguished part in one of the most important events which have occurred in the history of the British Colonies – the Confederation of the three leading Provinces of British North America.

> In all these matters you have exhibited a discretion, an uprightness of judgment, and a considerate and vigilant regard for the public interest, with which Her Majesty is entirely satisfied . . .
>
> I am to authorise you to communicate this despatch, in the most fitting manner, to the people of Canada.

The despatch was published in the *Ottawa Times*, whose Editor commented:

> We are sure that every man in the country will rejoice that Lord Monck has received such a tribute to the excellence of his administration of affairs in Canada, during very trying times.
>
> Despite the carpings of a few, it cannot be denied that Lord Monck's administration has been a continual success; that he has won the admiration of all political parties, and that he has set the example of modest and prudent social life which it would not be by any means unhealthy for people in more obscure positions to imitate. . .
>
> In the most trying times of political excitement, he held the impartial balance between contending parties, and never exposed himself to the reproof of having favoured one at the expense of the other.[2]

"The carpings of a few," referred to an article in *Le Pays* that implied that Monck was both negative and negligible and had left no mark on the pages of Canadian history. Unlike Queen Victoria who considered that Monck had borne "a distinguished part" in the bringing about of Confederation, the correspondent declared that his role had been that of spectator only. The reason for the embittered tone was betrayed by the allusion to the Lamirande case, which, according to *Le Pays*, demonstrated "*l'indécision et la faiblesse de Lord Monck*." The article ended with a sneer at the farewell dinners and addresses, at which the Ministers and other officials were said to have worn the stereotyped smiles they had been practising for three days before their mirrors while tying their ties.[3] Monck was well aware that the French-Canadians were dissatisfied with some aspects of the new political régime and that they blamed him for it, being ignorant of the many times he had brought their claims forward and done his best to protect their interests.

Two days before he left Canada, the *Montreal Gazette* reprinted a long article from a London periodical, *The Saturday Review*. The article described the "strong and prudent guidance," of Monck's seven years' administration. It recalled the doubts expressed at the time of Monck's appointment and paid a warm tribute to the "tact and judgement" with which he dealt with each crisis as it arose: strengthening the defences of

Canada; helping to unite the provinces in Confederation; and dealing with representatives of the United States, particularly during the "real peril" of the "Fenian menace."

> At times he was thought by many critics in England to have stretched courtesy to the republican and not over-friendly neighbours almost further than was compatible with dignity; but . . . a little excess of good breeding was, after all, not a bad example to set to the truculent politicians of New York and Washington.[4]

At the Monck's departure, even the discontented members of the Government signed a Testimonial in recognition of their regard for him.

"The house is getting a very *packy* look," Elizabeth wrote. "I dread the voyage and wish we were safe over. I have 3 evening receptions next week for farewells." To add to the confusion of their last weeks, she had insisted on sending home her great red cariole, although Charles had advised against it. "I do not think she will have much use for it in Ireland," he told Henry. As a result, they had to hire a cariole for their ceremonial departure on November 14. The snow came early that year, and wheeled vehicles were already laid up for the winter. "The sleigh we got at Gringras would not do for 4 horses," Elizabeth wrote, "so we had to go down with 2. Streets lined, guard of honour, guns, band, etc. *Everybody* you can think of came on board to take leave. Very fine, calm & bright."

They were escorted to the place of embarkation by members of the Dominion and local cabinets, with other officials, both civil and military; while a guard of honour from the 53rd regiment received Monck on the wharf. As the steamship *Nestorian* left the shore, a salute of seventeen cannons was fired from the citadel.

Elizabeth began writing an account of their last voyage home during their first evening on board the *Nestorian*. The weather changed as they passed the Gaspé coast, entered the Gulf of St. Lawrence, then the Straits of Belle Isle, where they saw "2 or 3 large icebergs". After "November 18th – into the Atlantic," there were no more entries until the 22nd, when she wrote that there had been "a desperate week of rough weather . . . Your Father, who has crossed so often, says it is the worst *he* ever had." It was just over seven years since their first crossing of the Atlantic, and during that time Charles had spent a total of only nine months away from Canada.

On the evening of Tuesday, November 24, 1868, Elizabeth triumphantly wrote her last entry: "Just going to land!"

Epilogue

In 1861, when the news of Monck's appointment to Canada was published, most Canadians had never heard of him, nor of anything he had done to justify such an important post. To a lesser extent, there was the same ignorance about his subsequent career, which was described by C. P. Stacey as having been "in no way remarkable".[1] There was a general feeling that the Governorship of Canada should lead on to something spectacular, such as the Viceroyalty of India or of Ireland, or at least to a very senior Government post though this had not always happened in the past. Some Governors did not long survive their term of office. O. D. Skelton noted that Sir Charles Metcalfe had been "the third Governor to whom Canada had proved fatal in five years."[2]

Neither of these fates awaited Charles Monck. Instead, he had been earmarked for a post which was about to come into existence for the first time – Commissioner for (Irish) Church Temporalities. Owing to its newness, the significance of the appointment was not immediately apparent, and it is not surprising that, to the majority of the people of Canada, the unknown Irishman seemed to have disappeared into the obscurity from which he came. In fact, the Disestablishment of the (Protestant) Church of Ireland was the chief topic of the day; and with the Liberals in power, it hit the headlines of the London newspapers.

From early 1868, Monck had pressed the Colonial Office for his release from his post in Canada. It has been suggested by a Canadian author that his anxiety to get home was motivated by his fear of being left out if a change of Government should bring about a reshuffle of political appointments. There may have been some truth in this theory; but all Monck's private correspondence clearly shows that he was mainly actuated by an intense desire to be on the spot at a time when it seemed possible that, as last, something was going to be done for Ireland.

As early as 1867, Monck received private letters from his political friends in England and Ireland requesting information on the organisation of the Anglican Church in Canada since its disestablishment by the Clergy Reserves (Canada) Act of 1853. After corresponding with Canadian bishops and other leading Churchmen, he summed up his findings in a reply to William Monsell.[3] His letter gave details of statistics and method of organisation and ended with his approval of the system. He was convinced that its effect on the clergy was favourable, while "unalloyed benefit" to the laity was produced "by the sense that the Church is *their own*."[4]

In January, 1868, after reading some of Gladstone's recent speeches on the "Irish Question," Monck wrote him a long letter, setting out his "strong convictions" with regard to the Irish problems of Church, Land, and Education: "I have always felt bound by every obligation of duty and interest to give my most earnest consideration to this subject," was his excuse for writing at such length; "... also because the condition of affairs in Lower Canada is, in many respects, analogous to that which exists in Ireland." He admitted that he felt deep sympathy with the hostility felt by Irish Catholics to the Established Church. "... a Church which is looked upon by them as alien ... whose creed is professed only by a small minority, is by Law the religion of the country, and ... deprives the great mass of the people of all benefits from the funds set apart for the maintenance of religion." In the same letter, he was very outspoken on the need for reform of the landlord-tenant laws in Ireland and for a system of secular education that would not attempt to force on the people anything opposed to their religious convictions.[5]

During the next few years, Monck expressed these views in the House of Lords. There is no doubt that his views on Church Disestablishment, together with his detailed information on Canadian Church management, played their part in the drawing up of Gladstone's Irish Church Bill. In March, 1868, Gladstone introduced a resolution for Irish Church Disestablishment. To Monck it seemed a definite step towards the achievement of what he and other members of the "Dublin Committee" had worked for twenty years earlier. He knew Gladstone was right to put Church Disestablishment first, and that reform of the land laws would follow as a natural sequence.

It was infuriating not to be at Westminster when the resolution was introduced. Monck knew only too well the strength of the opposition it would meet from those with vested interests and the vital necessity for supporters who had the courage of their convictions. Otherwise, the resolution would either be defeated, or whittled down to a half-hearted compromise of its original form. Monck later described the latter alternative as "the vice which has damaged every previous concession to justice in Ireland."[6]

The resolution was passed by the House of Commons but defeated in the House of Lords. At the end of the same year, the Liberal party came into power, with Gladstone as Prime Minister. Immediately upon taking office, he again brought forward the Irish Church Bill; and after several months of controversial debate, it became law in July, 1869. Monck had arrived in London in time to take a vigorous part in the debates in the House of Lords; and in seconding the Speech from the Throne, expressed himself forcibly on the injustice of confining State provision to the Church of the Protestant minority in Ireland at the expense of the Catholic majority.

To the general public, the storm created by the controversy somewhat obscured the complications involved in effecting the provisions of the Act; the administration and re-allocation of the immense property of which the "Church of Ireland" was now to be disendowed. The difficult and extremely delicate problem of redistributing this great wealth created the need for a new Government office. For this, Monck was the obvious choice, and that not only because he had proved himself to be a capable and trustworthy administrator, had been a Lord of the Treasury, and was known to be an ardent supporter of church and land reform in Ireland. The chief reason was his detailed knowledge of the system by which the Anglican Church in Canada had been organised since its disestablishment.

The work of the Irish Church Commission was not confined to the distribution of £5,000,000 of hard cash among such public works as national education, the relief of distress, and support of sea-fisheries. The historical significance of the Irish Church Act lay in the fact that a large part of Church property had consisted of land. This was now used by the Commissioners for an experimental scheme of state-aided purchase of the land by tenants, who were given first refusal before it was offered for sale elsewhere. In fact, the Church Commissioners paved the way and laid the foundation for both the 1870 and the 1881 Irish Land Acts.

Monck had been offered alternatives: nothing came of Lord Granville's suggestion that he should be sent as Ambassador to Constantinople; and when offered the Governorship of Madras, he refused it because a hot climate would injure his wife's health.[7] Also it would have entailed another long absence from Ireland.

Monck belonged to the Liberal party, but his private correspondence and Parliamentary speeches show that he was never in complete agreement with its leader. There was no open breach; in fact, during the last years of Monck's life, Gladstone was still trying to win his support. Monck's lack of confidence in him seems to have dated from the latter's famous pronouncement on first becoming Prime Minister: "My mission is to pacify Ireland." During the next twenty years, Monck fought a losing battle against the administering of palliatives to Ireland, rather than the removal of injustices. He was severely criticised for his views which, forty years later, would have been labelled "Bolshie," and even today might be considered slightly left-wing.

The House of Lords was then largely composed of big landowners. The greater part, if not all, of their wealth was derived from land-rents. Only a few shared Monck's views and aims; to most, all Irish patriots were rebels, and the formation of nationalist movements was an act of disloyalty to the British Empire. That the Irish had never accepted British rule, that they considered their country to be under enemy occupation, that to them every act of violence was a blow struck in the cause of freedom: all this was entirely beyond the scope of the majority of land-owners. They considered that "the rights of property" were threatened by the Irish Land Acts, as well as by Monck's speeches in the House of Lords.

The work of a Commissioner involved travelling all over Ireland, investigating grievances, and setting up special courts to deal with thousands of landlord-tenant disputes. As a landowner in six counties, Monck himself set a personal example by voluntarily reducing his own rents during bad years, refusing to evict for non-payment, and encouraging his tenants to purchase their own land at an agreed rate.

Although they did not all agree with him, Cabinet Ministers and others often consulted him on Irish problems, and if it had not been for his persistence, the slow progress of land reform in Ireland would have been still slower. Because of the experience he had gained in Canada, he was attended to when he spoke on such subjects as Church Disestablishment and national education.

What is more remarkable is that it was apparently considered quite natural that he should be allowed to make an extremely long speech during a debate on "The Military Force of the Kingdom," pointing out the defects in the present system, and suggesting a scheme for amending it. He had never served in the army, yet owing to the thoroughness with which he had studied the subject in Canada, his speech was replied to respectfully and later published as a pamphlet, a copy of which is now in the British Museum.

The Elementary Education Act, providing state-aided non-sectarian schools in Ireland, was passed in 1870. Monck, who had strongly supported the measure in Parliament, was appointed Commissioner for National Education. Among his many voluntary works, he was one of three official Visitors to Convict Prisons of Dublin, who were given free access to all prisoners and all parts of the prisons. To these and other commitments in Ireland, his duties as Lord Lieutenant of County Dublin, and his work on the Irish Church, Land, and Education Commissions, were now added directorships and subsequent chairmanship of the National Bank in London and the Anglo-American Telegraph Company. The latter directorship occupied a great deal of his time, but it also increased his income. Mainly by selling property, he had already reduced the debt of £90,000 inherited from his uncle and father-in-law, Lord Rathdowne, to £27,000; but he would not feel easy until the estate was solvent. The Monck children were of no help financially. Henry married Lady Edith Scott, a charming but penniless girl, in 1874. After serving with the Coldstream Guards through the two Egyptian campaigns, he left the army with the intention of becoming the wage-earner of the family, thus relieving his father of some of the pressure of overwork. But it became apparent that, while Henry had many good qualities, the ability to earn a living was not one of them. Consequently his father continued to be the bread-winner, and took over Henry's little house in London, while the young couple and their children settled at Charleville.[8]

Meanwhile, Louise, or "Puss," married her father's agent, Jack Royse. He was extremely handsome and an excellent agent, but unfortunately a compulsive gambler. He and Puss had a child every year, and she later trained her seven daughters as a ladies' string orchestra that won local fame at amateur performances in aid of charity. Stanley, the spoilt baby of the family, was no more help. Perpetually in debt and a constant source of anxiety to his parents, at the age of twenty-two he secretly married a lady who was said to be "of a certain profession." He died fourteen years later, having spent most of his married life overseas with his regiment, his wife accompanying him.

Naturally, it had been taken for granted that the eldest of the family, the deaf-mute Fan, was destined to be the permanent "daughter-at-home." When she was forty-four, she met Richard Pearce, a deaf and dumb clergyman. He was the first deaf man ordained in England; and either on the strength of this distinction, or because of his "wonderful ministry" among the deaf in the diocese of Winchester, had been presented to Queen Victoria.

He and Fan could "talk on their fingers" with great rapidity; and by this means he proposed to her and was promptly accepted. Fan had always had an inner source of happiness that could not be quenched even by her handicap. She and her Richard lived to a ripe old age and are remembered as being a very happy couple. For those among their visitors who had not learned the deaf and dumb language, there were always piles of pencils and blocks of paper in their house, along with many souvenirs of Canada. Fan always remembered Canada as a place where she had been treated with great kindness.

With his Government posts, attendance in the House of Lords, Lord-Lieutenancy, charitable works in Ireland, and chairmanships in London, Monck had been working at full stretch. At last his health broke under the strain. In 1876, he collapsed during a meeting in Dublin; for several months his severe illness caused anxiety among his friends who were all convinced that it was the result of overwork. He recovered sufficiently to be able to carry on with his many activities, which took him backwards and forwards across the Irish Sea. A few years later another attack left him unable to walk. Diagnosis was vague in those days. It is impossible now to tell if Monck was a victim of rheumatic fever, rheumatoid arthritis, or a stroke. This last is unlikely as, though he resigned all his Government appointments, and ceased to attend debates in the House of Lords, or to meet his friends in the Athenaeum Club, he wrote quantities of letters in which his handwriting is unimpaired.

He had retired from public life, but he continued to exert "back seat" influence on Irish affairs through correspondence with his many friends in the Government who constantly wrote to consult him. Gladstone and his colleagues counted on having his support for the Irish Home Rule Bill.

Gladstone described Monck as "in essence a Home Ruler,"[9] for he had always upheld the principle of self-government for any country that was ready for it. Monck withheld his support from the first Home Rule Bill; although the British Government proposed to concede a separate Parliament in Dublin, the concession was to be attended by restrictions and conditions which no Irishman could accept. The conditions could only be imposed by force, "the country meanwhile being ruined by agitation,"[10] in other words, by civil war. As he had expected, the Home Rule Bill proposed that a form of local government should be conceded to Ireland in a Dublin Parliament, while the reins would still be in the hands of the "Imperial Parliament" in which Ireland would not be represented. The Parliament at Westminster would control foreign affairs, the army and navy, the customs and excise duties, while Ireland would still contribute towards "Imperial expenses." Gladstone used Lord Spencer as go-between to enlist Monck's support; but no persuasive letters could shake Monck's conviction that the proposed measure would result in "anarchy." He was not unduly agitated about the Bill since he was certain that it would not pass. In this, he was correct. He consented to give his support to the subsequent amended Home Rule Bill which included Irish representatives to the Westminster Parliament, but he still felt that the provisions of the Bill granted "Home Rule" in name but not in fact.

Monck would never have thought of calling himself a visionary, but he was clear-sighted. He had said that the concession to Ireland of what was merely a form of local government, while calling it independent self-government, would eventually result in civil war and in partition, because the Protestants in the North would never consent to be under a Dublin Parliament. In fact, all the disasters he had foretold took place; and one by one all the reforms he had demanded were carried out, though not before many lives had been lost in the process, and not till many years after his death.

"It will not come in my lifetime, nor in yours," his great friend John Robert Godley had written to Monck, referring to "social revolution" as being the only remedy for the situation existing in Ireland in 1847; and Monck himself later declared, during a Parliamentary debate, that the effect of "centuries of neglect" on the part of the British Government could not be repaired in one generation. Neither he nor Godley had visualised the precise form the "social revolution" was to take; but in dedicating himself to Ireland's interests in general, and to tenant-right and tenant-ownership in particular, he had known that each step forward helped to lay a foundation for reform on a national scale. Although he did not live to see the end for which he had worked, he believed that it was in sight and that Ireland was on the verge of true self-government.

He had another severe illness in 1890 and between that time and his death four years later, he was not always fully conscious. "I hope that dear Lord Monck may be mercifully hardly conscious of his loss," a friend wrote when Elizabeth died in 1892; and the same kindly oblivion saved him from the foreknowledge that twenty-seven troubled years were to pass before Ireland achieved Home Rule.

He had always been ready to acknowledge the debt he owed to Canada. The seven years he spent there had influenced his ideas, besides gaining him a hearing at Westminster which he might not otherwise have been given. His sons and daughters looked back on that period of their lives with nostalgic affection; and as the result of two of his grand-daughters marrying and settling in Canada, there are several of Monck's descendants now living in British Columbia.

Chapter One

1 Most people refer to the post, inaccurately, as "Governor General". Previous to the Act of Confederation, "Captain-General and Governor-in-Chief" was the correct term.

Canada, meaning "British North America", was a loose term applied to six independent governments: Upper and Lower Canada, Newfoundland, the three maritime provinces (Prince Edward Island, New Brunswick, Nova Scotia), Rupert's Land, and the wild Northwest governed by the Hudson's Bay Company; these were linked to the British Crown by the State Governor-in-Chief or Governor General.

2 *The Daily Globe*, Toronto, November 2, 1861, copied from *Downshire Protestant*, September 13, 1861.

3 Edward Watkin was sent out from England to reorganise the Grand Trunk Railway Line and support the project for an Intercolonial Railway.

4 From the Templemore parish records, quoted in *A History of the Parish of Templemore*, by Mr. Lea Harden Johnstone, M.A.

5 Created Baron Emly in 1874.

6 C. E. Carrington, *John Robert Godley of Canterbury*.

7 Sir William Gregory to Lady Elizabeth Monck, 1847. From letter owned by W. W. McCann, Foxrock, County Dublin.

Chapter Two

1 Newcastle to Delane, September 1, 1861. Quoted in *John Thadeus Delane* by Sir George Dasent, London, 1908.

2 Sidney Herbert, 1810-61. Politician. Second son of Earl of Pembroke. Led movement for medical reform in the army and was primarily responsible for Florence Nightingale going to the Crimea. Created Baron Herbert of Lea, 1860. *D.N.B.*

3 Edward Cardwell, 1813-86. Statesman and Peelite. Secretary for Ireland, 1859-61. Secretary for the Colonies, 1864-86. Withdrew. British troops from colonial stations. Abolished transportation. Abolished purchase of army commissions. Created Viscount Cardwell, 1874. *D.N.B.*

4 Charles Adderley. Politician. Under-Secretary of State for Colonies, 1866-68. Created Baron Norton, 1878.

5 Chichester Fortescue, 1823-98. Statesman. Under-Secretary of State for Colonies, 1857-58 and 1859-65. Chief Secretary for Ireland, 1865-66 and 1868-70. Created Baron Carlingford, 1874. *D.N.B.*
6 Robert Lowe, 1811-92. Politician, Vice-President of Committee of Council on Education, 1859-64. Created Viscount Sherbrooke, 1880. *D.N.B.*
7 *Morning Chronicle*, 1861.
8 Joseph Pope, *Memoirs of the Rt. Hon. Sir John A. Macdonald*, Toronto: 1930; Edward Arnold, 1894.
9 Queen Victoria to the Duke of Newcastle, August 30, 1861.
10 J. R. Godley to C. Adderley, August 28, 1861. British Museum.
11 R. Lowe to E. Ellice, September 8, 1861.
12 "In 1860, in England, 550,000 depended directly, and many others indirectly, on the cotton industry; about 4/5 of the raw cotton came from America." Greville the diarist maintained that Britain's outcry against slavery was mainly hypocritical. *The Age of Reform* by Sir Llewelyn Woodward.

In the United States, the North wanted protection, *i.e.*, high tariffs, for their developing industries; the South wanted low tariffs to allow their exports to flow.

13 Letters of J. Godley to C. Adderley. British Museum.

Chapter Three

1 *Lord Monck and the Canadian Nation*, by C. P. Stacey.
2 *Ibid.*
3 W. L. Morton, *The Critical Years*, Toronto: McClelland and Stewart Limited, p. 99.
4 *Ibid.*
5 *Memoirs of Sir John A. Macdonald* by Sir Joseph Pope, *op. cit.*, Vol. I, p. 325.

Chapter Four

1 Lyons to Monck, November 25, 1861. Copy in Monck Papers.
2 Monck to Williams, November, 1861, New Brunswick Museum.
3 Colonel (later General Sir Daniel) Lysons, 1816-98. Had served in Barbados, Halifax (Nova Scotia), and in the Crimea. Assistant Adjutant General at H.Q. in England *D.N.B.*
4 *Oxford History of England*, "The Age of Reform", p. 308. Letter of Queen Victoria. British Museum.
5 Palmerston to Queen Victoria, November 29, 1861. *Ibid.*
6 Russell to Queen Victoria, November 29, 1861.
7 Queen Victoria to Lord Russell, December 1, 1861.
8 Monck to Newcastle, December 20, 1861. Newcastle Papers, Nottingham University Library.
9 Monck to Newcastle, December 28, 1861. Newcastle Papers.
10 Monck to Lyons, January 22, 1862. Lyons Papers, County Record Office, Sussex. By kind permission of His Grace the late Duke of Norfolk.
11 Donald Creighton, *The Road to Confederation*, Macmillan of Canada, 1964, p. 5.

12 *Correspondence of Sir John Macdonald* by J. Pope. O.U.P. Canadian Branch, Toronto.
13 General Sir Hastings Doyle, Commander of H.M. Forces in Nova Scotia, 1861; Lieutenant-Governor of Nova Scotia, 1867-73. *D.N.B.*
14 Personal letter, Doyle to Monck, Monck Papers.
15 Monck to Gordon, February 1862. Stanmore Papers. New Brunswick University Library.
16 " . . . We are confident, dear brothers, that there will be, everywhere, an immediate response to the appeal of the Representative of our gracious Sovereign . . . . The duty of serving so noble a cause should be near the hearts of all our young people . . . . Even though the present alarm may subside, we should face the fact that new difficulties may arise at any moment, and oblige us to take up arms."
17 *My Canadian Leaves* by Frances Monck.
18 Monck to Hodson, April 11, 1862. Hodson Papers, National Library of Ireland.

Chapter Five

1 Monck to Gordon, April 19, 1862.
2 Monck to Gordon, February 24, 1862. Stanmore Papers. Quoted by Donald Creighton in *The Road to Confederation*, *op.cit.*
3 *My Canadian Leaves* by Frances Monck, *op. cit.*
4 Monck to Newcastle, May 23, 1862. Newcastle Papers.
5 Monck to Ellice, October 21, 1862.
6 Newcastle Papers.
7 Adderley to Monck, 1862. Unpublished letter, Monck Papers.
8 Adderley to Monck, August 29, 1862, and December 11, 1862. Monck Papers.
9 Monck to Gordon, August 9, 1862.
10 The *Globe*, October 20, 1862.
11 Monck to Ellice, October 21, 1862.
12 Charles's younger brother, Richard Monck.
13 *My Canadian Leaves* by Frances Monck, *op. cit.*
14 George Augustus Sala (1828-1895). "Things I have seen and people I have known" by G. A. Sala, published 1894.

Chapter Six

1 Edward Ellice, who died later in that year (1863), was now aged eighty-two. He had held various governmental offices and was a supporter of Lord Palmerston. In 1821 he had amalgamated the North-West, X.Y., and the Hudson's Bay Companies. *D.N.B.*
2 John Rose, Canadian banker and politician; later Minister of Public Works in Canada.
3 Monck to Ellice, July, 1863.
4 Robert Lowe, Member for Colne, was in 1863 Vice-President of the Council for Education, later Chancellor of the Exchequer, then Home Secretary.
5 Robert Lowe to Monck, unpublished letter, 1863.

6 J. M. S. Careless, *Brown of the Globe*, Macmillan Company of Canada, Limited.
7 Monck to Lyons, British Minister at Washington, April 13, 1863. Lyons Papers.
8 Imperial troops were finally withdrawn in 1871. The Canadian Royal Military College was established in 1874. A Canadian force fought with the British army in the Boer War in 1899. In the 1914-18 war, Canada contributed "nearly three-quarters of a million men". Arthur Lower, *Colony to Nation*, Longmans, 1946.
9 Gordon to Newcastle, September 14, 1863. Quoted by Donald Creighton in *The Road to Confederation, op. cit.*
10 Gordon to Monck. Unpublished letter, Monck Papers.
11 Doyle to Monck. Unpublished letter, Monck Papers. Mr. Dundas was Governor of Prince Edward Island.
12 *The Road to Confederation*, by Donald Creighton, *op. cit.*, p. 24.
13 Monck to Gordon, October 15, 1863.
14 Monck to Gordon, October 16, 1863.
15 Creighton, *op. cit.*
16 Monck to Gordon, November 3, 1863.
17 Normanby (Mulgrave) to Monck, August 23, 1864. Unpublished letter, Monck Papers.
18 The 1670 Charter of the Hudson's Bay Company, of which Newcastle was now Chairman, had given them "the exclusive monopoly of trade and rights in land, fisheries and mines . . . and full jurisdiction, under the British Crown, for the maintenance of law and order." Their territory originally covered the Basin of Hudson Bay; but "where their own Government ended, they were to have the right of trade in all waters into which they could find a passage" – in fact, to the Pacific. The discovery of gold in the Fraser River, the consequent American gold rush, and the North-West potential for agrarian settlement, all helped to prove that – "a fur company could no longer continue as the government of half a continent." W. L. Morton. *The Critical Years*.
19 The Intercolonial Railway, begun in 1869 was completed in 1876. The Canadian Pacific Railway was completed in 1885, and opened in 1886.
20 Adderley to Monck. Unpublished letter. Monck Papers.
21 Lowe to Monck. Unpublished letter, November 11, 1863, Monck Papers.

Chapter Seven

1 By the Reciprocity Treaty of 1854 Between America and Canada, each country exported certain products to the other free of tariff.
2 A Letter of Marque was a commission given to a private ship to make reprisals on vessels of another state. *Chambers' Dictionary.*
3 Lyons to Monck. Unpublished letter, 1863, Monck Papers.
4 Stuart to Monck. Private unpublished letter, September 18, 1863, Monck Papers.
5 General Sir Hastings Doyle.
6 Monck to Lyons. Private letter, January 9, 1864, Lyons Papers.
7 Letter from George Brown to his wife, February 25, 1864, Brown Papers. Quoted in *Brown of the Globe* by J. M. S. Careless, *op. cit.*, p. 117. Brown was a member for South Oxford, Canada.

8 *The Critical Years* by W. L. Morton, p. 140.
9 *Ibid.*
10 Monck to Chichester Fortescue (Lord Carlingford) April 21, 1864. Public Record Office 42/641.
11 Monck to Lord Lyons, April 1864, Lyons Papers.
12 The minute in council referred to the transfer of the seat of government from Quebec to Ottawa.
13 Taché to Monck, August 30, 1864.
14 Brown Papers. Quoted in *Brown of the Globe, op cit.*
15 Monck to Taché, June 16, 1864, 5:00 p.m. Copy in Monck Papers.
16 *Canadian Historical Review*, 1922. Quoted in an article by R. G. Trotter.
17 Personal letter, Monck to Brown, June 21, 1864. Copy in Monck Papers.

Chapter Eight

1 Chief Justice C. A. W. Bowen to Lady Monck, May 23, 1864. Monck Papers in possession of Mr. J. J. McCann.
2 *My Canadian Leaves* by Frances Monck.
3 Queenstown, now Cobh, the harbour at Cork was so named when Queen Victoria landed there in 1849.
4 William Price, 1789-1867. A timber merchant, founder of the present firm of Price Bros. of Quebec.
5 W. L. Morton, *Monck Letters and Journals*, McClelland and Stewart. Feo would be surprised to find one of the original copies of her "journal" in the British Museum today, and " *My Canadian Leaves* by Frances Monck" included in the bibliographies of twentieth century works by Canadian historians, as well as in the entry on Monck in the *Dictionary of National Biography.* When the journal was printed, many of the proper names were discreetly replaced by an initial.
6 Private unpublished letter, Cardwell to Monck, May 13, 1864, Monck Papers.
7 Since the signing of the Reciprocity Treaty in 1854, great progress had been made in Canadian industries. The duties placed on their products were a grievance with the United States.
8 Monck to Lyons, February 20, 1864, Lyons Papers.
9 Copy of a private letter, Monck to Cardwell, May 30, 1864, Lyons Papers.
10 Brown Papers. Quoted in *Brown of the Globe, op. cit.*
11 W. L. Morton, *The Critical Years*, pp. 147-151.
12 Private unpublished letter, Cardwell to Monck, 1864, Monck Papers.
13 Cardwell to Monck, July-August, 1864. Private unpublished letters, Monck Papers.
14 David Graham Drummond Ogilvy, 10th Earl of Airlie.

Chapter Nine

1 Private letter, Monck to Cardwell, November 14, 1864. Windsor Castle Archives.
2 Private letters, Monck to Cardwell, November 1864 to January 1865. Windsor Castle Archives.

3 *Memoirs of Sir John Alexander Macdonald*, by Joseph Pope, *op. cit.*
4 *Ibid.*
5 Private despatch, Monck to Cardwell, December 16, 1864. Copy in Monck Papers.
6 Cardwell to Monck. Private unpublished letter, December 16, 1864. Monck Papers.
7 Cardwell to Gordon, November 12, 1864. P.R.O. 30/48/6/39. Quoted in *Documents on Federation of British North America* by G. P. Browne, McClelland and Stewart Limited, Toronto and Montreal.
8 Copy of Private despatch, Monck to Cardwell, November 7, 1864. Monck Papers.
On the subject of the proposed constitution of the Senate, Monck wrote, in the same private despatch: "What is required in practice is some body, which, by the greater permanence of its tenure of Legislative authority, will be . . . comparatively independent of the temporary fluctuations of popular opinion . . . The objection to a nominated Upper Chamber holding its position for life and restricted in point of numbers, is that it affords no means in the event of collision in opinion between itself and the representatives of the people, of bringing the two bodies into harmony; while as it would really be nominated by the responsible advisers of the Governor, there would be a risk that it would represent only one political party.
"On the whole, the leaning of my own opinion would be to adopt the principle embodied in the resolution of the Conference to the extent of appointing the Members of the Upper Chamber by Crown nomination, but only for a limited time – say eight years – and to provide that one eighth of the number should go out of office each year, and be eligible for reappointment if it should be considered desirable."
9 Monck to Cardwell, November 14, 1864. Windsor Castle Archives.
10 Private unpublished letters, Cardwell to Monck. October, November, and December, 1864.
11 *Ibid.*
12 *Ibid.*
13 Private letter, Monck to Cardwell, November 11, 1864. Windsor Castle Archives.
14 Private unpublished letter, Cardwell to Monck, December 24, 1864.
15 Private letter from Monck to Cardwell, February 3, 1865. Windsor Castle Archives.
16 Gordon to Cardwell, undated letter. P.R.R. 30/48/6/39; December 5, 1864. Quoted from *Documents on Federation, op. cit.*
17 Dr. Tupper was Prime Minister for Nova Scotia.
18 Private unpublished letters, MacDonnell to Monck. October and November, 1864. Monck Papers.
19 Letters from Monck to Cardwell, December 24, 1864 and January 21, 1865. Windsor Castle Archives.
20 Monck to Henry, April, 1865. Canadian Public Archives.
21 Cardwell to Monck, April, 1865. Monck Papers.
22 "Lord Monck and the Canadian Nation", *Dalhousie Review*, July, 1934.
23 Public Record Office, C.O. 188/143.
24 Quoted by Donald Creighton in *The Road to Confederation, op. cit.*
25 Ottawa, situated on the river from which it took its name, has been described by W. L. Morton in *The Critical Years* as "an Irish shanty town"

populated by "rough lumber magnates". Its remote situation was a kind of no-man's-land, and had been chosen to succeed Quebec as the seat of Canadian government to avoid jealousy between Upper and Lower Canada.

26 27 Private unpublished letters from Sir Richard MacDonnell to Monck, February 19, March 3, 9, and 20, 1865. Monck Papers.

28 From Monck Papers, in possession of Mr. J. J. McCann.

29 Sir Julius Benedict, 1804-85. Conductor and composer. Conducted in Vienna, Naples, Lyceam, and Drury Lane, London. Accompanied Jenny Lind on American tour, 1850. For many years conducted the Norwich Festival. *D.N.B.*

30 Private unpublished letters, Cardwell to Monck. Monck Papers.

31 Cardwell to Gordon. Stanmore Papers, New Brunswick University Library.

32 Monck to Gordon, June 22, 1865. Stanmore Papers.

33 General Hastings Doyle was to act as Administrator.

34 Cardwell to Monck, June 17, 1865. Unpublished private letter.

35 As in the previous year, the Coalition Government was to be led by a "figure-head". Sir Narcisse Belleau was a *Bleu* (Conservative French-Canadian), and had been leader of the Legislative Council since 1857. He was subsequently appointed Lieutenant-Governor of the Province of Quebec after the Confederation Act passed. W. L. Morton, *The Critical Years*.

36 Letter from Macdonald to Brown, August 5, 1865. Quoted in *Sir John Macdonald* by Joseph Pope, Appendix IX, *op. cit.*

37 *The Life and Times of Sir Alexander Tilloch Galt*, O. D. Skelton, Toronto, McClelland and Stewart Limited, 1920.

38 W. L. Morton, *The Critical Years, op. cit.*

39 Cardwell to Monck, July 8 and 15, 1865. Private unpublished letters. Monck Papers.

40 Private letters, MacDonnell to Monck, January 16, 1865, and February 19, 1865. Monck Papers.

41 Cardwell to Monck, August 11, 1865. Private unpublished letter. Monck Papers.

42 Cardwell to Monck, August 11, 1865. Private unpublished letter. Monck Papers.

43 Cardwell to Monck, September 9 and 15, 1865. Private unpublished letters. Monck Papers.

Chapter Ten

1 Monck to Williams, March 2, 1866. New Brunswick Museum.

2 Monck to Cardwell, April 16, 1866. Windsor Castle Archives.

3 *Ibid.*, May 7, 1866.

4 *North America*, by Anthony Trollope, 1869.

5 Brown to Macdonald, August 15, 1864. *Sir John Macdonald* by Joseph Pope, *op. cit.*

6 *My Canadian Leaves* by Frances Monck.

7 The last two words were in quotation of the stock press comment.

8 Monck to Cardwell, May 7, 1866. Public Records Office.

9 A legend has persisted that Monck went to Ottawa in a "disgruntled" frame of mind, and that his attitude affected subsequent actions for which he has been criticised. In support of this theory a modern writer (R. H. Hubbard, author of *Rideau Hall*) has quoted the 1864 entry in *My Canadian Leaves* as the opinion of "the Monck family", overlooking the fact that the diarist's companions who were "disgusted" with Ottawa, were Lord Lyons and his staff.
10 Careless, *Brown of the Globe, op. cit.*
11 Bruce to Monck. Private unpublished letters, February 17 and March 11, 1866. Monck Papers.
12 Bruce to Monck. Private unpublished letters. Monck Papers.
13 Hope to Monck, March 21 and April 11, 1866. Private unpublished letters, Monck Papers.
14 Careless, *Brown of the Globe, op. cit.*
15 Bruce to Monck, March 11, 1866. Private letters, Monck Papers.
16 Bruce to Monck, April 9, 1866. Monck Papers.
17 Monck to Cardwell, June 4, 1866. Public Records Office.
18 Creighton, *The Road to Confederation, op. cit.*
19 Monck to Cardwell, June 14, 1866. Public Records Office.
20 Copy of telegram in Monck Papers in possession of J. J. McCann.
21 McGee to Lady Monck, June 4, 1866. Monck Papers in possession of J. J. McCann.

Chapter Eleven

1 Cardwell to Lady Monck, June 30, 1866. Monck Papers in possession of J. J. McCann. Until this time, Monck had been an Irish peer; an English peerage would make him eligible to sit in the House of Lords.
2 Letter from Queen Victoria to Lord Russell, June 28, 1866. *Letters of Queen Victoria*, British Museum.
3 The British North America Act (March 29, 1867) was to provide a guarantee of separate schools in both Upper and Lower Canada.
4 Monck to Macdonald, June 21, 1866, *Sir John Macdonald* by Joseph Pope, *op. cit.*
5 Macdonald to Monck, June 22, 1866. *Ibid.*
6 Monck to Williams, July 14, 1866. *Ibid.*
7 Monck to Carnarvon, July 21, 1866. Carnarvon Papers, Public Record Office.
8 Carnarvon to Monck, August 10, 1866. Private letter. Monck Papers.
9 Monck to Carnarvon, August 10, 1866. Private letter. Public Records Office.
10 General in Command of British North American Forces.
11 Monck to Carnarvon, August 24, 1866. Public Records Office.
12 Carnarvon to Monck. Private unpublished letter. Monck Papers.
13 Monck to Carnarvon. August 27, 1866. Private letter. Public Records Office.
14 Carnarvon to Monck, August 31 to September 28, 1866. Private unpublished letters. Monck Papers.
15 J. A. Macdonald to Monck, October 8, 1866. Private letter. Monck Papers.

16 Letter from J. A. Macdonald to Tilley, October 8, 1866. Copy in Monck Papers.
17 Monck to Macdonald, June 22, 1866. *Sir John Macdonald* by Joseph Pope.
18 Monck to Carnarvon, September 22, 1866. Private letter in Carnarvon Papers. Public Records Office.
19 Sir Frederick Bruce to Monck, September 26, 1866. Private unpublished letter. Monck Papers.
20 American Secretary of State.
21 Macdonald to Monck, private letter. Monck Papers.
22 Carnarvon to Monck, November 9, 1866. Monck Papers. Unpublished letter.
23 General Sir John Michel to Monck, October 1 and 2, 1866. Private letters, Monck Papers.
24 Monck to Carnarvon, October 8, 1866. Carnarvon Papers. Public Records Office.
25 Pierrepont Edwards to Monck, November 14, 1866. Private letter. Monck Papers.
26 *Letters of Queen Victoria*, 2nd Series, edited by G. E. Buckle, 1926. British Museum.
27 Bruce to Monck, September 1866. Private letter. Monck Papers.
28 The Bill inserted a clause in the Confederation Act guaranteeing separate schools for the Protestant minority in Catholic Lower Canada, where the educational system consisted of denominational "confessional" schools. The Roman Catholic minority in Upper Canada demanded an equal right to separate schools, although the State Schools there were undenominational, and it was considered that the establishment of separate schools for Catholics would dislocate the educational scheme.
29 Macdonald to Monck, October 20, 1866. Private letter. Monck Papers.
30 Letters from Galt to Monck, October 1 and 6, 1866. Private letters, Monck Papers.
31 Galt to Monck, October 23, 1866. Private letter. Monck Papers.
32 Macdonald to Monck, 1866. Private letter. Monck Papers.
33 Carnarvon to Monck, October 5, 1866. Private letter. Monck Papers.
34 Copy of Despatch, Carnarvon to Monck, November 24, 1866. Monck Papers.
35 Carnarvon to Monck, November 23, 1866. Private unpublished letter. Monck Papers.
36 Galt to Mrs. Galt, December, 1866. Quoted in *Life and Times of Alexander Tilloch Galt*, by O. D. Skelton, *op. cit.*
37 *Ibid.*
38 H. L. Langevin to Mgr. Jean Langevin, December 4, 1866. Quoted in W. L. Morton, *The Critical Years, op. cit.*
39 Monck to Carnarvon, October 25 and November 3, 1866. Private letter. Carnarvon Papers. Public Records Office.

Chapter Twelve

1 Pierrepont Edwards to Monck, November 15, 1866. Private letter. Monck Papers.

2 *A Short History of the Irish People*, by M. Hayden and G. Moonan. Hayden Press, Dublin.
3 Carnarvon to Monck. Private letter. Monck Papers.
4 Lord Grey to Lord Carnarvon, February 5, 1867. *Letters of Queen Victoria*, British Museum Reading Room.
5 Francis Brooke of Summerton County, Dublin, died in March, 1867.
6 Monck to Carnarvon, September 7, 1866. C.O. 42. Vol. 656. Quoted by Donald Creighton, *The Road to Confederation, op. cit.*
7 Macdonald to Lord Knutsford, July 18, 1889. *Sir John Macdonald* by Joseph Pope, *op. cit.*
8 Quoted in *The Road to Confederation*, Donald Creighton, *op. cit.* p. 428.
9 Buckingham to Monck, May 29, 1867. P.A.C. Quoted in *The Critical Years*, by W. L. Morton, p. 219.
10 Monck to Carnarvon, September 15, 1866. Carnarvon Papers. Public Records Office.

Chapter Thirteen

1 W. L. Morton, *The Critical Years, op. cit.*, p. 220.
2 Monck to Macdonald. Quoted from *Sir John Macdonald* by Donald Creighton, p. 475. note 20.
3 O. D. Skelton, *Life and Times of Alexander Tilloch Galt.*
4 *Canada's Governors General* by John Cowan, 1952.
5 E. A. Meredith, *Private Journals*, Vol. 13, No. 5, M.S. Group 29.13.18. Public Archives of Canada.
6 The North West Territory was included in the Confederation in 1870; Prince Edward Island in 1873; and Newfoundland in 1949.
7 Tom Cullen, *The Empress Brown*, Bodley Head, p. 124.
8 Colonel Hawley commanded the Rifle Brigade.
9 Adderley to Monck, November 8, 1867. Private letter. Monck Papers.
10 Adderley to Monck, February 29, 1868. Private letter. Monck Papers.
11 Tupper to Monck, February 29, 1868. Private letter. Monck Papers.
12 Adderley to Monck, March 7, 1868. Private letter. Monck Papers.
13 The Duke of Edinburgh was Queen Victoria's son, Prince Alfred, then making a tour in Australia.
14 Adderley to Monck, February 29, 1868. Private letter. Monck Papers.
15 The "burnt house" was the name given to the wood which had grown up on the site of the old Charleville House, burned in 1792.
16 *D.N.B.*
17 Joseph Pope, *Sir John Macdonald*, Vol. II, *op. cit.*
The measure to reduce the Governor General's salary to £6,500 was subsequently disallowed by the Imperial Parliament, on the grounds that it would place Canada "in the third class among colonial governments, and thus restrict Her Majesty's Ministers in their choice of Governors General."
18 Joseph Pope, *Sir John Macdonald, op. cit.* Vol. II.
19 *Ibid.*
20 Carnarvon to Monck. Private unpublished letter. Monck Papers.
21 *Montreal Herald*, October 17, 1861.
22 R. H. Hubbard, *Rideau Hall,* Ottawa, 1967. Quoting from the diaries of E. A. Meredith.

Chapter Fourteen

1 Lord Lisgar.
2 *The Ottawa Times*, November 18, 1868. P.A.C.
3 *Le Pays*, November 16, 1868. P.A.C.
4 *The Montreal Gazette*, November 12, 1868. P.A.C.

Epilogue

1 *The Dalhousie Review*, 1934.
2 Sir Charles Metcalfe, Governor General, 1843-45. *Life and Times of Alexander Tilloch Galt*, by O. D. Skelton, *op. cit.*
3 William Monsell, 1812-94. M.P. for Limerick, Under-Secretary for the Colonies. Cr. Baron Emly, 1874.
4 Monck to Monsell, October 24, 1867.
5 Monck to Gladstone, January 8, 1868. Gladstone Papers, British Museum.
6 Hansard Parliamentary Reports, 1869. Institute of Historical Research.
7 Mountstewart Grant Duff to Monck, October 18, 1886. Monck Papers.
8 Henry Monck's eldest son, Captain, the Hon. Charles Monck, Coldstream Guards was killed in action in 1914. He was the father of the present Viscount, and of the author.
9 Gladstone to Spencer, May, 1886. Monck Papers (copy).
10 Monck to Henry Monck, 1886. Monck Papers.

Acknowledgments

I would like to thank the many people who helped me with this biography; especially Mr. Michael Meaney, who gave me the Monck Papers on which the book is based; and Professor W. L. Morton, without whose help and innumerable kindnesses it could not have been written. I am very grateful to Mrs. Kate Atterton who typed and retyped it, corrected the proofs, and compiled the index and bibliography.

Index